D1579725

Circular Motion

Motion in a Circle

Uniform circular motion is the motion of an object travelling at a constant velocity on a circular path. Circular motion is described using angles rather than distance moved. These angles are usually expressed in **radians** (symbol rad). One complete cycle is $360° = 2\pi$ radians. The velocity of a rotating object is the angle that an object moves through per second (i.e. radians per second or rad s^{-1}) and is called **angular velocity**, ω (omega), where $\omega = \frac{\theta}{t}$ is the instantaneous angular velocity and $\omega = \frac{\Delta\theta}{\Delta t}$ represents the average angular velocity. The angle described by a rotating object, θ, is called the **angular displacement**. Angular velocity is a vector quantity with its direction along the axis of rotation.

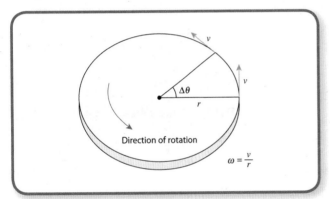

$$\omega = \frac{v}{r}$$

Direction of rotation

Angular speed is simply the magnitude of the vector quantity angular velocity. Since there are 2π radians in one complete revolution, the angular speed is related to the **period of rotation**, T, by $\omega = \frac{2\pi}{T}$. The **linear speed**, v, of an object moving in a circle of radius r is the distance the object travels per unit time. Its direction is tangential to the circular path and is determined by dividing the circumference by the period, i.e. $v = \frac{2\pi r}{T}$. Since $\omega = \frac{2\pi}{T}$, this can be expressed by

$$v = r\omega \text{ or } \omega = \frac{v}{r}$$

Objects that are rotating are often described as completing a number of **revolutions per second** (rps) or **revolutions per minute** (rpm). The former is simply the **frequency**, f, and this is usually given in hertz (Hz), or s^{-1} in terms of SI units. For circular motion, frequency $= \frac{\text{number of rotations}}{\text{time taken}}$; it therefore follows that $f = \frac{1}{T}$ or $T = \frac{1}{f}$. Hence angular speed can also be expressed as $\omega = 2\pi f$ and is therefore known as **angular frequency**.

Centripetal Acceleration and Centripetal Force

Objects that rotate at a constant speed are also constantly changing direction. This means that the velocity (which is a vector quantity) must also be constantly changing and therefore, according to the definition of acceleration, the object is accelerating. This acceleration is called the **centripetal acceleration**, which always acts towards the centre of rotation. It is given by

$$a = \frac{v^2}{r} = \frac{(r\omega)^2}{r} = r\omega^2$$

From Newton's Second Law $F = ma$, there must be a corresponding **centripetal force** $F = \frac{mv^2}{r} = mr\omega^2$ that also acts towards the centre. It is this centripetal force that keeps objects moving in a circle. The circle of rotation may be horizontal, vertical or at an angle. Removing the force would result in the object flying off at a tangential velocity v. For a car cornering on a level road, the only force acting between the tyres and the road is the frictional force and it is this frictional force that provides the centripetal force. The nature of this centripetal force in other rotating systems is shown in the table. In situations where the object describes a circle at an angle θ, such as an aeroplane banking or a car on a banked circuit, it is the component of the lift towards the centre of the circle or the component of the friction towards the centre that provides the centripetal force.

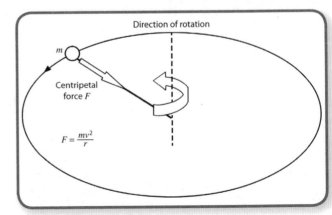

Direction of rotation

m

Centripetal force F

$$F = \frac{mv^2}{r}$$

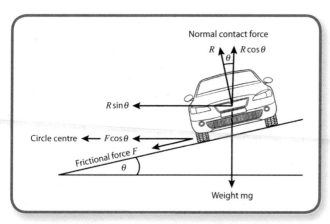

Rotating object	Centripetal force
Orbiting planet	Gravitation
Orbiting electron	Electrostatic force
Car moving on a roundabout	Friction between tyres and road
Hammer (in track and field athletics)	Tension in wire

Motion in Vertical Circles

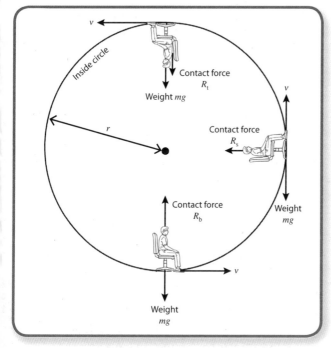

Motion in a vertical circle, such as cars travelling over a humpback bridge, aeroplanes carrying out loop-the-loops, and roller coaster rides, involves forces that act on the person moving in a loop. For vertical circles two additional forces need to be considered: the **weight** mg of an object or person, and the **contact** force R that the seat exerts on the person or the object. It is the direction of the contact force that is important as the loop is completed. For objects or persons **inside a loop** there are three key positions. **At the top** of the loop, both the weight and the contact force R_t act downwards and together provide the centripetal force: $R_t + mg = \frac{mv^2}{r}$. **At the side** it is only the contact force that provides the centripetal force and so $R_s = \frac{mv^2}{r}$ (there is no component of mg towards the centre). However, **at the bottom** of the loop the weight and the contact force act in opposite directions so that $R_b - mg = \frac{mv^2}{r}$. In this case, $R_b = \frac{mv^2}{r} + mg = m(a + g)$ and this apparent contribution to a person's weight makes a person 'feel' heavier at the bottom and 'lighter' at the top of a loop. If the contact force at the top of a loop were zero then the **minimum speed** required to just complete a loop would be $g = \frac{v^2}{r}$ or $v \geq \sqrt{rg}$. At this precise moment, the person would feel '**weightless**'. In vertical rides where the object or person is **outside the loop**, at the top the forces involved are $mg - R_t = \frac{mv^2}{r}$, giving $R_t = m(g - a)$, with a person feeling 'weightless' when $a = g$.

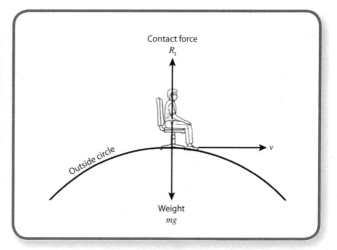

Conservation of Energy

The principle of **conservation of energy** can be applied, for example, to roller coaster rides and used to determine the speed of the roller coaster car. For a car starting at the top of the roller coaster (at a height h), the loss of gravitational potential energy E_p is equal to the gain in kinetic energy E_k throughout the entire ride, provided that no energy is lost from the system. The velocity of the car can be found at any point by equating the kinetic and potential energies, $\frac{1}{2}mv^2 = mg\triangle h$, giving $v = \sqrt{2g\triangle h}$.

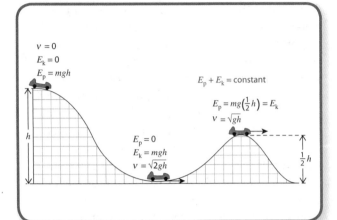

$v = 0$
$E_k = 0$
$E_p = mgh$

$E_p + E_k = $ constant

$E_p = mg(\frac{1}{2}h) = E_k$
$v = \sqrt{gh}$

h

$E_p = 0$
$E_k = mgh$
$v = \sqrt{2gh}$

$\frac{1}{2}h$

SUMMARY

- Frequency, f, is the reciprocal of the period, T, i.e. $T = \frac{1}{f}$

- Angular speed, ω, is the angle (in radians) an object rotates through in one second and linear speed, v, is the speed of an object at any instant of time (this has a direction that is tangential to the circular path)

- Angular velocity is the rate of change of angular displacement, $\omega = \frac{\theta}{t} = \frac{2\pi}{T} = 2\pi f$, in the direction of rotation; it has units of rad s^{-1}

- Angular speed is the magnitude of angular velocity

- Centripetal acceleration is $a = \frac{v^2}{r} = \omega^2 r$ and is always directed towards the centre of rotation; centripetal force is therefore $F = ma$ and thus $F = \frac{mv^2}{r} = m\omega^2 r$

- For vertical circles, consideration must be given to the weight of the object and the contact force; also, the centripetal acceleration and force varies for objects that are inside a loop or outside a loop

- For vertical rotations, the loss in gravitational potential energy equals the gain in kinetic energy: $mg\triangle h = \frac{1}{2}mv^2$

QUICK TEST

1. What SI unit is used in circular motion to describe the size of angles?

2. What is the direction of the linear velocity at any instant for an object undergoing circular motion?

3. Give the equation and the SI units for angular speed.

4. What equation connects linear speed with angular speed?

5. What does the number of revolutions per second represent?

6. What is the expression that links period with frequency and with angular speed?

7. The second hand on a wrist watch is 1.2 cm long. Calculate the frequency and the angular frequency of the second hand.

8. In the above question, determine the linear speed of the tip of the second hand.

9. What provides the centripetal force in rotating objects such as a rotating mass at the end of a length of string?

10. What is the equation for the centripetal force and what is the direction of this force?

11. What would happen to an object if the centripetal force were removed?

12. What is the centripetal force that keeps planets in orbit around the Sun?

13. What is the strength of the centripetal force required to keep a car of mass 1200 kg following a curve of radius 50 m when travelling at 25 m s^{-1}?

14. What is the minimum speed for a roller coaster ride to complete a loop that has a radius of 15 m with the car travelling inside the loop?

PRACTICE QUESTIONS

1. The figure shows the basic configuration of the
Large Hadron Collider (LHC), which propels protons
around its 27 km of evacuated stainless steel tubing.
The protons circulate the ring at 1.1×10^4 rps.

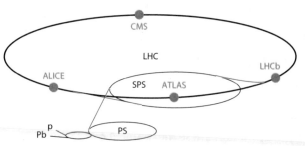

    a) Calculate the time period for a proton to make one complete revolution. [1 mark]

    b) Determine the angular velocity of the orbiting protons. [1 mark]

    c) The protons travel close to the speed of light. Determine the orbital velocity as a fraction
of the speed of light to two decimal places [the speed of light is $3.0 \times 10^8\,\mathrm{m\,s^{-1}}$]. [3 marks]

    d) Determine the size of the centripetal force on one proton [use the relativistic proton mass
$m_\mathrm{p} = 3.94 \times 10^{-23}\,\mathrm{kg}$]. [3 marks]

2. The International Space Station (ISS) orbits 400 km above the Earth at a speed of $7.68\,\mathrm{km\,s^{-1}}$.
[radius of the Earth $R_\mathrm{E} = 6400\,\mathrm{km}$]

    a) Calculate the angular speed of ISS. [2 marks]

    b) Determine the time, in minutes,
to complete one complete orbit
and hence find the number of
orbits made by ISS each day. [3 marks]

    c) Calculate the centripetal
acceleration of ISS and compare
this to the gravitational field
strength using the empirical relation

$$g \approx 9.81 \left(\frac{R_\mathrm{E}}{R_\mathrm{E} + h} \right)^2$$

[4 marks]

3. A pilot of mass m is performing a vertical loop-the-loop in a plane. The plane is flying at a constant
speed of $215\,\mathrm{m\,s^{-1}}$ and the radius of the loop is 3.0 km.

    a) Calculate the contact force exerted by the seat on the pilot at the top of the loop in terms of mg. [3 marks]

    b) Calculate the contact force exerted by the seat on the pilot at the bottom of the loop
in terms of mg. [3 marks]

    c) Describe what the pilot experiences at these two positions. [2 marks]

    d) Determine the speed of the plane at the top of the loop when the contact force is zero. [3 marks]

    e) Explain the significance of this speed. [3 marks]

Simple Harmonic Motion

Fundamentals of Simple Harmonic Motion (SHM)

An object that oscillates or vibrates repeatedly and constantly about an equilibrium position undergoes periodic motion. These **mechanical oscillations** require the action of a force that is directed towards this equilibrium position, and such a force is known as a **restoring force**. A restoring force that is directly proportional to the object's **displacement**, x, provides the conditions necessary for an object to oscillate with a special periodic motion called **simple harmonic motion**. Mathematically, this can be expressed as $F = -kx$, where k is a positive constant. Applying Newton's Second Law of motion provides for an alternative expression $a = -\omega^2 x$, where a is the acceleration, x is the displacement and ω is a constant defined by $\omega = \frac{2\pi}{T}$, where T is the period. The solution to the simple harmonic motion equation is $x = A \sin(\omega t)$, where A is the amplitude of the oscillation, i.e. its maximum displacement. If f is the number of oscillations per second, i.e. the **frequency**, then the constant ω can be written as $\omega = 2\pi f$, and this is called the **angular frequency**, measured in rad s^{-1}. The solution above can then be given in terms of frequency by $x = A \sin(2\pi ft)$. The solution states that the displacement from the equilibrium position is sinusoidal, with an amplitude given by A, and with period $T (= \frac{1}{f})$. Two examples of such motion are the behaviour of a mass–spring system and the behaviour of a mass at the end of a light string or rod, i.e. a **simple pendulum**; both can be used to practically demonstrate simple harmonic motion.

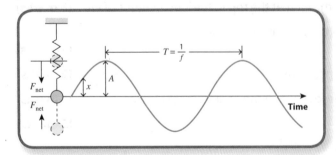

Displacement, Velocity and Acceleration

The solution found for the **displacement** x is shown graphically. The gradient function of x can then be used to find the **velocity** (velocity is the gradient of the displacement–time graph) and this leads to a velocity–time graph that has a maximum value of $(2\pi f)A$ and is out of phase with the displacement curve by 45° or $\frac{\pi}{4}$. The velocity equation is

$$v = 2\pi fA \cos(2\pi ft) = \omega A \cos(\omega t)$$

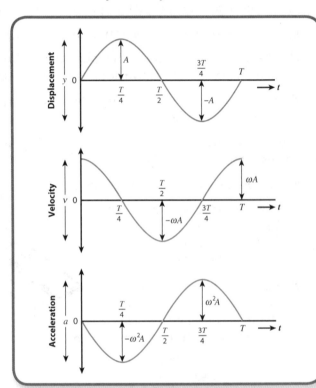

Acceleration is the gradient of the velocity–time graph, and this has a maximum value of $(2\pi f)^2 A$ and is out of phase by π or is in antiphase with the displacement–time graph. The acceleration is therefore given by

$$a = -(2\pi f)^2 A \sin(2\pi f)t = -\omega^2 A \sin(\omega t) = -\omega^2 x$$
$$\text{or simply } a = -\omega^2 x$$

It is this equation that defines simple harmonic motion. It is important to note that:

- The frequency (f) is independent of the amplitude (A) of the oscillation
- The **maximum displacement** $x_{max} = \pm A$
- The **maximum velocity** $v_{max} = \pm \omega A$
- The **maximum acceleration** $a_{max} = -\omega^2 A$
- The **velocity** at any displacement can be re-written as $v = \pm\omega\sqrt{A^2 - x^2}$

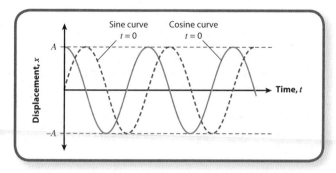

The above equations have been formulated on the basis that if $t = 0$ then $x = 0$ and the displacement follows a sine function. However, if at time $t = 0$ the displacement is $x = A$ then the displacement equation becomes $x = A\cos(\omega t)$ and the above equations for v and a are modified as shown in the table.

	If $x = 0$ when $t = 0$		If $x = A$ when $t = 0$	
Displacement	$x = A\sin(\omega t)$	$x = A\sin(2\pi ft)$	$x = A\cos(\omega t)$	$x = A\cos(2\pi ft)$
Velocity	$v = A\omega\cos(\omega t)$	$v = 2\pi fA\cos(2\pi ft)$	$v = A\omega\sin(\omega t)$	$v = 2\pi fA\sin(2\pi ft)$
Acceleration	$a = -\omega^2 A\sin(\omega t)$	$a = -4\pi^2 f^2 A\sin(2\pi ft)$	$a = -\omega^2 A\cos(\omega t)$	$a = -4\pi^2 f^2 A\cos(2\pi ft)$

The Restoring Force and Energy

A **freely oscillating** object has no external varying driving force acting on it other than the impulse that initiated its motion. It will therefore oscillate with a **constant amplitude**. The only force acting on it is the **restoring force**. Any frictional forces present would reduce the amplitude and cause the object to eventually stop oscillating. Throughout the motion there is a continuous transfer of energy, with **kinetic energy**

$$E_k \propto \left(A^2 - x^2\right)$$

being exchanged for **potential energy**

$$E_p \propto x^2$$

and vice versa. The type of potential energy depends on what is providing the restoring force.

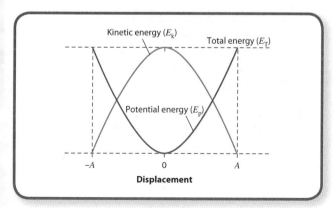

For a mass on the end of a **spring** it is the **elastic potential energy** (the energy stored in the spring

together with any gravitational potential energy) and for a mass on the end of a **pendulum** it is the **gravitational potential energy**. In both systems, as the object moves towards the midpoint, the restoring force does work on the object transferring potential energy to kinetic energy. At the midpoint the object's potential energy is zero but it possesses maximum kinetic energy. As the object reaches its greatest displacement, its kinetic energy becomes zero but it possesses maximum potential energy. The shape of the curves for the kinetic and potential energies are **parabolic** (both x^2-type functions), and the sum of the potential and kinetic energies, i.e. $E_T = E_k + E_p$, is called the **mechanical energy** of the system and remains constant throughout the motion (**conservation of energy**). For an object oscillating with a frequency f and amplitude A the energies involved for a displacement x are shown in the table.

	In terms of angular frequency	In terms of frequency of oscillation
Potential energy, E_p	$\frac{1}{2}m\omega^2 x^2$	$2m\pi^2 f^2 x^2$
Kinetic energy, E_k	$\frac{1}{2}m\omega^2(A^2 - x^2)$	$2m\pi^2 f^2(A^2 - x^2)$
Total energy, E_T	$\frac{1}{2}m\omega^2 A^2$	$2m\pi^2 f^2 A^2$

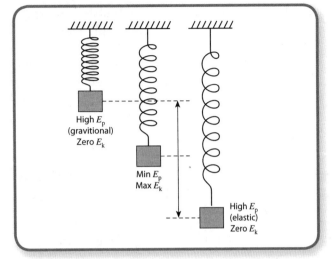

High E_p
(gravitional)
Zero E_k

Min E_p
Max E_k

High E_p
(elastic)
Zero E_k

SUMMARY

● **Simple harmonic motion occurs when the acceleration (or restoring force) on an object is directly proportional to its displacement from the equilibrium position and in a direction towards the equilibrium position**

● **The equation for simple harmonic motion is $a = -\omega^2 x = -(2\pi f)^2 x$; the negative sign indicates that a is in the opposite direction to x**

● **A mass on a spring and a simple pendulum are two examples of systems that can demonstrate simple harmonic motion**

● **The equations for the displacement x are given by a cosine or sine function, depending on whether $x = A$ or $x = 0$ when $t = 0$.**

● **A freely oscillating object has no external varying driving force acting on it and oscillates at a constant amplitude**

● **The total energy of a simple harmonic system is equal to the sum of the kinetic and potential energies**

● **The total energy is proportional to the square of the amplitude $E \propto A^2$**

QUICK TEST

1. Define what is meant by simple harmonic motion.

2. What is meant by 'restoring force' when an object oscillates with simple harmonic motion?

3. Give one equation that represents an object oscillating with simple harmonic motion.

4. What is angular velocity and how is it connected to frequency?

5. How is the period of oscillation defined?

6. The pendulum of a grandfather clock oscillates once every 2.2 s. Calculate the frequency and hence determine the acceleration when the pendulum is 60 mm from the midpoint.

7. An object oscillates with simple harmonic motion and its motion can be described by the equation $x = 0.16\sin(8\pi t)$. What is the amplitude and the period of the oscillations?

8. Use the equation in question 7 to calculate the displacement when (a) $t = 0.0625$ s (b) $t = 0.125$ s. (Note: calculator should be in radians mode.)

9. A body oscillates with simple harmonic motion at a frequency of 5 Hz and an amplitude of 2.5 cm. Calculate (a) the maximum velocity (b) the maximum acceleration.

10. An object of mass 0.02 kg is oscillating with simple harmonic motion at a frequency of 3.4 Hz and an amplitude of 8 cm. Calculate the potential energy when (a) $x = 0$ (b) $x = 8$ cm.

11. In the above example, calculate the kinetic energy of the object when (a) $x = 0$ (b) $x = 8$ cm (c) $x = 5$ cm.

PRACTICE QUESTIONS

1. Tides are generally sinusoidal and their oscillations can be modelled by simple harmonic motion. At one particular harbour, the time between consecutive high tides is 12 hours and the height difference between high tide and low tide is approximately 6.0 m. The mean sea level occurred at midnight followed by a high tide.

    a) Sketch a diagram to show the height of tides between midnight and 24 hours later. **[3 marks]**

    b) Calculate the angular frequency of the tide's motion. **[1 mark]**

    c) A small ship requires a minimum depth of 4.0 m to enter the harbour. Determine the time after midnight when the ship can start to enter the harbour. **[3 marks]**

    d) What is the velocity (rate of rise) of the tide at this time. Give your answer in m per hour. **[3 marks]**

2. A tuning fork is vibrating at 440 Hz. Each tip or prong of mass 0.0136 kg is vibrating with simple harmonic motion with an amplitude of 0.62 mm. At $t = 0$ the amplitude is zero.

    a) What is meant by simple harmonic motion? **[2 marks]**

    b) Write an equation for the displacement of the tuning fork prong as a function of its frequency. **[2 marks]**

    c) Calculate (i) the maximum velocity and (ii) the maximum acceleration of the tip of the prong. **[4 marks]**

    d) Determine the mechanical energy of the system. **[2 marks]**

    e) What type of vibration does the tuning fork undergo? **[1 mark]**

3. The graph shows the variation of kinetic energy with displacement of a particle of mass 0.85 kg undergoing simple harmonic motion.

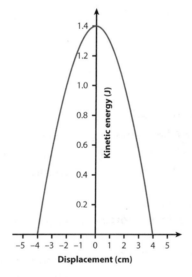

Use the graph to:

    a) determine the total energy of the particle. **[1 mark]**

    b) hence, find the maximum speed of the particle. **[3 marks]**

    c) determine the potential energy of the particle and hence calculate the period of oscillation. **[4 marks]**

Simple Harmonic Oscillators

Harmonic Oscillators

In its simplest form a **harmonic oscillator** is just a system that oscillates with **simple harmonic motion**. There are many systems in physics that are a good approximation to a harmonic oscillator and it is therefore a good starting point for solving their behaviour. In **classical mechanics** the simple pendulum is a good example, while in **quantum physics** the way atoms vibrate about their mean positions is another.

A Simple Mass–Spring Oscillator

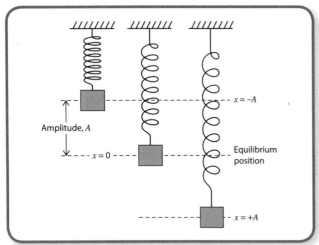

A mass vibrating with small oscillations at the end of a spring is a good example of a **simple harmonic oscillator**. The mass will extend the spring and, if left, will reach an equilibrium position where there is no net force acting on the mass. Displacing the mass from this equilibrium position by a small amount requires the spring to exert an **elastic restoring force** that obeys **Hooke's Law**; the motion exhibited is **sinusoidal** in time and the mass oscillates with simple harmonic motion. In this case the restoring force F is given by $F = -kx$, where k is the **spring constant** and x is the **displacement** from the equilibrium position. Provided that there is no energy loss due to friction, the mass will continue to oscillate. The acceleration of the mass is obtained from **Newton's Second Law** to give $a = \frac{F}{m} = -\frac{kx}{m}$ and this can be re-written in terms of the oscillating frequency f as $a = -\left(2\pi f\right)^2 x$ if $\left(2\pi f\right)^2 = \frac{k}{m}$.

Using this equation and making f the subject gives

$$f = \frac{1}{2\pi}\sqrt{\frac{k}{m}} \text{ and therefore } T = 2\pi\sqrt{\frac{m}{k}}$$

⬤ Adding extra mass increases the inertia of the system and the oscillations take longer and the frequency is reduced.
⬤ If the spring constant is less, i.e. a weaker spring, the oscillations take longer and the frequency is reduced.
⬤ The period is independent of the amplitude.

Carrying out an experiment to measure the oscillation time for various masses allows the spring constant k to be determined. This is achieved by plotting a graph of T^2 (on the y-axis) against m (on the x-axis), which should give a straight line with slope $\frac{4\pi^2}{k}$.

A Two-Spring Oscillator

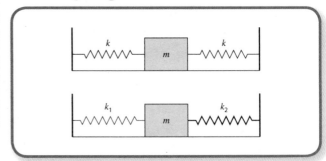

A mass can be connected between **two springs** with the same spring constant. In this situation the **restoring force** from the left-hand spring is $F_L = -kx$ and the restoring force from the right-hand spring is $F_R = -kx$, giving a net restoring force of $F_{net} = F_L + F_R = -2kx$. The acceleration can be found from $-2kx = ma$ and hence $a = -\frac{2kx}{m}$. If the system is oscillating with simple harmonic motion then $\omega = \sqrt{\frac{2k}{m}}$ and the period for the oscillations is given by $T = 2\pi\sqrt{\frac{m}{2k}}$. If the springs have different spring constants, say k_1 and k_2, then $T = 2\pi\sqrt{\frac{m}{k_1+k_2}}$. Copper ions in a crystal lattice vibrate in a similar way because the **interatomic forces** act in a similar way to the forces exerted by springs. For copper ions the spring constant is $\sim 200\,\mathrm{Nm^{-1}}$ and the mass is $10^{-24}\,\mathrm{kg}$. The frequency of oscillation is $\sim 10^{13}\,\mathrm{Hz}$ and the copper ions move at a maximum velocity of $\sim 630\,\mathrm{ms^{-1}}$.

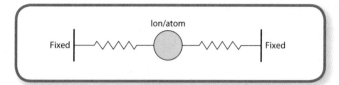

Fixed — Ion/atom — Fixed

The Simple Pendulum

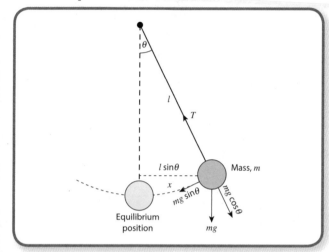

Equilibrium position

Mass, m

Another example of a harmonic oscillator is a mass attached to the end of a wire that is displaced from its equilibrium position, i.e. a **simple pendulum**. After it is released, the mass oscillates back and forth through the equilibrium position with simple harmonic motion. While the precise mathematical derivation is not needed, it is important to state that the derivation does require that the angle between the release position and the vertical does not exceed about 10° in order for the small angle approximation to be valid. If the angle is less than this then $a = -\frac{gx}{l} = -(2\pi f)^2 x$ as long as $(2\pi f)^2 = \frac{g}{l}$. This leads to a period of oscillation given by $T = 2\pi\sqrt{\frac{l}{g}}$. Note that:

- if l is increased then the time period also increases
- the period is independent of the amplitude
- when the mass passes through its equilibrium position, the tension in the wire acts directly upwards and the resulting force on the mass is given by $T - mg = \frac{mv^2}{l}$.

	Spring	**Pendulum**
Angular velocity (ω)	$\sqrt{\frac{k}{m}}$	$\sqrt{\frac{g}{l}}$
Period (T)	$2\pi\sqrt{\frac{m}{k}}$	$2\pi\sqrt{\frac{l}{g}}$

Carrying out an experiment to measure the oscillation time for varying length of wire allows the acceleration g due to gravity to be determined. This is achieved by plotting a graph of T^2 (on the y-axis) against l (on the x-axis), which should give a straight line with slope $\frac{4\pi^2}{g}$.

Quantum Harmonic Oscillator

A **quantum harmonic oscillator** is the quantum analogue of a classical oscillator and is an important model system in quantum physics. The expressions derived for the classical simple harmonic oscillator can also be used where the spring constant is replaced by a **bond force constant**, k, and the mass is replaced by a **reduced mass**, m_r, that depends on the masses in the diatomic molecule. This leads to the angular frequency being given by $\omega = \sqrt{\frac{k}{m_r}}$. The most important difference between the two systems is that the quantum case gives rise to a **zero-point vibration**, which implies that the molecules are never completely at rest even at absolute zero. The quantum oscillator also has numerous implications that aid our understanding of complex modes of vibration and in the theory of heat capacity.

In all cases above it has been assumed that the harmonic oscillator vibrates freely with no external forces acting on it. **Free vibration** is a condition where there are **no dissipative forces** (such as friction or drag) and **no periodic forces** acting on the system. The frequency of oscillation is then called the **natural frequency** of the system.

SUMMARY

- A **harmonic oscillator** is a system that oscillates with simple harmonic motion
- A **mass–spring system** is a simple example of a system that exhibits simple harmonic motion
- A **two-spring system** provides a model for the motion of atoms/ions in a rigid lattice
- A **simple harmonic oscillator** is a system that shows simple harmonic motion that has found application in many areas of physics
- The **harmonic oscillator** is a good representation of the **bonding** in a **crystal lattice**
- A **simple pendulum** undergoes simple harmonic motion provided that the displacement angle is less than 10°
- **Free vibrations** are vibrations without the influence of forced periodic vibrations or dissipative forces

QUICK TEST

1. Explain what is meant by a harmonic oscillator?

2. Why is a mass between two springs a good model for an atom/ion?

3. In both the simple pendulum and the mass–spring system the period is independent of what parameter?

4. What experiment can be used to determine the acceleration due to gravity, and why?

5. Calculate the period of a simple pendulum of length (a) 0.5 m (b) 1.0 m.

6. What would be the effect on the period if the simple pendulum were on the Moon?

7. A spring has a natural length of 30 cm. A mass of 0.3 kg is attached to the spring and it stretches 8.0 cm. Determine the spring constant.

8. In the above question, determine the period when the mass is displaced and set in simple harmonic motion.

9. A mass is tethered between two springs and displaced 10 cm before being released. The mass then oscillates with simple harmonic motion with a frequency of 0.8 Hz. Calculate the maximum velocity of the mass.

10. In the above question, determine the velocity of the mass when it is 7.0 cm from its equilibrium position.

11. The spring constant for an oxygen molecule is 1180 N m^{-1}. Calculate the frequency of vibration of an oxygen atom, given the mass as 2.66×10^{-26} kg.

PRACTICE QUESTIONS

1. A spring is attached to a fixed point and suspended vertically using a mass of 0.1 kg. The mass is pulled downwards a distance of 5 mm and then released. The spring constant is $40\,\mathrm{N\,m^{-1}}$.

   a) Calculate the extension produced in the spring. **[2 marks]**

   b) Assuming the spring undertakes simple harmonic motion, determine the period of oscillation and hence the frequency of oscillation. **[3 marks]**

   c) Calculate (i) the maximum velocity and (ii) the maximum acceleration of the spring. **[2 marks]**

   d) Determine the net force acting on the mass when it is 2 mm below the equilibrium position. **[1 mark]**

2. The bonding of copper ions in a crystal lattice can be modelled by a set of springs that connect the copper ions together, as shown in the figure. The mass of a copper ion is $1.2 \times 10^{-25}\,\mathrm{kg}$ and the spring constant of each of the interatomic 'bonds' is $220\,\mathrm{N\,m^{-1}}$.

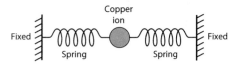

   a) Why are springs a good model for bonds between atoms? **[1 mark]**

   b) Calculate the frequency of vibration of a copper ion. **[3 marks]**

   c) If the amplitude of vibration of a copper ion is about $1.1 \times 10^{-11}\,\mathrm{m}$, determine (i) the maximum kinetic energy of a copper ion and (ii) its maximum speed of vibration. **[5 marks]**

3. A simple pendulum consists of a small mass of 0.15 kg attached to a thread of length l. The mass is then displaced from its equilibrium position through a height of 15 mm before being released. The mass oscillates with simple harmonic motion and the time recorded for 10 complete oscillations is 16.8 s.

   a) What is meant by simple harmonic motion? **[3 marks]**

   b) Determine the period of oscillation of the pendulum. **[1 mark]**

   c) Hence calculate the length of the thread. **[2 marks]**

   d) Determine the change in the potential energy of the mass before being released and hence calculate the maximum velocity of the mass during oscillation. **[3 marks]**

Forced Oscillations and Resonance

Forced Oscillations

Forced vibrations occur when there is an **external driving force** applied to the system. Without the driving force, the system would oscillate at its **natural frequency**; however, when an **external periodic force** is applied, the system undergoes **forced oscillations**. The response to this force depends on the frequency of this periodic force. The experimental set-up shown demonstrates the effect of applying an external periodic force to a system. Without the vibration generator, the frequency of the oscillations with the mass m and springs with spring constant k is $f = \frac{1}{2\pi}\sqrt{\frac{k}{m}}$. This frequency is called the **natural frequency** of the system and is independent of the amplitude of vibration. If this system is now coupled to the vibration generator and the frequency generated increases from zero through and past the natural frequency of the system, two key effects are observed:

- the **amplitude** of the oscillations increases rapidly and dramatically as the natural frequency is approached and decreases sharply once past the resonance condition
- the **phase difference** changes from zero at low frequencies to exactly $\frac{\pi}{2}$ at resonance and then to π beyond resonance. This phase change is continuous.

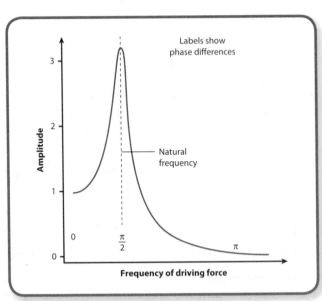

The change in amplitude is due to the mass gaining more and more energy from the driving system (vibration generator) and, at its natural frequency, the energy gained is a maximum and the system is said to be in **resonance**.

Resonance

Resonance occurs when the frequency at which an object is forced to vibrate is equal to the natural frequency of vibration of the object. The **amplitude of vibration** is a maximum at this frequency as the system is allowed to store and transfer energy between the object and driver. Resonance phenomena occur in many areas in physics where there are vibrations, such as acoustic resonance, nuclear magnetic resonance and mechanical resonance. More familiar examples of resonance include:

- **acoustic resonance** of musical instruments and the phenomenon of shattering a piece of crystal glass when a sound wave at the correct frequency (pitch) matches the natural frequency of the wineglass
- **mechanical resonance** is displayed when a playground swing resonates if the person pushing the swing does so in time with the natural frequency, thereby making the swing go higher and higher

to achieve maximum amplitude; the energy the swing absorbs is a maximum when the frequency of the driving force (push) is identical to the swing's natural frequency

● **electrical resonance** arises when radios and TVs are tuned to precise radio frequencies that match the selected station frequency.

Barton's Pendulum

The effect of resonance can be demonstrated using **Barton's pendulum**, a simple device connecting about six small but equal masses at the ends of threads of different lengths hanging from a supporting wire. A **single driver pendulum**, of generally greater mass, is adjusted to be the same length of one of the other pendulums. As the driver pendulum is displaced, the energy of the oscillation motion is transmitted along the support thread to the pendulum that has the same natural frequency as the driver pendulum but 90° out of phase with it.

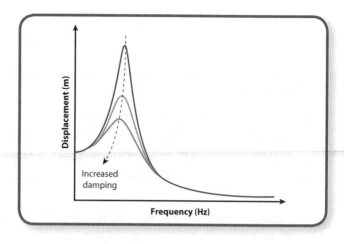

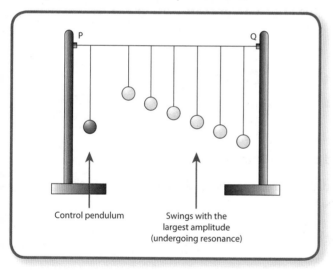

Control pendulum

Swings with the largest amplitude (undergoing resonance)

Effects of Damping

At resonance, the amplitude of vibration is a maximum and is limited only by the degree that the system is damped. **Damping** occurs in all real systems as any oscillating system loses energy to its surroundings through **frictional forces** such as air resistance. Other systems may be deliberately damped to either prevent them from oscillating or to reduce vibration and hence prevent resonance. The effects of increased damping on a system are to:

● **reduce the amplitude** of vibration at all frequencies
● **reduce the sharpness** at resonance and hence flatten the response to cover more frequencies
● **shift the resonance** peak towards lower frequencies.

Degrees of Damping

There are several degrees of damping and this depends on the application to which it is being applied. A system that is not damped would reflect a sinusoidal response to its displacement over time, showing a constant amplitude. **Light damping** gradually transfers energy to the surroundings and the amplitude of oscillation slowly diminishes in time. **Heavy damping** significantly reduces the amplitude towards zero in a much shorter time and perhaps only two or three periods of oscillation are seen. When only a quarter of a cycle or so is used to reduce the amplitude to zero, the system is said to be **critically damped**. This kind of damping is used in car suspension systems and in moving coil meters to avoid any oscillations and to return the system to its equilibrium condition in the shortest time possible. Beyond critical damping, a system is said to be **overdamped** if the time taken to reach zero amplitude is extended beyond a full period, for example heavy doors closing slowly to let people through.

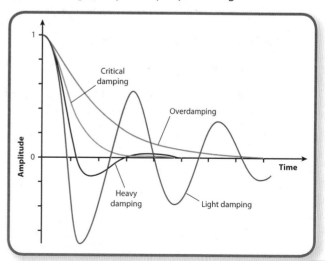

SUMMARY

- A forced frequency of vibration is the periodic frequency at which a object or mass is made to vibrate

- Resonance is a physical phenomenon that occurs when the frequency at which an object is being forced to vibrate (the periodic force) is equal to the object's natural frequency; there is a phase difference between the driving and driven systems of 90° ($\frac{\pi}{2}$)

- When an object or mass freely vibrates (i.e. no external or periodic forces acting), it does so at its own natural frequency

- Oscillations or vibrations that diminish with time are said to be damped due to dissipative forces that reduce the total energy of the system

- Damped oscillations range from light damping to overdamping

- Critical damping reduces the displacement or amplitude to zero in the minimum time possible without any oscillations

- At resonance, increased amounts of damping move the resonance conditions to lower frequencies

- Barton's pendulum is a device that demonstrates the effects of resonance using a set of pendulums and a driving pendulum

QUICK TEST

1. Define what is meant by a natural frequency.

2. What is the difference between a free vibration and a forced vibration?

3. When a system is oscillating at its maximum amplitude, what is the phase difference between the displacement and the periodic force causing resonance?

4. What is meant by critical damping?

5. What is resonance and when does it occur?

6. Give two examples of resonance in a physics context.

7. What is meant by a damping force?

8. Give an example of where critical damping is used.

9. A simple mass–spring system undergoes simple harmonic motion. A large circular sheet of negligible mass is then placed on the mass and lies horizontally. Describe the nature of the oscillations.

10. What is meant by the term 'overdamping' and give an example.

PRACTICE QUESTIONS

1. a) State what is meant by light damping, heavy damping and critical damping. **[3 marks]**

A person of mass 65 kg is undertaking a bungee jump from a bridge. They are attached to an elastic nylon rope of length 10 m and spring constant of 200 N m^{-1}; the other end is attached to a bridge and the initial amplitude of oscillation is 8.6 m.

b) Assuming that the motion can be described as simple harmonic, calculate the period and frequency of the oscillations. **[2 marks]**

c) Determine the maximum velocity and maximum acceleration during one of these initial oscillations. **[2 marks]**

d) The oscillations encountered by a bungee jumper do not continue in this way and eventually the jumper comes to rest in the equilibrium position. Determine the distance of the jumper below the bridge in this position. **[3 marks]**

e) Explain the processes that occur from the initial jump to when the jumper finally stops oscillating. **[3 marks]**

2. Infrared radiation is strongly absorbed by carbon monoxide molecules. As a result of this absorption, the oscillations of the carbon atoms or oxygen atoms increase significantly, depending on their orientation as they sit on a platinum surface.

a) What is the name given to this phenomenon? **[1 mark]**

b) What condition must be fulfilled for it to occur? **[2 marks]**

c) The range of wavelengths of infrared radiation extends from 2.0 μm to 20 μm but the above phenomenon only occurs at 2.7 μm. Determine the frequency of this particular value of infrared radiation. **[1 mark]**

d) If the mass of a carbon atom is 2.0×10^{-26} kg, determine the stiffness of the carbon monoxide bond, assuming that it can be modelled by a spring. **[3 marks]**

Thermal Energy

Heat, Temperature and Thermal Equilibrium

Temperature, T, is a simple way of expressing the 'hotness' of a body using a numerical scale. This may involve a thermometer based on degrees Celsius or Fahrenheit but, in thermal physics and particularly thermodynamics, the **absolute temperature** scale is used. This is based on the **kelvin scale** where 0 K is **absolute zero** and equivalent to −273°C; an interval in temperature of 1°C is identical to 1 K. Even at absolute zero, atoms have a small amount of energy, including thermal energy, called their **zero point energy**. **Heat** is the amount of **energy transferred** from one body to another as a result of a difference in temperature. Heat (often referred to as **thermal energy**, ΔQ) flows from hot bodies to colder bodies when in contact until they are at the same temperature, called **thermal equilibrium**. Under these conditions, the thermal energy lost by one body must equal the thermal energy gained by the other body.

Internal Energy and Thermodynamics

The **internal energy**, U, of a system is one of the most fundamental properties of **thermodynamics**, a topic that looks at the large-scale or macroscopic behaviour of a system. The internal energy is the sum of the random **kinetic** and **potential energies** of all the individual particles (atoms or molecules) that make up the system (the kinetic energy component may also include rotational and vibrational energy, as in the case of molecular gases). As explored later, the kinetic energy depends on the temperature of the system whereas the potential energy depends on the **intermolecular forces** between particles and hence on the state of the system (e.g. liquid/solid). The internal energy of a system can therefore change as a result of heat being added or taken away from the system. The **first law of thermodynamics** states that an increase in internal energy of a system (ΔU) is equal to the heat added (ΔQ) minus the work done by the system (ΔW), i.e. $\Delta U = \Delta Q - \Delta W$. This interplay between heat energy and work done lies at the heart of thermodynamics. A change in the mean kinetic energy of a system (a microscopic property) can therefore be directly related to its temperature (a macroscopic and measurable property) of the system.

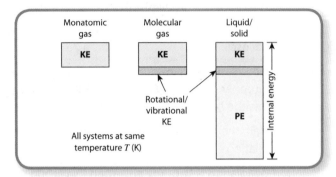

All systems at same temperature T (K)

Specific Heat Capacity

When a system (e.g. a gas in a cylinder) is heated, the gas may expand and do work against an external pressure. If the gas is not allowed to expand, its internal energy may increase, leading to a change in temperature. This change in temperature may also result in a change of state. The magnitude of the change in temperature, ΔT, is dictated by several macroscopic properties.

The amount of thermal energy, ΔQ, required to raise the temperature of a substance depends on its mass, m, the temperature rise, ΔT, and the nature of the substance or material itself. This property of a material which dictates how much energy is needed is called the **specific heat capacity**, c, of that substance. This means

$$\text{specific heat capacity} = \frac{\text{heat supplied (J)}}{\text{mass (kg)} \times \text{temperature rise (K)}}$$

or $c = \frac{\Delta Q}{m \Delta T}$. This is often expressed in the form $\Delta Q = mc\Delta T$.

Material	c (J kg^{-1} K^{-1})
lead	130
copper	390
aluminium	910
ice	2200
water	4200

The SI unit of specific heat capacity is $J\,kg^{-1}\,K^{-1}$, although often the more convenient unit $kJ\,kg^{-1}\,K^{-1}$ is used. The table shows specific heat capacities of some common materials. Note that ice and water are significantly different because they are in two very different states of matter. When more than one material is involved, for example heating water in a metal container (as in a calorimeter), the total heat capacity of the water and the metal container is needed. For a calorimeter of mass m_{cal} and specific heat capacity c_{cal} with water of mass m_{water} with specific heat capacity c_{water}, the total heat capacity is $C = m_{cal}c_{cal} + m_{water}c_{water}$ and the amount of thermal energy required is then $\Delta Q = C\Delta T$. This transfer of energy as heat occurs up to the melting point in solids and the boiling point in liquids. Beyond these limits, there is a change in state but without a corresponding change in temperature.

Measuring Specific Heat Capacities

The specific heat capacity of a solid can be determined using an electrical method. A heater within the material supplies a known amount of electrical energy given by current $(I) \times$ heater p.d. $(V) \times$ heating time (t), or IVt. A thermometer within the material is used to measure the temperature rise ΔT. Assuming that the material is well insulated from heat loss to the surroundings, $mc\Delta T = IVt$ and hence $c = \frac{IVt}{m\Delta T}$. It is common practice to measure the temperature at regular time intervals and to plot a graph of T against t to determine the change in temperature.

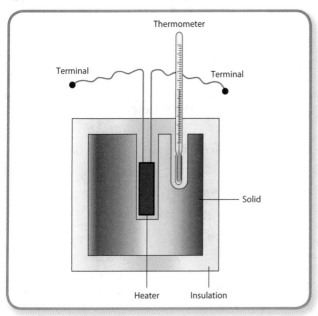

In the case of a liquid, a copper calorimeter of known mass and specific heat capacity is used and a similar set-up adopted as that used for a solid. Assuming that there is no heat loss to the surroundings, $IVt = m_1c_1\Delta T + m_{cal}c_{cal}\Delta T$, and hence c_1 can be determined.

Specific Latent Heat

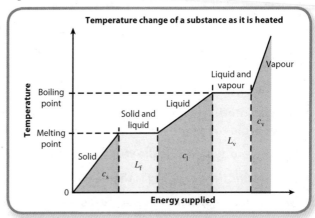

Temperature change of a substance as it is heated

At both the **melting point** and **boiling point** of a substance, the thermal energy supplied is used to **change the state** of the substance without a change in temperature. This thermal energy is called **latent heat** ('hidden' heat) and is given by $\Delta Q = mL$. The heat required to melt a unit mass of material at its melting point is called the **specific latent heat of fusion**, L_f. No temperature change occurs during a change of state as the energy is instead used to make or break bonds, for example to separate the bonds in a solid so that the substance becomes a liquid. The amount of energy required during this stage is

$$\text{specific latent heat} = \frac{\text{heat transferred (J)}}{\text{mass (kg)}}$$

or $L_f = \frac{\Delta Q}{m}$ and $\Delta Q = mL_f$. Similarly, the amount of heat required to vaporise a unit mass at its boiling point is called the **specific latent heat of vaporisation**, L_v. In this case, the amount of energy required is $\Delta Q = mL_v$. Both specific latent heats have units of $J\,kg^{-1}$, or often $kJ\,kg^{-1}$. The specific latent heat of a substance is therefore the sum of the energy needed to increase the potential energy of its particles and to do work against external pressure as the substance expands, i.e. leading to an increase in internal energy.

	Melting point (°C)	Specific latent heat of fusion, L_f (kJ kg^{-1})	Boiling point (°C)	Specific latent heat of vaporisation, L_v (kJ kg^{-1})
oxygen	−219	14	−183	210
water	0	334	100	2260
iron	1810	289	3020	6340

SUMMARY

- **Heat** is the amount of energy transferred as a result of a difference in temperature; **temperature** is a measure of how 'hot' a system is and is based on a numerical scale

- The **absolute** or **kelvin scale** of temperature uses absolute zero (−273.15°C) as its lower fixed point

- The **internal energy** of a system is the sum of both the randomly distributed kinetic and potential energies of all the individual atoms or molecules that make up the system

- **Thermodynamics** is the study of energy transfer by heat and work

- **Specific heat capacity** is the heat needed to raise the temperature of 1 kg of a material by 1 K

- An **electrical method** can be used to determine specific heat capacities by raising a known mass through a measured or known temperature difference

- The **specific latent heat** is the quantity of heat absorbed or released when a material changes its physical state at constant temperature; units of specific latent heat are J kg^{-1}

- The **specific latent heat of fusion** occurs at the melting point, and the **specific latent heat of vaporisation** occurs at the boiling point

QUICK TEST

1. What is meant by specific heat capacity?

2. What are the units of specific heat capacity?

3. Give the equation for the specific heat capacity of a material and explain the symbols used.

4. What is meant by thermal equilibrium?

5. How much thermal energy is required to raise the temperature of 1.2 kg of water from 50°C to 100°C? [$c_{water} = 4200$ J kg^{-1} K^{-1}]

6. What is meant by the term 'specific latent heat' and define those at the melting point and the boiling point of a material.

7. What is the equation for determining the amount of energy required through latent heat?

8. What is the energy required to transform 0.5 kg of ice into water? [$L_{ice} = 334$ kJ kg^{-1}]

9. A pan of boiling water is boiled for a further 25 seconds on a 2.7 kW hot plate before being removed from the heat. Neglecting heat losses and the specific heat capacity of the pan, determine how much water is converted into steam during these 25 seconds. [$L_v = 2260$ kJ kg^{-1}]

PRACTICE QUESTIONS

[Use the specific heat and specific latent heat values in the tables opposite.]

1. a) What is meant by the specific heat capacity of a solid? **[2 marks]**

An aluminium pan is being used to bring some water up to its boiling point from room temperature of 22°C.

  b) Calculate the energy required to heat a pan of mass 0.25 kg from room temperature to 100°C. **[3 marks]**

  c) Calculate the energy needed to heat 1.75 kg of water from room temperature to 100°C. **[2 marks]**

  d) Determine the time (in minutes) required to bring a pan of water to the boil if it is placed on a 2.5 kW hot plate. **[4 marks]**

  e) What key assumption is made in arriving at your answer in part **d)**? **[1 mark]**

2. a) Explain what is meant by the specific latent heat. **[2 marks]**

Ice cubes of total mass 40 g are taken out of a freezer at −8°C and placed into a glass of water of mass 250 g at room temperature (23°C).

  b) Determine how much energy is needed to bring the ice cubes up to 0°C. **[2 marks]**

  c) Calculate the energy needed to then turn the ice cubes into water. **[2 marks]**

  d) The water in the glass reduces to a temperature T after the ice cubes have been added. Determine the temperature T. **[6 marks]**

3. The specific heat capacity of a block of metal was measured using a known quantity of energy delivered by an electrical heater. The figure shows the results of the measurements taken every minute.

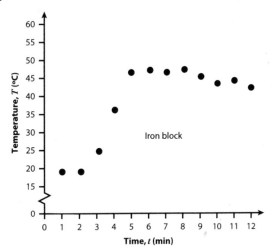

  a) Draw appropriate lines through the measurements that allow the change in temperature to be determined. **[2 marks]**

  b) What is the value of ΔT in kelvin? **[2 marks]**

  c) The electrical heater used a stabilised 12.0 V power supply delivering 4 A and was used for only 5 minutes before being switched off. Determine the amount of energy supplied to the metal block. **[2 marks]**

  d) If the metal block had a mass of 0.954 kg, calculate the specific heat capacity of the block. **[2 marks]**

  e) Suggest two experimental factors that would lead to possible errors in determining the specific heat capacity of the metal. **[2 marks]**

Ideal Gases

An Ideal Gas

A monatomic gas is composed of a large collection of particles (molecules) of the same single atom that are rapidly moving about, colliding with each other and with the side of the container that holds them together. The **internal energy** of a gas is the sum of both the randomly distributed **kinetic energies** as well as the **potential energies** (i.e. energies associated with the **intermolecular forces**) of all the individual atoms or molecules that make up the gas. In an ideal gas these intermolecular forces are assumed to be zero as the molecular distances are large. This is a valid assumption as many real gases (monatomic, diatomic, …) show behaviour that is very close to an ideal gas. The quantity of a gas is usually expressed not in terms of **molecular mass**, m, but in the number of **moles**, n, that the gas contains. 1 mole of any substance contains the same number of molecules, called the **Avogadro constant**, i.e. $N_A = 6.02 \times 10^{23}$ molecules mol^{-1}. The number of moles of a gas is then $n = \frac{N}{N_A}$, where N is the total number of molecules in the gas. Molecular mass is related to the Avogadro constant through the **molar mass**, M_m, which is the mass of one mole (N_A) of molecules of a substance, and is $M_m = N_A m$. For example, the molar mass of nitrogen is 0.028 kg and of helium is 0.004 kg. The physical state of a fixed mass of gas can be described by three physical quantities: pressure, temperature and volume, via a series of laws.

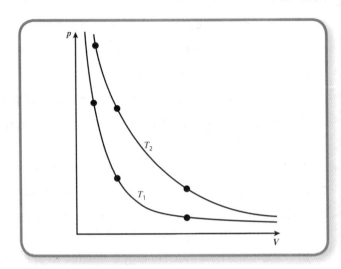

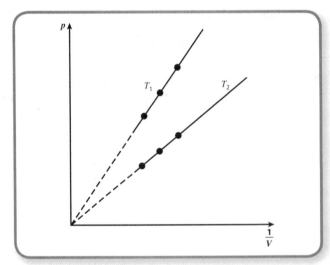

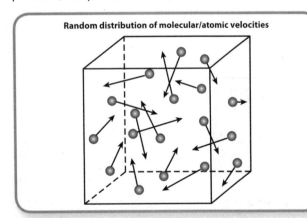

Random distribution of molecular/atomic velocities

Boyle's Law

When a gas is placed under pressure, its volume decreases; for a fixed mass of an ideal gas at constant temperature, its volume is inversely proportional to

its pressure, i.e. $p \propto \frac{1}{V}$, and this is known as Boyle's Law. This is often expressed as

$$pV = \text{constant}$$

A plot of p against $\frac{1}{V}$ gives a straight line. All of the points on the curve or line are at the same temperature. Changing the temperature gives a set of new curves (lines) and these are called **isothermal** curves or lines. The higher the temperature, the further the isothermal curves are from the origin, e.g. $T_2 > T_1$. Because $pV = \text{constant}$ it follows that, for a change in either the pressure or the volume, the new value of the other property can be found using the equation $p_1 V_1 = p_2 V_2$.

Charles' Law

When the pressure remains constant, the volume of a fixed mass of an ideal gas is directly proportional to the temperature, i.e. $V \propto T$, a relationship known as **Charles' Law**. The gradient of the straight line changes if there is a different constant pressure, a different amount of gas, or a different gas. However, in all cases the volume of gas becomes zero at a unique temperature value called **absolute zero**; this is precisely $-273.15°C$ ($-273°C$ is taken as an appropriate value to use in numerical calculations). Plotting a V–T graph with T now as an **absolute temperature** in kelvin gives a straight line passing through the origin and it is this relationship that defines Charles' Law:

$$\frac{V}{T} = \text{constant}$$

The more useful equation $\frac{V_1}{T_1} = \frac{V_2}{T_2}$ can be used when values of volume and temperature change.

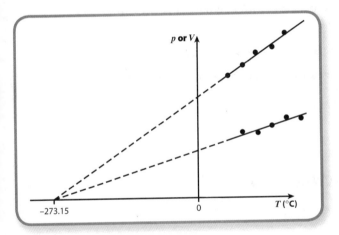

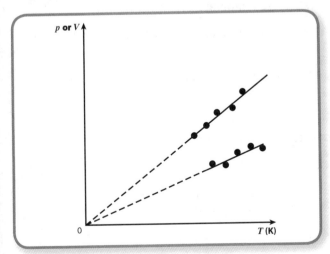

The Pressure Law

At constant volume, the pressure of a gas is directly proportional to its temperature, i.e. $p \propto T$. A similar graph to that used above for Charles' Law gives an intercept value at absolute zero. This **pressure law** is usually expressed as

$$\frac{p}{T} = \text{constant}$$

where T is the absolute temperature in kelvin. Using the equation $\frac{p_1}{T_1} = \frac{p_2}{T_2}$ provides a suitable method for evaluating new pressures or temperatures.

The Ideal Gas Equation

All three of the empirical gas equations above can be combined into one equation called the **Ideal Gas Equation** and given by

$$\frac{pV}{T} = \text{constant}$$

The 'constant' in this equation is dependent on the amount of gas used and hence on the number of moles, n. In this case, the equation becomes $\frac{pV}{nT} = \text{constant}$. This new 'constant' has the same value for all gases, i.e. it is a universal constant and is known as the **molar gas constant**, R. Its numerical value and SI unit are $R = 8.31\,\text{JK}^{-1}\text{mol}^{-1}$. The ideal gas equation (sometimes also referred to as the **equation of state**) can therefore be expressed as

$$pV = nRT$$

When one of the parameters changes, the equation $\frac{p_1 V_1}{n_1 T_1} = \frac{p_2 V_2}{n_2 T_2}$ can be used.

The above ideal gas equation has been derived empirically through the three gas laws and is a very good approximation as to how real gases behave. It is particularly valid for gases at low pressure or high temperature as the assumption of zero intermolecular forces becomes even more valid.

Boltzmann constant

The number of moles in a gas is given by $n = \frac{N}{N_A}$. Inserting this into the ideal gas equation gives $pV = N\left(\frac{R}{N_A}\right)T$. The ratio $\frac{R}{N_A}$ is the ratio of two fundamental constants and this new ratio k (also written as k_B) yields another fundamental constant in physics called the **Boltzmann constant**. The value of the Boltzmann constant is 1.38×10^{-23} JK^{-1}. In effect, the Boltzmann constant is just the gas constant for one molecule of gas. Rewriting the ideal gas equation in terms of the Boltzmann constant gives yet another useful version of this equation, i.e.

$$pV = NkT$$

It is this form of the ideal gas equation that is commonly referred to as the **equation of state**.

SUMMARY

- The absolute temperature scale is based on kelvins, where a change of 1 K equals a change of 1°C
- Absolute zero is 0 K or −273°C (−273.15°C)
- For a fixed mass of an ideal gas, Boyle's Law states that pV = constant for constant temperature
- For a fixed mass of an ideal gas, Charles' Law states that $\frac{V}{T}$ = constant at constant pressure
- For a fixed mass of an ideal gas, the pressure law states that $\frac{p}{T}$ = constant at constant volume
- All of the laws apply to an ideal gas
- An ideal gas is a gas that is modelled by ignoring any intermolecular forces
- The ideal gas equation combines all three laws to give $pV = nRT$, where R is the molar gas constant
- The equation of state involves the Boltzmann constant, where $pV = NkT$
- In all applications of the laws covered, the temperature should be expressed as an absolute temperature in kelvin

QUICK TEST

1. What is an ideal gas?

2. What is the temperature of a room at 22°C in terms of absolute temperature?

3. What is Charles' Law and what is plotted in order to obtain a straight-line graph that passes through the origin? Give the units associated with each variable.

4. The pressure of a gas is 2×10^5 Pa and the volume is 4.5 m^3. What is the new pressure if the volume is decreased to 0.6 m^3 at constant temperature?

5. The pressure of a gas is 1.5×10^5 Pa and its temperature is 300 K. The gas is heated and the pressure rises at constant volume to 1.8×10^5 Pa. Determine the new temperature of the gas.

6. How is a mole of a gas related to the Avogadro constant?

7. What is the mass of one mole of nitrogen-28?

8. What is the ideal gas equation?

9. Under what conditions does the ideal gas equation apply?

10. A flask contains 0.0004 kg of nitrogen gas. How many moles does it contain? (Use answer to question **7**.)

11. Calculate the number of nitrogen molecules in the flask given in question 10. [$R = 8.31 \, \text{JK}^{-1}\text{mol}^{-1}$]

12. A helium balloon has a volume of 2.1 m³ when released outside when the temperature is 293 K and pressure 1×10^5 Pa. When it reaches a particular altitude, the volume is 18 m³ and the temperature is 264 K. Calculate the new pressure in the balloon.

PRACTICE QUESTIONS

1. **a)** What is meant by the term 'ideal gas'?   **[1 mark]**

   b) A cylinder of propane gas has a volume of 0.1 m³ at a temperature of 25°C. If the pressure in the cylinder is 2.4×10^5 Pa, how many moles of propane gas are in the cylinder?   **[2 marks]**

   c) Determine the number of molecules of propane gas in the cylinder.   **[1 mark]**

   d) The cylinder is now moved into an environment where the outside temperature is −8°C. Calculate the pressure in the cylinder in this new environment.   **[3 marks]**

   e) The release valve is used to release propane gas at this temperature. What term is used to describe a change at constant temperature.   **[1 mark]**

2. **a)** For the ideal gas equation $pV = nRT$, explain what each of these symbols represents and give their SI units.   **[3 marks]**

   b) While non-SI units can be used for p and V, the units of T cannot be in degrees Celsius. With reference to one of the gas laws, explain why.   **[2 marks]**

   c) A car tyre when inflated to a pressure of 220 kPa at 290 K has a volume of 1.2×10^{-2} m³. Assuming that the air in the tyre behaves as an ideal gas, calculate the number of moles of air molecules.   **[2 marks]**

   d) If the molar mass of air is 2.9×10^{-2} kg, determine (i) the mass of air in the tyre and (ii) the density of air in the tyre.   **[3 marks]**

3. At sea level the atmospheric pressure is 1.0×10^5 Pa at an ambient temperature of 300 K. At altitude, both the pressure and temperature decrease so that at the height of Everest (8800 m) the pressure is 2.1×10^4 Pa and the temperature is 270 K.

   a) Calculate the number of moles of air in 1 m³ of air at (i) sea level and (ii) the summit of Everest.   **[2 marks]**

   b) Determine the number of air molecules per cubic metre at sea level.   **[1 mark]**

   c) The key components of air are oxygen (22%) and nitrogen (78%). How many more molecules of oxygen per cubic metre are there at sea level compared with the summit of Everest. Give your answer as a percentage difference.   **[3 marks]**

The Kinetic Theory of Gases

Brownian Motion

Molecules in a gas are too small to be observed individually but their effect can be seen in the behaviour of smoke particles observed under a microscope. The **erratic** and **random motion** seen in the smoke particles is due to each particle colliding with a gas molecule; the smoke particle's random behaviour reflects the impact forces of the gas molecules, which alter its direction and magnitude. This particular type of motion is called **Brownian motion** and it was first observed in the behaviour of pollen grains in water by Robert Brown. Visualising atoms and molecules as perfectly hard spheres that collide but otherwise do not interact with each other allowed Newton's laws of motion to be applied to the collisions, which led eventually to the gas laws outlined earlier.

The Kinetic Theory of Gases

The kinetic theory of gases is based on the notion that starting from a purely microscopic picture of matter, in which particles obey Newton's laws of motion, eventually leads to a macroscopic description of the way 'real' gases behave. The model that was developed, called the **kinetic theory of gases**, is based on several underlying assumptions or postulates:

- A gas comprises a very large number of identical molecules
- The molecules obey Newton's laws of motion
- Any collisions are treated as elastic collisions (i.e. no loss of energy) and the interaction time is negligible
- The size of the molecules is much smaller than the mean distance between molecules
- Intermolecular forces can be neglected
- The velocities and directions of the molecules are taken as random.

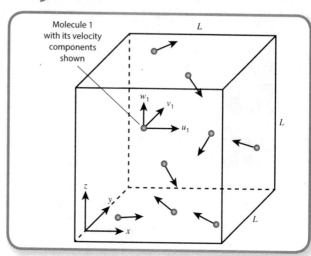

The Derivation of Pressure in One Dimension

The key features of the kinetic theory can be derived from a consideration of a gas contained in a cubic box of side length L. For a single gas molecule of mass m travelling at a velocity u_1 hitting one side of the container, there is a momentum change resulting from the reflection that is normal to the wall. Because momentum is a vector quantity, direction is important, so that the change in momentum $\Delta(mu) = mu_1 - (-mu_1) = 2mu_1$.

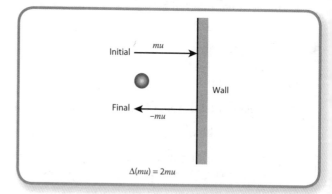

$$\Delta(mu) = 2mu$$

The total momentum change per second is therefore the change of momentum for a single molecule multiplied by the number of collisions per second. As a molecule will hit the wall again after it has travelled to the other side of the box and back again (a distance of $2L$), the time for this will be $\frac{2L}{u_1}$. Hence, the number of collisions per second will be given by $\frac{u_1}{2L}$. Therefore,

momentum change = $2mu_1 \times$ number of collisions
per second   per second

$$= 2mu_1 \times \frac{u_1}{2L} = \frac{mu_1^2}{L}$$

The **rate of change of momentum** is defined as a **force**. The force acting on one side wall by a number of molecules travelling with a set of random velocities is then given by

$$F = \frac{mu_1^2}{L} + \frac{mu_2^2}{L} + \frac{mu_3^2}{L} + \dots$$
$$= \frac{m\left(u_1^2 + u_2^2 + u_3^2 + \dots\right)}{L}$$

This collection of random velocities of say N molecules can be defined by just one velocity called the **mean square speed**, so that

$$\overline{u^2} = \frac{\left(u_1^2 + u_2^2 + u_3^2 + \dots + u_N^2\right)}{N}$$

and hence,

$$F = \frac{Nm\overline{u^2}}{L}$$

The pressure exerted by the gas at this end wall is $\frac{force}{area}$, i.e.

$$p = \frac{force}{area} = \frac{\left(\frac{Nm\overline{u^2}}{L}\right)}{L^2} = \frac{Nm\overline{u^2}}{L^3} = \frac{Nm\overline{u^2}}{V}$$

where V is the volume of the container (a cube).

Pressure in Three Dimensions

Extending the above treatment into three dimensions requires velocities not only along the direction of u but also along the other two perpendicular directions v and w. Using Pythagoras' Theorem gives $c_1^2 = u_1^2 + v_1^2 + w_1^2$ and treating all N particles in the same way allows an overall **mean square speed** to be defined as $\overline{c^2} = \overline{u^2} + \overline{v^2} + \overline{w^2}$. Since all particles are moving randomly, there is no special direction and so $\overline{u^2} = \overline{v^2} = \overline{w^2}$ or $\overline{c^2} = 3\overline{u^2}$. The equation for pressure above now takes the form

$$p = \frac{Nm\overline{c^2}}{3V} \quad \text{or} \quad pV = \frac{1}{3}Nm\overline{c^2}$$

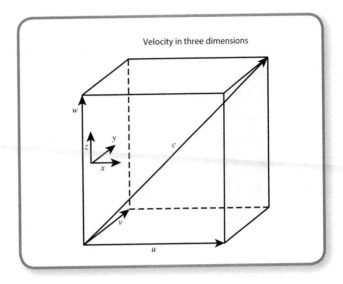

Velocity in three dimensions

Nm is the **total mass** of the gas inside the box and thus the **density of the gas** inside the box is given by $\rho = \frac{Nm}{V}$ so that $p = \frac{1}{3}\rho\overline{c^2}$. The mean square speed $\overline{c^2}$ has units of $m^2\,s^{-2}$ and represents the square of the speed of the 'average' molecule in the gas. To obtain this 'average' or mean speed, the square root of this speed is required; this is more commonly referred to as the **root mean square speed** or c_{rms}, i.e. $c_{rms} = \sqrt{\overline{c^2}}$ with units of $m\,s^{-1}$. Often the equation derived above is stated using this form, i.e. $pV = \frac{1}{3}Nmc_{rms}^2$. When using the ideal gas equation, it is often necessary to insert a value for the **molecular mass**, m.

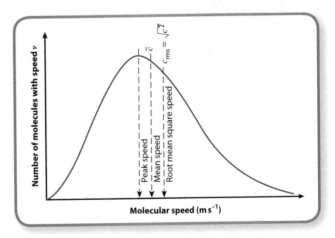

SUMMARY

- **Brownian motion** is the visible but erratic and random motion of small particles, such as smoke particles, caused by collisions with air molecules
- The **kinetic theory of gases** describes the macroscopic behaviour of gases from a microscopic picture based on Newton's laws of motion
- The kinetic theory of gases assumes that the **intermolecular forces** between molecules is zero
- There are several further assumptions or postulates in deriving the kinetic model, including **elastic collisions** with the walls of the container and **negligible collisions times**
- In three dimensions, the kinetic theory gives the equation $pV = \frac{1}{3}Nm\overline{c^2}$
- The **root mean square speed** is defined by $c_{rms} = \sqrt{\overline{c^2}}$
- The kinetic model can also be expressed in terms of the **gas density** as $p = \frac{1}{3}\rho c_{rms}^2$
- **Molecular mass, molar mass** and the Avogadro constant are related by $M_m = N_A m$

QUICK TEST

1. What is Brownian motion?

2. Give three assumptions used in the kinetic theory of gases.

3. What is the change in momentum of a molecule of mass m travelling at a speed v when it hits the wall of a container at $90°$?

4. Why is the root mean square speed rather than just the mean speed used in the kinetic theory of gases?

5. What equation connects the pressure with the root mean square speed?

6. What happens to the temperature if the value of the root mean square speed of a gas increases?

7. Four molecules in a gas have speeds of $320 \, m \, s^{-1}$, $375 \, m \, s^{-1}$, $225 \, m \, s^{-1}$ and $420 \, m \, s^{-1}$. Calculate (a) the mean speed and (b) the root mean square speed.

8. What is the effect on the root mean square speed of nitrogen molecules if the pressure is increased at constant temperature?

9. Calculate the rms speed of air particles if the density of air is $1.25 \, kg \, m^{-3}$ and the air pressure is $1.0 \times 10^5 \, Pa$.

10. Helium gas is contained in a volume of $0.00035 \, m^3$ at a pressure of $2.8 \times 10^5 \, Pa$. If there are 1.4×10^{22} helium molecules in the container each with a mass of $6.6 \times 10^{-27} \, kg$, determine the rms speed of the helium molecules to 2 s.f.

PRACTICE QUESTIONS

1. a) The kinetic theory of an ideal gas leads to the derived equation

$$pV = \frac{1}{3}Nmc_{rms}^2$$

Explain what each symbol in the above equation represents. **[3 marks]**

b) Why is it called the 'kinetic theory' of gases? **[2 marks]**

c) State two further assumption used in the derivation of the above equation. **[2 marks]**

d) Describe how the above equation can be used to explain how it is consistent with Boyle's Law. **[3 marks]**

2. A single molecule of a gas of mass m is moving in a cubic box of length L with a velocity u. The molecules collide elastically with the end face and at right angles to the face.

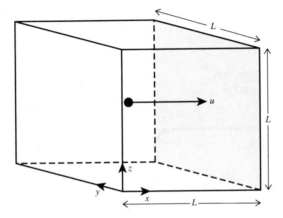

a) Explain what is meant by 'elastic collisions'. **[1 mark]**

b) Show that the time between collisions with the end face is $\Delta t = \frac{2L}{u}$. **[2 marks]**

c) Determine the change in momentum per collision and explain your reasoning. **[3 marks]**

d) Show that for a box containing N molecules the mean force F on the end face is $F = \frac{Nmu^2}{L}$ **[3 marks]**

e) Hence, derive an expression for the pressure on this end face. **[2 marks]**

f) A full derivation gives $pV = \frac{1}{3}Nmc_{rms}^2$. What other considerations have been made to arrive at this equation? **[4 marks]**

3. A sample of a gas is enclosed in a cylinder at a pressure of 1.4×10^5 Pa. The volume of the cylinder is $0.06\,m^3$ and there are 1.4×10^{25} molecules of gas with a root mean square speed of $392\,m\,s^{-1}$.

a) Calculate the mass of one molecule of gas. **[2 marks]**

b) Hence show that the density of the gas in the cylinder is approximately $2.7\,kg\,m^{-3}$. **[3 marks]**

c) If the pressure of the gas remains constant but the density is doubled, explain what the effect is on the root mean square speed. **[2 marks]**

d) Describe what would happen, in terms of the kinetic model, if the pressure became extremely high. **[4 marks]**

Energy and Temperature

Molecular Speeds

The molecules in an ideal gas have a continuous spread of speeds – some molecules travel very fast while others travel more slowly. The speed of any individual molecule also changes continually as it collides with other molecules and with the walls of the container. Provided the temperature remains constant, a typical distribution of molecular speed is shown in the diagram below (sometimes referred to as a **Boltzmann distribution**). As the **temperature** of the gas **increases**,

- the root mean square speed of the molecules increases
- the maximum molecular speed increases
- the distribution of molecular speeds become flatter and broader.

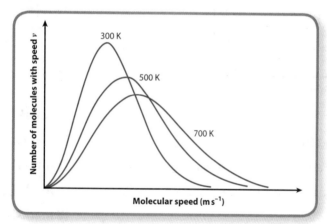

The **root mean square speed** c_{rms} is defined in the following way:

$$c_{rms} = \sqrt{\frac{\left(c_1^2 + c_2^2 + \ldots + c_N^2\right)}{N}}$$

where $c_1, c_2, \ldots, c_N$ represent the speeds of the individual molecules and N is the number of molecules in the gas. This is not the same as the mean speed, $\bar{c}$, which is the sum of the individual molecular speeds divided by the number of molecules. However, it should be understood that the **mean velocity** of molecules in a gas as a whole is zero.

The Kinetic Theory Equation

For an ideal gas consisting of N identical molecules, each of mass m, within a container of volume V, the pressure p of the gas can be calculated from the kinetic theory by

$$pV = \frac{1}{3} Nmc_{rms}^2$$

If the temperature remains constant and the volume is reduced then the time between collisions and impacts on the container walls is also reduced. As a consequence, there are more collisions taking place per second so the pressure increases, as the equation used in **Boyle's Law** states.

If the volume remains constant then the mean square speed increases and therefore the temperature increases. Molecular impacts on the walls of the container are more frequent and more energetic and the total force exerted on the walls of the container increases. It follows that the pressure also increases, as stated by the **pressure law**.

Kinetic Energy

The **mean kinetic energy** $(\overline{E_k})$ of a molecule in a gas is simply the total kinetic energy of all the molecules shared between the number of molecules in the gas, i.e.

$$\overline{E_k} = \frac{\frac{1}{2}mc_1^2 + \frac{1}{2}mc_2^2 + \ldots + \frac{1}{2}mc_N^2}{N}$$

$$= \frac{\frac{1}{2}m\left(c_1^2 + c_2^2 + \ldots + c_N^2\right)}{N}$$

$$= \frac{1}{2}mc_{rms}^2$$

The higher the gas temperature, the greater the value of c_{rms} and hence the greater the mean kinetic energy of a molecule in the gas.

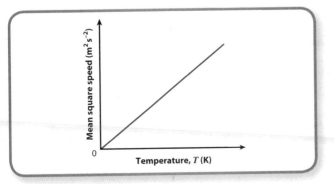

For an ideal gas, the ideal gas equation gives $pV = nRT$ and, according to the kinetic theory of gases, $pV = \frac{1}{3}Nmc_{rms}^2$. Equating these two equations results in

$$\frac{1}{3}Nmc_{rms}^2 = nRT$$

and multiplying by $\frac{3}{2}$ gives

$$\frac{3}{2} \times \frac{1}{3}Nmc_{rms}^2 = \frac{3}{2} \times nRT$$

giving

$$\frac{1}{2}Nmc_{rms}^2 = \frac{3}{2}nRT$$

Hence,

$$N\overline{E_k} = \frac{3}{2}nRT$$

where $N\overline{E_k}$ is the **total kinetic energy** of n moles of an ideal gas. For one mole of gas, it simply reduces to $\overline{E_k} = \frac{3}{2}RT$. Remembering that the Boltzmann constant $k = \frac{R}{N_A}$ and that $n = \frac{N}{N_A}$, a more succinct equation for the mean kinetic energy of a molecule of an ideal gas is

$$\overline{E_k} = \frac{1}{2}mc_{rms}^2 = \frac{3}{2}kT$$

It is this equation that can be used to determine the root mean square speed provided that the mass of a molecule is known.

It follows that the internal energy of a system, U, of an ideal gas with N molecules is just $N\overline{E_k}$, so $U = \frac{3}{2}NkT$. Since $pV = nRT$, it also follows that $U = \frac{3}{2}nRT = \frac{3}{2}pV$. The change in the internal energy due to a change in temperature is then given by

$$\Delta U = \frac{3}{2}nR\Delta T$$

This simply says that the internal energy of an ideal gas depends only on its temperature and not on the nature of the gas.

The Scope of the Kinetic Theory

In deriving these kinetic theory equations, we have assumed that there are no forces between gas molecules and that the volume of the molecules is small when compared with the volume of the gas. When the density of the gas is high, the molecules are much closer to each other and these assumptions are no longer valid.

SUMMARY

- The **root mean square speed** is defined as
$$c_{rms} = \sqrt{\frac{\left(c_1^2 + c_2^2 + \ldots + c_N^2\right)}{N}}$$

- The **distribution of speeds** among the molecules of a gas obeys a **Boltzmann distribution** and its shape depends on the temperature of the gas

- The **kinetic theory of gases** correctly predicts the behaviour of a gas as described by the gas laws

- The **total kinetic energy** of a gas containing n moles is $\frac{3}{2}nRT$ and for a gas containing one mole it reduces to $\frac{3}{2}RT$

- The **mean kinetic energy** of a molecule of a gas is $\frac{3}{2}kT = \frac{1}{2}mc_{rms}^2$

- The **internal energy** of a gas containing N molecules is $U = \frac{3}{2}NkT = \frac{3}{2}pV$

- The **kinetic theory** is not valid for gases under very high pressure or high density

QUICK TEST

1. Explain the change in the distribution of the molecular speed of a gas when its temperature is reduced?

2. What is the kinetic theory equation?

3. What is the value of the mean velocity of a set of N molecules in an ideal gas?

4. If the gas is said to be an ideal gas, what gas law is obeyed?

5. What is the internal energy of an ideal gas with N molecules?

6. Calculate the mean kinetic energy of a hydrogen molecule at 0°C.

7. Using the answer to question **6**, calculate the root mean square speed of a hydrogen molecule at this temperature. [molar mass of hydrogen = 0.002 kg]

8. Calculate the root mean square speed of an oxygen molecule at 20°C. [molar mass of oxygen = 0.032 kg]

9. A cylinder of oxygen has a volume of 0.025 m³ and contains oxygen gas at a pressure of 120 kPa. Calculate the total kinetic energy of all the oxygen gas molecules in the cylinder, assuming that they behave as an ideal gas.

PRACTICE QUESTIONS

1. The mass of one mole of nitrogen molecules (the molar mass) is 0.028 kg.

   a) Calculate the root mean square speed of nitrogen molecules at room temperature of 295 K. **[4 marks]**

   b) Explain why there is a distribution of molecular speeds in this gas. **[2 marks]**

   c) Determine the mean kinetic energy of a nitrogen molecule. **[2 marks]**

   d) The temperature of the nitrogen gas is increased to 365 K. Determine the value of the root mean square speed of the nitrogen molecules at this new temperature. **[2 marks]**

   e) Explain what effect this has on the speed distribution. **[1 mark]**

2. A helium balloon is being used to transport equipment to high altitude. The outside temperature is 298 K and the volume of the balloon is 0.06 m^3 measured at standard atmospheric pressure of 1.0×10^5 Pa.

   a) The balloon rises to a height of 15 km, where the pressure is 1.4×10^4 Pa and the temperature is 217 K. Calculate the volume of the balloon. **[3 marks]**

   b) Determine the mean kinetic energy of the helium molecules in the balloon at this height. **[2 marks]**

   c) Hence calculate the root mean square speed of the helium molecules. **[3 marks]**

   d) Using the value of the pressure at this altitude, calculate the density of helium inside the balloon. **[2 marks]**

3. In a simulated experiment, the following results were obtained for the distribution of molecular speeds for 100 neon gas molecules.

Speed, c (m s^{-1})	280	300	320	340	360	380	400
Number of molecules	5	17	23	25	14	9	7
c^2 (km^2 s^{-2})							

   a) Complete the table by calculating the square speeds of the neon molecules in km^2 s^{-2}. **[2 marks]**

   b) Using this information, determine the root mean square speed of the neon molecules. **[3 marks]**

   c) If the molar mass of neon is 0.0202 kg, determine the mean kinetic energy of the molecules of the neon gas. **[3 marks]**

   d) Use your answer to part c) to calculate the temperature of the neon gas in degrees Celsius. **[3 marks]**

Electric Fields

Electric Fields and Electric Field Strength

An **electric field** is a region in space where charged objects experience a force. For example, a point positive charge, $+Q$ (the simplest of charges), that is surrounded by an electric field that is the same in all directions is said to be in an **isotropic field**. As this electric field radiates outwards from the charge, it becomes weaker and this type of field is known as a **radial electric field**. The **electric field strength**, E, of an electric field is defined by the **force per unit charge**, $E = \frac{F}{Q}$, where

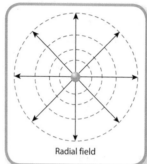

Radial field

F is the force in newtons (N) and Q is the charge in coulombs (C), with E in units of newtons per coulomb (NC^{-1}). This is similar to gravitational field strength, which is defined as the force per unit mass (see Day 4). Strictly, the electric field strength at a point is given (in terms of magnitude and direction) by the force per unit charge acting on a very small positive charge placed at that point. This point charge must be small enough so as not to distort the electric field in which it placed. The field points in the direction of the force on a positive charge.

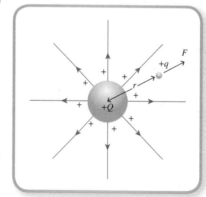

Coulomb's Law

In the case of two point charges Q_1 and Q_2, the **strength of the force** applied to a charge Q_2 by a charge Q_1 a distance r away is given by **Coulomb's Law**,

$$F = \frac{1}{4\pi\varepsilon_0} \frac{Q_1 Q_2}{r^2}$$

If the charges are **opposite** then the force is **attractive** and F will usually be taken to be negative; if the charges are **alike** then the force is **repulsive** and therefore taken to be positive; Coulomb's Law also obeys the inverse square law. The constant ε_0 is called the **permittivity of free space** and is equal to 8.85×10^{-12} Fm^{-1}, where F is the Farad, the SI unit associated with electrical capacitance. If there is a medium (rather than a vacuum) between the two charges then the value of the permittivity of the medium is used to determine F, which will be reduced because of this medium. Sometimes the initial term $\frac{1}{4\pi\varepsilon_0}$ is replaced by the constant k, resulting in Coulomb's Law being expressed as $F = \frac{kQ_1Q_2}{r^2}$, where $k = 9.0 \times 10^9$ F^{-1} m. The format of this equation for Coulomb's Law is very similar to that for Newton's Law of Gravitation, except that the gravitational force between two masses is always attractive (see Day 4).

For charges that are not point-like but are **charged over the surface of a sphere**, Coulomb's Law is still valid provided that the distance r (the distance between the centres of the spheres) is greater than the sum of the radii of the two spheres. In these situations the charge is spread uniformly over the surface of the spheres.

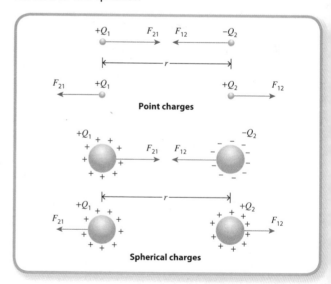

Point charges

Spherical charges

In the case of a very small charge q within the field created by a charge Q, the force is given by $F = Eq$ and hence the electric field strength E a distance r away from a positive charge Q is given by the equation

$$E = \frac{1}{4\pi\varepsilon_0}\frac{Q}{r^2}$$

A plot of the electric field strength as a function of r is an inverse square law relationship and shows both positive and negative values of E.

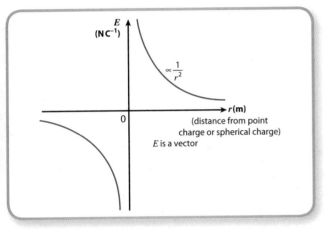

The **gradient of the potential** at r gives the **electric field strength**; the electric field lines are always at right angles to the equipotential surfaces. Like gravitational potential (see Day 4), the electrical potential can be negative ($V \propto -\frac{1}{r}$ around a negative charge). However, unlike gravitational potential, it can also be positive ($V \propto +\frac{1}{r}$ around a positive charge).

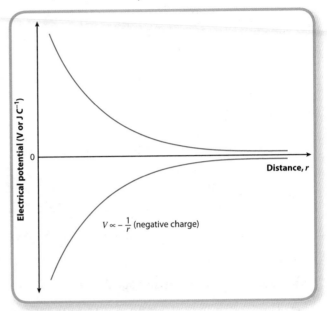

Electrical Potential

The **electrical potential**, V, at a point that is a distance r from a positive charge Q is the work done in moving a very small positive charge from infinity to that point, and is given by

$$V = \frac{Q}{4\pi\varepsilon_0 r}$$

Moving further away from the charge that is creating the field reduces the electrical potential. A spherical charge is therefore surrounded by spherical potential surfaces (represented by concentric circles when viewed in cross-section, known as **equipotentials**) and these surfaces are linked to the electric field strength through the equation

$$E = -\frac{\Delta V}{\Delta r}$$

The **work done** against the electric field in moving a charge from a lower potential (at r_2) to a higher potential (at r_1) defines the **potential difference**, i.e.

$$\Delta V = \frac{Q}{4\pi\varepsilon_0}\left(\frac{1}{r_2} - \frac{1}{r_1}\right)$$

The work done is $\Delta W = \Delta VQ = F\Delta r$. When a charge moves along an equipotential surface, $\Delta V = 0$ so no work is done in moving a charge.

Uniform Electric Fields

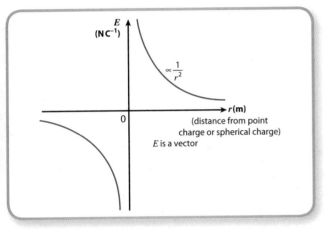

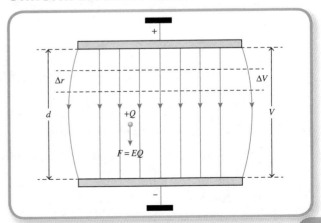

Electric field lines and equipotentials

A **uniform electric field** is one where the electric field strength is the same at all points. This occurs for example between **two parallel charged plates** (although not at the end of the plates). The work done in moving a positive charge, Q, from one plate to the other plate is $\Delta W = Fd = EQd$, and this is the same as the energy gained by the charge in moving through the potential difference V, i.e. VQ, giving $EQd = VQ$ and hence

$$E = \frac{V}{d}$$

in units of $V\,m^{-1}$. A **charged particle**, e.g. an electron, travelling at a constant velocity entering a uniform vertical electric field at right angles to the field lines will experience a force. It continues with a constant horizontal component of velocity but will experience

an acceleration vertically upwards due to the field; it will therefore undergo a **parabolic trajectory** when traversing a uniform electric field. On leaving the field, the path resumes as a straight line. This is the principle behind all **electron beam tube** devices.

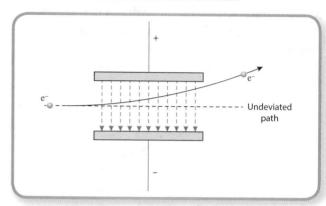

SUMMARY

- An electric field is a region in space where a charged object experiences a force

- Any object that has a charge has an electric field surrounding it

- A point charge, Q, is surrounded by a radial electric field

- The electric field strength, E, from a point charge or spherical charge in a radial field obeys the inverse square law, i.e. $E = \frac{Q}{4\pi\varepsilon_0 r^2}$

- The strength of the force of attraction or repulsion between two charges (in a vacuum) is given by Coulomb's Law, $F = \frac{Qq}{4\pi\varepsilon_0 r^2}$

- The electric field strength, E, in a radial field is defined as the force per unit charge, i.e. $E = \frac{F}{Q}$, and is equal in magnitude to the potential gradient but in the opposite direction

- Electrical potential is the potential difference between a point at a distance r and a point at infinity that is at zero potential; work is done in moving the point charge from infinity to the point r.

- Potential difference is the work done against an electric field in moving a unit charge from a lower potential to a higher potential

- Within a uniform electric field, the electric field strength is constant and given by $E = \frac{V}{d}$

QUICK TEST

1. State Coulomb's Law.

2. What does ε_0 refer to in Coulomb's Law and what are its units?

3. Does Coulomb's Law work if each charge is distributed all over the surface of a sphere?

4. What is the force of attraction between two point charges X and Y if $X = +3\,\mu C$, $Y = -2\,\mu C$ and their separation is $0.25\,m$?

5. What is meant by a uniform electric field?

6. Electric field strength can be given as NC^{-1} or Vm^{-1}. Show that these are equivalent.

7. A small charge of $+4\,\mu C$ is placed in a uniform electric field of $600\,Vm^{-1}$ directed vertically up. What force does the charge experience and in what direction?

8. How is electrical potential defined?

9. What is the defining equation for electrical potential a distance r from a positive charge Q in a radial field and what are its units?

PRACTICE QUESTIONS

1. a) Define what is meant by work done when moving a charge through a potential difference and give the equation. **[2 marks]**

   b) The potential at a point is given by $V = \frac{Q}{4\pi\varepsilon_0 r}$. State what V, Q, r and ε_0 represent and give their units. **[4 marks]**

   c) A small charge of $+1.5\,nC$ lies at a distance of $3.0\,m$ away from a charge of $+0.080\,\mu C$. It is moved to a distance of $2.0\,m$ from the larger charge.

   (i) Show that the change in potential is $120\,V$. **[3 marks]**

   (ii) Hence determine the work done in moving the small charge. **[2 marks]**

2. In an electron beam tube, electrons are accelerated and enter a uniform electric field generated by a set of deflecting plates as shown in the figure.

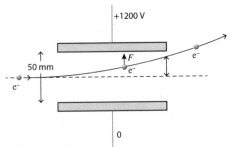

   a) Calculate the electric field strength between the plates. **[2 marks]**

   b) Determine the upward acceleration of the electrons. $[m = 9.1 \times 10^{-31}\,kg, q = 1.6 \times 10^{-19}\,C]$ **[3 marks]**

   c) If electrons traverse the length of the plates in $2.4\,ns$, show that their upward displacement is $12\,mm$. **[2 marks]**

3. a) What is the electric field and electrical potential (i) on the surface of a metal sphere and (ii) inside a metal sphere. **[4 marks]**

   The dome sphere of a Van de Graaff generator has a radius of $0.1\,m$ and a charge of $22.2\,nC$.

   b) Calculate the electric field strength on the surface of the dome and determine the field strength at a distance of $0.5\,m$ from the centre of the dome. **[4 marks]**

   c) Calculate the electrical potential at the surface of the dome and also at a distance of $0.5\,m$ from the centre of the dome. **[4 marks]**

Capacitors

Capacitance

Capacitors are components of electrical circuits that can temporarily store and then release **electrical charge** and **energy**. The ability of an object to store charge is called **capacitance**, C, and is given by $C = \frac{Q}{V}$, where Q is the stored charge and V is the potential difference between the two conductors. Capacitance is measured in farads (F) where $1F = 1CV^{-1}$ (one coulomb per volt). The above equation is often more conveniently expressed as $Q = CV$. Although the farad is the unit of capacitance, microfarads are a more commonly used unit for practical purposes. Modern capacitors consist of two rolled parallel plate conductors separated by an insulating layer known as a **dielectric**. Different insulating materials have a different dielectric constant (also known as the **relative permittivity**). The amount of charge stored in a capacitor for each volt applied across it depends on the area of the plates, the thickness of the dielectric and the relative permittivity of the dielectric insulating material. Capacitors in parallel give an equivalent capacitor as $C = C_1 + C_2$ while for capacitors in series this is $\frac{1}{C} = \frac{1}{C_1} + \frac{1}{C_2}$. They have numerous applications in both electrical and electronic circuits.

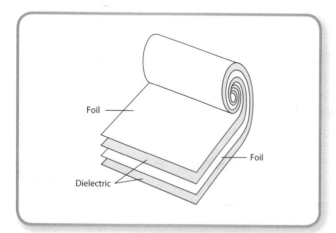

Foil

Foil

Dielectric

Energy Stored in a Capacitor

When a capacitor is charged, the **energy is stored** in the electric field between the plates and the amount of charge is directly proportional to the potential difference across it. When the capacitor is allowed to discharge, the **work done** or **energy transferred**

is $\Delta W = \Delta E = \Delta QV$. Thus when both V and Q fall to zero the total energy transferred is the area under the line, i.e. $E = \frac{1}{2}QV$, and this must be equal to the original energy stored in the capacitor. Since $Q = CV$, two further expressions can also be used, i.e.

$$E = \frac{1}{2}CV^2 \quad \text{or} \quad E = \frac{1}{2}\frac{Q^2}{C}$$

Which equation to use depends on what values are given in the question.

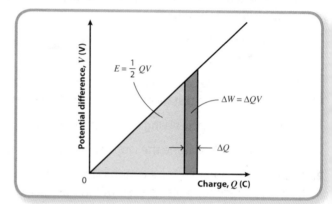

Charging a Capacitor

When a capacitor is connected to a battery (switch connected to A), electrons flow from the negative terminal to plate X of the capacitor; **simultaneously** electrons leave plate Y and flow back to the positive terminal. This process builds up charge on X and Y until the potential difference across the capacitor is identical to the supply voltage. During the charging process, **no charge** has crossed the **insulating dielectric material**. The charging (and discharging) processes are **exponential** although this shape is not readily seen as these processes occur almost instantaneously; they can be slowed down by placing a **resistor** in series with the

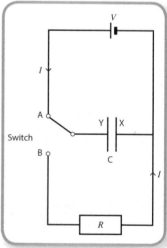

capacitor. The **time taken to charge** (and discharge) a capacitor depends on both the capacitance (C) of the capacitor and the resistance within the circuit (R). Combined together, the value of RC gives the **time constant** (τ) for the charging and discharging process of a capacitor. If Q_0 is the final charge on a capacitor and Q is the charge on a capacitor after a time t then the amount of charge is given by

$$Q = Q_0\left(1 - e^{-t/RC}\right)$$

If $t = RC$ then $Q = Q_0\left(1 - e^{-1}\right)$ and $\frac{Q}{Q_0} = \left(1 - \frac{1}{e}\right) \approx 0.63$, i.e. the time constant, RC, is the time taken to charge a capacitor to 63% of its final value. In practical situations, the time taken to fully charge (or discharge) a capacitor is taken to be about **5RC**. Naturally, the larger the resistance, the longer it takes to charge (or discharge) a capacitor. As current is the flow of charge ($I = \frac{\Delta Q}{\Delta t}$), the equation for current at a given time t is $I = I_0 e^{-t/RC}$ (and this is the same for either charging or discharging). In this case, the value of RC is the time taken for the charging (or discharging) current to decrease to $\frac{1}{e}$ of its original value. The potential difference, V, across a capacitor follows a similar equation to that of charge and is given by $V = V_0\left(1 - e^{-t/RC}\right)$.

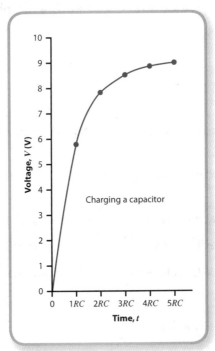

Discharging a Capacitor

The circuit above can also be used to **discharge a capacitor**. By positioning the switch to B, the capacitor starts to discharge through the resistor R. This discharge follows an exponential curve, $Q = Q_0 e^{-t/RC}$, and this is also true for the potential difference as $Q \propto V$, so that $V = V_0 e^{-t/RC}$.

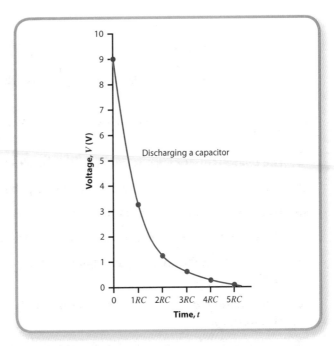

Measuring the Charging and Discharging of a Capacitor

The circuit shown provides a good example of a circuit that can be used to record the charging and discharging of a capacitor. Because both graphs are exponential functions, it is necessary to perform some mathematical manipulation in order to obtain a straight-line graph. For the current equation

$$I = I_0 e^{-t/RC}$$

rearranging and taking natural logarithms (i.e. to the base e) gives

$$\ln\left(\frac{I}{I_0}\right) = \ln\left(e^{-t/RC}\right) = -\frac{t}{RC}$$

and

$$\ln I - \ln I_0 = -\frac{t}{RC}$$

Hence

$$\ln I = -\frac{1}{RC}t + \ln I_0$$

A plot of $\ln I$ against t should give a **straight line** with **gradient** $-\frac{1}{RC}$ and **intercept** $\ln I_0$. As R is known, C can be determined and I_0 obtained from the intercept value c via e^c.

SUMMARY

- **Capacitors** are components of electrical circuits that can temporarily store and then release electrical charge and energy

- **Capacitors in parallel give an equivalent capacitor as** $C = C_1 + C_2$ **while for capacitors in series it is** $\frac{1}{C} = \frac{1}{C_1} + \frac{1}{C_2}$

- **The overall capacitance is given by** $C = \frac{Q}{V}$, **which is often more conveniently expressed as** $Q = CV$

- **The energy stored in a capacitor is given by the area under a** V–Q **curve**

- **The discharge of a capacitor follows an exponential curve,** $Q = Q_0 e^{-t/RC}$

- **The value of** RC **gives the time constant** (τ) **for the circuit**

- **In practical situations, the time taken to fully charge (or discharge) a capacitor is taken to be about** $5RC$

- **The equation for current at a given time** t **is** $I = I_0 e^{-t/RC}$ **(and is the same for either charging or discharging)**

- **The equation for the current at time** t **can be expressed as** $\ln I = -\frac{1}{RC} t + \ln I_0$ **and a plot of** $\ln I$ **against** t **should give a straight line**

QUICK TEST

1. Link the electrical symbols C, I, V and F with the quantities charge, potential difference, current and capacitance.

2. Capacitors C_1 (400 μF) and C_2 (200 μF) are connected in series. What is the value of the equivalent capacitor?

3. If the above two capacitors are connected in parallel, what is the equivalent capacitor?

4. What is the equation for the energy stored in a capacitor in terms of charge and potential difference?

5. A capacitor stores a charge of 5.8 mC at a p.d. of 6.0 V. Calculate the value of the capacitance.

6. What is meant by the dielectric constant?

7. What is the energy stored in a capacitor in terms of C and V?

8. Calculate the capacitance of a capacitor that stores 0.50 J of energy when a p.d. of 12 V is connected across it.

9. Show that the time constant τ has units of seconds.

10. If $C = 500$ μF and $R = 56$ kΩ, calculate the time constant for the circuit.

11. A 2000 μF capacitor is charged up to a potential difference of 12 V. Calculate the energy stored in the capacitor.

PRACTICE QUESTIONS

1. The circuit shows a 12 V supply source that is used with a 3.3 kΩ resistor to charge a capacitor of 0.68 μF when the switch is closed. The capacitor is initially uncharged.

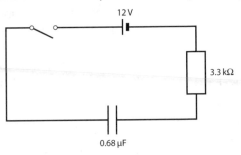

12 V

3.3 kΩ

0.68 μF

a) Find the time constant for this circuit. **[2 marks]**

b) Determine the initial charging current and describe the charging current when the time is in excess of 5 × the time constant. **[3 marks]**

c) Calculate the maximum charge that can be stored in the capacitor. **[2 marks]**

d) Calculate the maximum amount of energy that can be stored by the capacitor. **[2 marks]**

2. A camera flash uses a 33 μF capacitor to power its function. The duration of the flash is 2.0 ms which produces a mean power output of 2.5 kW.

a) Show that the energy output of each flash is 5 J. **[2 marks]**

b) Assuming that all the stored energy is used in a single flash, determine the potential difference between the plates of the capacitor immediately before the flash. **[2 marks]**

c) Determine the maximum charge stored by the capacitor. **[2 marks]**

d) Hence calculate the mean current provided by the capacitor during a single flash. **[2 marks]**

3. a) What is meant by the time constant in a capacitor circuit and what effect does a larger time constant have on the way a capacitor charges or discharges? **[3 marks]**

b) Sketch graphs to show how the voltage varies for a (i) charging and (ii) discharging capacitor of capacitance 47 μF that is in series with a resistor of value 5.6 kΩ and a supply voltage of 6 V. Label the voltage values after 1 time constant and only plot graphs up to 5 time constants. **[4 marks]**

c) Determine how much energy is stored in the capacitor after 1 s. **[6 marks]**

Magnetic Fields

Magnetic Flux Lines

Magnets are objects that provide, and are therefore surrounded by, an external magnetic field. Bar and horseshoe magnets that retain appreciable magnetisation have regions (poles) from which the magnetic forces appear to originate, termed **north** and **south poles**. All magnets have opposite poles and are referred to as dipole magnets. A **magnetic field** is a region around a magnetic material where a moving charge may experience a force. This field of force is represented by a series of **flux lines** that indicate the direction and strength of the field; the closer the lines are together, the stronger the field. The **magnetic field strength** can be represented by the **magnetic flux density**, B, defined as the force per unit current per unit length on a wire placed at right angles to the direction of the magnetic field, i.e. $B = \frac{F}{Il}$. The unit for magnetic flux density is the **tesla** (T), where 1 T causes a force of 1 N on a 1 m wire carrying a current of 1 A at right angles to the flux; 1 T is equal to 1 weber per square metre ($Wb\,m^{-2}$), where the weber is the unit of **magnetic flux**, denoted by the symbol Φ. Magnetic flux density can be measured using a **Hall probe**, which contains a semiconductor material that generates a potential difference across the material that is directly proportional to the flux density.

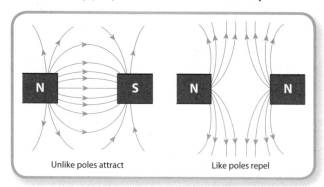

Unlike poles attract   Like poles repel

Current-carrying Wires

A length of wire that carries a current (I) induces a magnetic field around the wire. The direction of the magnetic flux is clockwise for a current flowing into the page (denoted by $\otimes$) and anticlockwise for a current flowing out of the page (denoted by $\odot$). The magnetic flux density, B, is directly proportional to the current in the wire and inversely proportional to the distance from the wire, i.e. $B = \frac{kI}{r}$, where k is a constant that depends on the material around the wire. The magnetic flux therefore forms a **series of concentric circles**. Generally, $k = \frac{\mu}{2\pi}$, where μ is the **permeability** of the material; it is a measure of its effect on the strength of the magnetic field. For a vacuum (including air), μ is replaced by μ_0, the **permeability of free space,** where $\mu_0 = 4\pi \times 10^{-7}\,T\,m\,A^{-1}$. The magnetic flux density is then given by

$$B = \frac{\mu_0 I}{2\pi r}$$

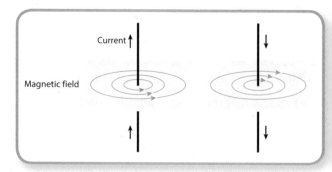

For a single loop of wire, the flux lines are strongest along the core of the loop. This is even more pronounced for multiple-loops systems such as the current-carrying coil of wire called a **solenoid**. The magnetic flux outside the solenoid behaves like a bar magnet with north and south poles determined by the current direction, while the magnetic flux is **uniform** inside the solenoid and is given by

$$B = \mu_0 n I$$

where n is the number of turns per metre.

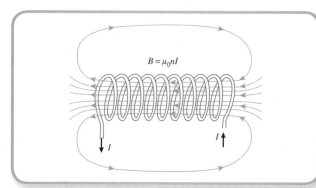

Forces on Current-carrying Wires

When a wire carrying a current is placed in a magnetic field, the wire experiences a force due to the interaction between the field and the moving charges in the wire (which create a magnetic field around the wire). The magnetic field making the wire move is called a **catapult field**. The direction of the force is always perpendicular to both the current direction and the magnetic field and can be found using **Fleming's left-hand rule**. The **F**irst finger points in the direction of the **F**ield, the se**C**ond finger points in the direction of the **C**urrent, and the **T**humb points in the direction of the **T**hrust or force. The size of the force depends on the current (I), the length of the wire **in the field** (l) and the strength of the magnetic field (B), and is given by

$$F = BIl$$

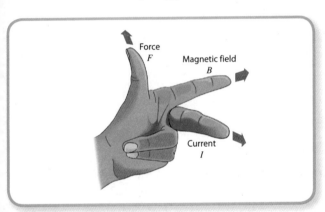

Force
F

Magnetic field
B

Current
I

If the wire is at an angle θ to the magnetic flux lines then the equation becomes $F = BIl \sin\theta$ so that if the current is parallel to the flux lines then no force acts on the wire. The size of this force can be measured using a current-carrying loop of wire suspended over a top-pan electronic balance that holds a U-shaped magnet; the electronic balance reading changes when a current flows in the wire. The change in the reading of the balance will indicate the magnetic force on the magnet.

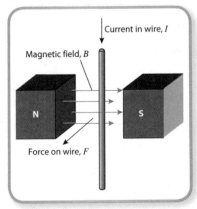

Current in wire, I

Magnetic field, B

N   S

Force on wire, F

Charged Particles in Magnetic Fields

A **beam of charged particles** moving in a magnetic field also experiences a force. If a charge q travels a distance l in time t then it is moving with a velocity $v = \frac{l}{t}$. Since current $I = \frac{q}{t}$, it follows that

$$F = BIl = B \times \frac{q}{t} \times vt = Bqv$$

and Fleming's Left-Hand Rule allows the direction of the force to be determined. The sign of the charge is important as positive and negative charges will move in opposite directions. The force on a moving charged particle in a magnetic field is always **perpendicular** to its **direction of travel**. The charged particle follows a circular path and the **centripetal force** must equal the force exerted by the magnetic field:

$$F = Bqv = \frac{mv^2}{r}$$

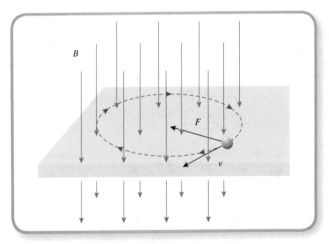

B

F

v

This effect is used in particle accelerators, including **cyclotrons** and **synchrotrons**, to provide for a circulating and highly focussed charged beam. If B and q (usually the charge is for electrons but not always) are constant then $r = \frac{mv}{Bq} \propto mv$, i.e. the radius of the orbit is proportional to the particle's momentum. Alternatively, a **mass spectrometer** keeps both v and B constant, allowing ions with different charge-to-mass ratios to give distinct radii. It is therefore able to separate ions of different mass-to-charge ratios and determine their relative abundances in a graph known as a **mass spectrum**.

SUMMARY

- A magnetic field arises from the magnetic effects of electric currents within materials
- The strength of a magnetic field can be represented by the magnetic flux density
- Fleming's left-hand rule gives the direction of the force on a current-carrying conductor in a magnetic field
- The magnetic flux is uniform inside a solenoid and given by $B = \mu_0 n I$
- A wire carrying a current placed in a magnetic field experiences a force due to the interaction between the field and the moving charges in the wire given by $F = BIl \sin \theta$
- A beam of charged particles moving in a magnetic field also experiences a force given by $F = Bqv$
- Charged particles move in circular paths in an external magnetic field and this effect is used in particle accelerators including cyclotrons and synchrotrons
- Mass spectrometers utilise the circular motion to exploit differences in the mass of ions

QUICK TEST

1. What is meant by magnetic flux density?

2. What is the name of a probe that is used to measure the strength of magnetic fields?

3. What does the equation $B = \frac{\mu_0 I}{2\pi r}$ represent? Define the symbols used.

4. If a wire is carrying a current of 2 A, what is the magnetic flux density 0.03 m from the wire? $[\mu_0 = 4\pi \times 10^{-7} \, \mathrm{T\,m\,A^{-1}}]$

5. In Fleming's Left-Hand Rule, what does the thumb represent?

6. A solenoid has a length of 0.18 m and has 270 turns of wire. Determine the number of turns per metre and hence calculate the flux density at the centre of the solenoid if it carries a current of 1.4 A.

7. What is the equation for the force acting on a length of wire in an external magnetic field?

8. A wire of length 0.2 m is placed at an angle of 30° to a uniform magnetic field of 0.08 T. If the current in the wire is 2.0 A, calculate the size of the force on the wire.

9. How does an electron move in an external magnetic field if it enters the field at right angles? Give its equation.

10. What is measured in a mass spectrometer and what two key parameters have to be kept constant to achieve this?

PRACTICE QUESTIONS

1. The force on a beam of charged particles moving at a velocity v at 90° to an external magnetic field, B, is given by $F = Bqv$, where q is the charge on the particles.

a) Show that the radius of the circular path is given by $r = \frac{mv}{Bq}$.   **[2 marks]**

b) State the direction of the force if the magnetic field is into the paper.   **[1 mark]**

An electron enters a uniform magnetic field of flux density 2.2×10^{-4} T at right angles to the field at a speed of 5.0×10^{6} m s^{-1}.

c) Determine the radius of the electron's path. [$m = 9.1 \times 10^{-31}$ kg, $e = 1.6 \times 10^{-19}$ C]   **[2 marks]**

d) What would be the effect if a positron entered the same field?   **[1 mark]**

2. In a practical experiment, a sensitive top-pan balance is used to measure the force on a current-carrying conductor. As the current along XY is varied, the change in mass is recorded by the balance and the results are shown in the table.

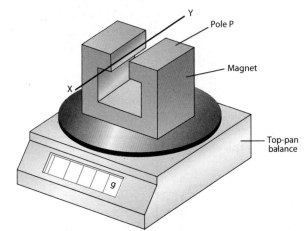

Current (A)	−2.0	−1.5	−1.0	−0.5	0	0.5	1.0	1.5	2.0
Change in mass (g)	1.49	1.14	0.78	0.41	0.00	−0.42	−0.81	−1.18	−1.57
Force (N)									

a) Complete the table and plot a graph to show the relationship between the force on the wire (along the y-axis) and the current flowing through the wire (along the x-axis).   **[4 marks]**

b) Determine the gradient of the line of best fit.   **[2 marks]**

c) What does the gradient of the line represent?   **[1 mark]**

d) If the length of wire within the magnetic field is 50 mm, calculate the magnetic flux density.   **[2 marks]**

Electromagnetism

Magnetic Flux

The **strength of a magnetic field** is defined in terms of its **magnetic flux density**, B, which is measured in tesla (T). This can be visualised by the number of **magnetic flux lines** that pass at

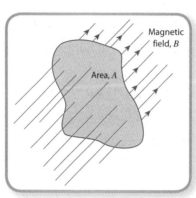

right angles through an area of $1\,m^2$. Multiplying the magnetic flux density by the surface area, A, through which the magnetic field passes yields the **magnetic flux**, Φ, i.e. $\Phi = BA$. The unit of magnetic flux is the **weber** (Wb), where $1\,Wb = 1\,Tm^2$. When the area is not perpendicular to the magnetic field (or the magnetic field is not perpendicular to the area of interest), the equation becomes $\Phi = BA\cos\theta$, where θ is the angle as shown.

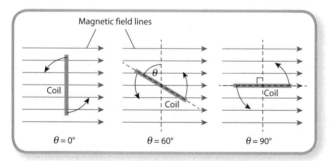

$\theta = 0°$ $\theta = 60°$ $\theta = 90°$

Magnetic Flux Linkage

When an object passes through a magnetic field, it is said to 'cut' through the lines of magnetic flux. For example, a length (l) of wire that moves with a constant velocity (v) perpendicular to the magnetic flux lines will 'cut' through more flux lines if (a) the wire is longer, (b) the wire moves faster, or (c) the magnetic flux density is greater. Moving a wire that is **parallel** to the flux lines does not 'cut' them at all. Extending this idea to a loop of wire, the magnetic flux is $\Phi = BA$ for a single loop. For a coil of wire with N turns, each turn of the coil has a flux Φ linking it so the total **magnetic flux linkage** (the magnetic flux linked by the loop) is

$$N\Phi = BAN$$

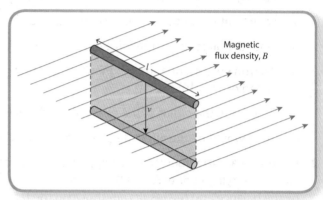

Magnetic flux linkage is strictly measured in **weber-turns** to distinguish it from magnetic flux. If the area is set at an angle to the magnetic field then the equation is modified to $N\Phi = BAN\cos\theta$. Magnetic flux linkage depends on the magnetic flux density, the coil's cross-sectional area, the orientation of the coil and the flux lines, and the number of turns on the coil.

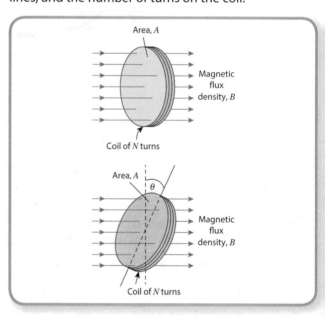

Electromagnetic Induction

When a moving length of wire or a coil of wire moves through a magnetic field or vice versa, an **induced electromotive force** is produced. This can be explained by the relative movement between the coil and the field or by how the magnetic flux linkage changes. The magnitude of the **emf induced** (in volts) is equal to the rate of change of the magnetic flux linkage, i.e.

$$\varepsilon = \frac{\Delta(N\Phi)}{\Delta t}$$

For a coil with a fixed number of turns, N, this gives

$$\varepsilon = N\frac{\Delta\Phi}{\Delta t}$$

The direction of the induced current is given by **Fleming's right-hand rule** where the forefinger, second finger and thumb represent field, induced current and force or motion.

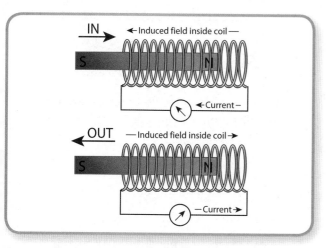

This expression for the magnitude of the induced emf is known as **Faraday's Law**. The direction of the induced emf is determined by **Lenz's Law**, which states that the direction of the induced emf **opposes** the change in magnetic flux that is producing it. This law is a consequence of the law of conservation of energy. Lenz's Law introduces a negative sign into the equations above and can be easily demonstrated using a small powerful magnetic cylinder that descends down a copper tube compared with either an aluminium tube or by using a non-magnetic cylinder and observing the difference in the time taken to travel the length of the tube.

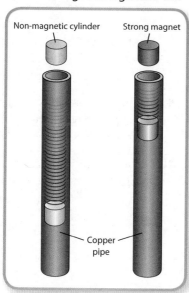

A Fixed Coil in a Changing Magnetic Field

This is an example of $\Delta\Phi = \Delta\boldsymbol{B} \times A$. A current-carrying solenoid containing N turns produces a uniform magnetic field within it. If the current is altered then there is a corresponding change in the field. This change in magnetic field, detected using a search coil (a device in which a current can be induced to detect and measure a magnetic field), causes a change in the magnetic flux linkage and hence an induced emf given by Faraday's equation

$$\varepsilon = N\frac{\Delta\Phi}{\Delta t} = NA\frac{\Delta B}{\Delta t}$$

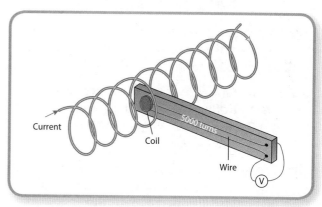

A Moving Conductor in a Magnetic Field

This is a case where $\Delta\Phi = \boldsymbol{B} \times \Delta A$. If the length of the moving conductor is l and it is travelling at a speed v then the area swept out per second is $\Delta A = lv$. Hence Faraday's Law gives the magnitude of the induced emf as (with $N = 1$)

$$\varepsilon = \frac{\Delta\Phi}{\Delta t} = Blv$$

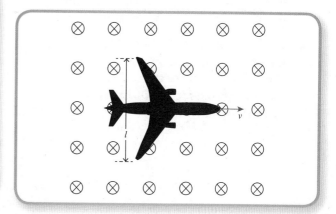

An interesting example to consider is an **aircraft moving at right angles to the Earth's magnetic field** where l represents the length of the wingspan. Another example is of a **search coil of N turns** and area A in a uniform magnetic field of flux density B. If the search coil is rapidly pulled away from the field then the area that is linked by the flux also changes and the induced emf can be determined using Faraday's Law $\varepsilon = N\frac{\Delta\Phi}{\Delta t}$, where $\Delta\Phi = B\Delta A$.

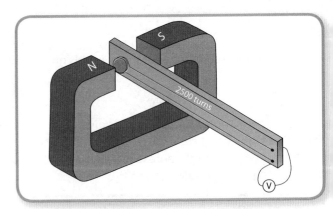

SUMMARY

- The strength of a magnetic field is defined in terms of its magnetic flux density, B, measured in tesla (T)

- Magnetic flux, Φ, is the product of the magnetic flux density and the area, i.e. $\Phi = BA$; the unit of magnetic flux is the weber (Wb), where $1\,\text{Wb} = 1\,\text{T m}^2$

- The total magnetic flux linkage is given by $N\Phi = BAN$ and measured in weber-turns to distinguish it from magnetic flux

- If the area is set at an angle to the magnetic field then the equation for magnetic flux linkage is modified to $N\Phi = BAN\cos\theta$

- The induced electromotive force is produced due to the relative movement between a wire or coil and the magnetic field or because the magnetic flux linkage changes

- Faraday's Law states that the induced emf is given by $\varepsilon = \frac{\Delta(N\Phi)}{\Delta t}$; for a coil with a fixed number of turns, N, this gives $\varepsilon = N\frac{\Delta\Phi}{\Delta t}$

- The direction of the induced emf is determined by Lenz's Law, which states that the direction of the induced emf opposes the change in flux that is producing it

QUICK TEST

1. What term is used to describe the strength and direction of a magnetic field, and what are its units?

2. What is magnetic flux?

3. What is the unit of magnetic flux?

4. What is magnetic flux linkage?

5. A coil of cross-sectional area $0.08\,\text{m}^2$ has 250 turns and is placed at right angles to a magnetic field of flux density $4.2 \times 10^{-3}\,\text{T}$. Calculate the magnetic flux linkage.

6. State Faraday's Law of electromagnetic induction.

7. What is Lenz's Law?

8. A rectangular coil measures $4\,\text{cm}$ by $6\,\text{cm}$ and is placed at $90°$ to a magnetic field of flux density $1.2\,\text{T}$. If the coil has 200 turns, what is the magnetic flux linkage?

9. Using the data above, determine the magnetic flux linkage when the coil is parallel to the magnetic flux.

10. A wire of length $12\,\text{cm}$ moves through a horizontal magnetic field of flux density $1.5\,\text{T}$ at a speed of $0.05\,\text{ms}^{-1}$. Calculate the induced emf in the wire.

PRACTICE QUESTIONS

1. **a)** What is the difference between magnetic flux and magnetic flux density? **[4 marks]**

   A coil has an area of $18\,cm^2$ and is placed at right angles to a magnetic field of 2×10^{-3} T.

   b) Determine the magnetic flux passing through the coil. **[2 marks]**

   c) If the coil has 500 turns, calculate the magnetic flux linkage in the coil. **[2 marks]**

   d) The magnetic flux density is reduced uniformly to 1.2×10^{-3} T in 2.0 s. Calculate the magnitude of the induced emf across the ends of the coil. **[3 marks]**

2. **a)** State Faraday's Law of electromagnetic induction, defining the quantities involved. **[2 marks]**

   A large aircraft is flying at 630 km per hour over the UK. The vertical component of the Earth's magnetic field is 5.0×10^{-5} T and the wing tips are 34 m apart.

   b) Calculate the area swept out by the aircraft's wings in 1 second. **[2 marks]**

   c) Hence determine the emf generated between the wing tips. **[3 marks]**

   d) State how the direction of the induced emf is determined. **[1 mark]**

3. **a)** State what is meant by magnetic flux linkage and give its units. **[2 marks]**

   A search coil is being used to measure the magnetic flux density between the poles of a U-shaped magnet. The search coil comprises 3000 turns in an area of $1.2\,cm^2$.

   b) If the search coil is removed from the poles of the magnet in 0.20 s and the induced emf generated is 0.45 V, calculate the flux density of the magnet. **[4 marks]**

A.C. Generators and Transformers

Alternating Current

An **alternating current** (a.c.) is a current that repeatedly and continuously reverses its direction with a constant frequency. If the form of a current–time graph is a sine wave then the current is said to be **sinusoidal**. A prime example of an a.c. is mains electricity, which has a frequency of 50 Hz with each cycle taking 0.02 s. The **peak value** of an a.c. (or of its associated alternating voltage) is the maximum current (or voltage) measured from the zero position. It is the same in either direction and can be measured as half the **peak-to-peak** current (or voltage); it is equivalent to the amplitude of the waveform. For mains (household) electricity the peak value (V_0) is 325 V but for light and heavy industrial usage this value will be appreciably higher.

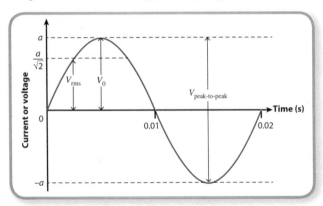

Root mean Square Current and Voltage

Since a.c. currents and voltages vary continuously, the question arises as to what value should be taken when undertaking calculations. This is determined via the equivalent direct current (d.c.) or voltage and is called the **root mean square (rms)** current or voltage: it is based on the heating effect or power that either an a.c. or a d.c. supply would produce in the same resistor. The mean power for an a.c. supply is just $\frac{1}{2}I_0^2 R$ and this is equivalent to a d.c. supply of $I_{rms}^2 R$. Equating these two expressions gives $I_{rms} = \frac{1}{\sqrt{2}}I_0$ and this is also true for the alternating voltage $V_{rms} = \frac{1}{\sqrt{2}}V_0$.

This means that household a.c. has a nominal voltage of $\frac{325}{\sqrt{2}} = 230$ V. The **root mean square** value of an **a.c. current or voltage is $\frac{1}{\sqrt{2}} \times$ the peak current or peak voltage**. This means that the mean a.c. power is

$$P_{mean} = I_0 V_0 = \frac{I_0}{\sqrt{2}} \times \frac{V_0}{\sqrt{2}} = \frac{I_0 V_0}{2} = \frac{P_{peak}}{2}$$

In other words, the **mean power dissipated** through a fixed resistor by an a.c. supply is equal to **half the peak power dissipated**.

Generating an Alternating Current

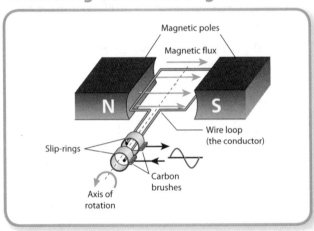

An **a.c. generator** (also called a **dynamo**) is a device that converts kinetic energy into electrical energy. This is achieved by rotating a coil in a magnetic field which induces an electrical current in the coil. Slip-rings on a **split commutator** (or static carbon brushes) allow a continuous current to be generated. This current (or voltage) changes direction every half of a rotation, thereby producing an alternating current or voltage. A cross-sectional view through the device shows that at a particular angle the amount of flux 'cut' by the coil (the flux linkage) is given by $\Phi = BAN \cos\theta$. As the coil rotates, the flux linkage will vary sinusoidally between $+BAN$ and $-BAN$. The induced emf depends on the rate of change of flux linkage and this can be seen also to vary sinusoidally. If the coil is rotating with an angular speed (angular frequency) ω then $\theta = \omega t$ and the flux linkage varies as $\Phi = BAN \cos \omega t$ with the **induced emf** given by $\varepsilon = BAN\omega \sin \omega t$.

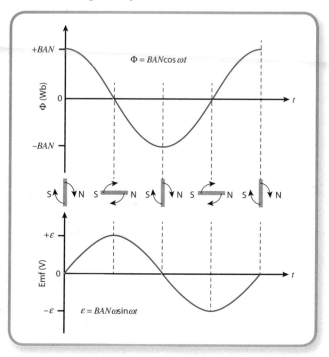

Transformers

A **transformer** is an electrical device by which an alternating supply may be changed from a low potential difference to a high potential difference and vice versa. They only work with an alternating current (voltage) since with a direct current there would be no change in magnetic flux linkage. They are used extensively in the transmission of electrical energy via the **National Grid** as well as in charging devices such as mobile phones and camera batteries. Transformers are based on electromagnetic induction where an alternating current (voltage) applied to a **primary coil** produces an alternating magnetic field in the iron core. This alternating magnetic field 'cuts' the **secondary coil** thereby inducing an emf across it at the same frequency. The emf of the primary coil is $V_p = N_p \frac{\Delta \Phi}{\Delta t}$ and that of the secondary coil is $V_s = N_s \frac{\Delta \Phi}{\Delta t}$. Combining these equations gives the more simple expression $\frac{V_p}{V_s} = \frac{N_p}{N_s}$, where N is the number of turns in the primary (p) or secondary (s) coil. Step-up transformers increases the voltage by having more turns on the secondary coil and step-down transformers reduce the voltage by having fewer turns on the secondary coil.

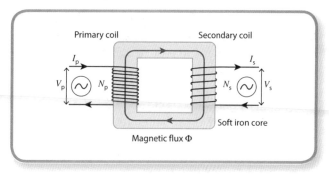

Transformer Power and Efficiency

In an ideal transformer (where no energy is lost), the input power would be equal to the output power, i.e.

$$P = I_p V_p = I_s V_s$$

These equations can be combined into just one expression:

$$\frac{N_p}{N_s} = \frac{V_p}{V_s} = \frac{I_s}{I_p}.$$

In practice there are (small) power losses from the transformer, mostly in terms of heat. This is produced by **eddy currents** in the transformer's iron core as well as by the **resistance** within the coils. To reduce these losses, the iron core is produced from a series of laminated sheets that are insulated from each other, and thicker copper wire that has a lower resistance is used. The **efficiency** of a transformer is just the ratio of power out to power in, i.e. $\eta = \frac{\text{power out}}{\text{power in}} = \frac{I_s V_s}{I_p V_p}$.

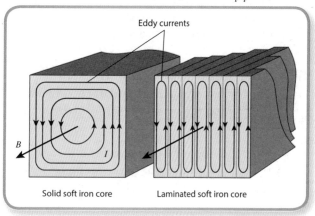

The National Grid

Electricity generated from power stations (coal or nuclear) is transmitted around the UK via the **National Grid** at the lowest current possible so as to minimise the resistance losses and reduce ohmic heating in the overhead power lines, which are proportional to $I^2 R$. Lower current means higher voltage and so the electricity generated is **stepped up** to about 400 kV for transmission and then reduced to 230 V for domestic use via **step-down** transformers. Light and heavy industry usually require much larger voltages.

SUMMARY

- An alternating current (a.c.) is a current that repeatedly and continuously reverses its direction every half cycle

- The root mean square (rms) voltage or current is based on the heating effect or power that an a.c. and a d.c. current would produce in the same resistor

- The root mean square value of an a.c. current or voltage is $\frac{1}{\sqrt{2}} \times$ the peak current or peak voltage

- Slip-rings on a split commutator allow a continuous current to be generated

- The induced emf of an a.c. generator is given by $\varepsilon = BAN\omega \sin \omega t$

- In an a.c. transformer, the ratio of the secondary voltage to the primary voltage is the same as the ratio between the number of turns in the respective coils, i.e. $\frac{V_p}{V_s} = \frac{N_p}{N_s}$

- Power losses from a transformer are mostly in terms of heat and are produced predominantly by eddy currents within the iron core

- The efficiency of a transformer is just the ratio of power out to power in, i.e. $\eta = \frac{\text{power out}}{\text{power in}} = \frac{I_s V_s}{I_p V_p}$

QUICK TEST

1. How does the voltage or current of an a.c. generator vary?

2. What is the equation that connects the root mean square current with its peak value?

3. The root mean square voltage in the UK is nominally 230 V. Calculate the peak value, V_0.

4. What is the phase difference between the magnetic flux linkage and the induced emf?

5. A rectangular coil of area 0.05 m^2 and 500 turns rotates at 20 rad s^{-1} in a uniform magnetic field of 1.5×10^{-3} T. Calculate the maximum value of the emf induced in the coil.

6. Briefly explain how a transformer works.

7. A step-down transformer has a primary coil with 1200 turns and transforms a mains voltage supply of 240 V a.c. to 12 V a.c. How many turns are there are on the secondary coil?

8. What is the main cause of energy loss in a solid soft iron core and how is this overcome?

PRACTICE QUESTIONS

1. A transformer has a laminated soft iron core with a primary coil consisting of 250 turns.

    a) What is the purpose of the soft iron core being laminated?   **[3 marks]**

    b) If an input voltage of 12V a.c. is supplied, how many turns on the secondary coil are needed to produce a step-up voltage of 132V a.c.?   **[2 marks]**

    c) The current in the primary coil is 1.65 A. Assuming the transformer is 100% efficient, calculate the current in the secondary coil.   **[2 marks]**

    d) If the measured output power of the transformer is 18W, calculate its efficiency.   **[2 marks]**

    e) What other effect apart from those mentioned in part **a)** causes a loss of efficiency in transformers?   **[1 mark]**

2. The figure shows the orientation of a rectangular coil in a magnetic field. The coil is 3 cm by 2 cm and contains 1000 turns of wire. The strength of the magnetic field is 0.05 T.

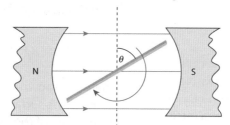

    a) Write an equation that relates the magnetic flux linkage with the angle between the coil and the field.   **[1 mark]**

    b) If the coil is rotated with an angular speed of $30\pi\,\text{rad}\,\text{s}^{-1}$, calculate (i) the maximum value of the magnetic flux linkage and (ii) the maximum value of the induced emf.   **[6 marks]**

    c) On the figure below, sketch a graph of the way the magnetic flux linkage and induced emf behave in one complete cycle.   **[5 marks]**

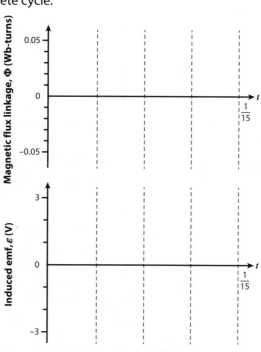

Gravitational Fields

Force between Two Masses

Newton showed that there is always an attractive force acting between two masses, M and m, that is proportional to their respective masses but inversely proportional to the square of the distance between them. Mathematically, $F \propto \frac{Mm}{r^2}$, where r is the distance between the centres of mass. The expression is another example of the **inverse square law**, where doubling the distance of separation decreases the force by a factor of 4. A full analysis of the forces leads to the equation

$$F = -\frac{GMm}{r^2}$$

where the constant of proportionality, G, is called the **gravitational constant** (often referred to as 'Big G'). It is this equation that is known as **Newton's Law of Gravitation**. Although the law is shown as a force between two masses, it applies to all particles in the universe that possess mass, irrespective of how far that distance stretches, i.e. the **gravitational force** has an **infinite range**.

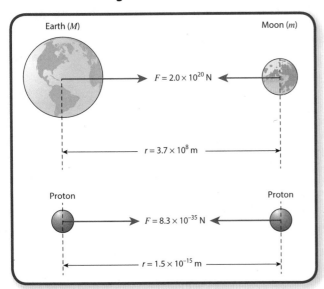

The constant of proportionality, G, was determined accurately by Cavendish in 1798 and is equal to $6.67 \times 10^{-11}\,\text{Nm}^2\,\text{kg}^{-2}$. The more massive the objects (e.g. moons, planets and stars), the larger the force of attraction between them; smaller masses (e.g. electrons and other sub-atomic particles) result in forces that are very small or insignificant, but not zero.

Gravitational Field Strength

The application of Newton's Law of Gravitation to a person (say of mass $m = 70\,\text{kg}$) standing on the surface of the Earth (mass $M = 5.97 \times 10^{24}\,\text{kg}$, radius $R = 6.37 \times 10^6\,\text{m}$) gives a resultant force of gravitational attraction of $F = 687\,\text{N}$. Although the force on the Earth and on the person are of course exactly the same, the force on the person has a much larger effect than the force on the Earth does because the Earth is so massive. The force that acts downwards on the person is simply $F = mg$ and this is known as **weight**. Equating these two forces leads to

$$g = \frac{F}{m} = \frac{687\,\text{N}}{70\,\text{kg}} = 9.8\,\text{Nkg}^{-1}$$

where g is known as the **gravitational field strength**; at the Earth's surface, it is $9.81\,\text{N kg}^{-1}$. It depends both on the mass of the object creating the field and on the distance between the centres of each object.

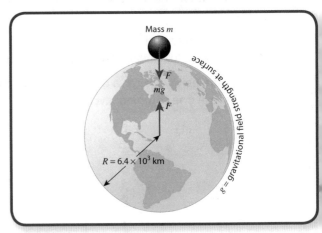

Gravitational Fields

A **gravitational field** is therefore a region of space where a mass experiences a force. For spherical masses, the field diminishes with increasing distance from its centre, and is known as a **radial field**. For large spherical and massive objects, such as the Earth, the gravitational fields generated are significant. The gravitational field can be pictured as a series of **field lines** or **lines of force** similar to a magnetic field. A small mass, sometimes referred to as a test mass (so small that its own gravitational field does not affect the more dominant field), placed within the field will be attracted towards the centre of mass of the larger object. The direction of this attractive force is represented by an arrow pointing towards the centre of the Earth. As the small mass is moved further away, the lines of force spread further apart so that the density of field lines becomes less, representing the diminishing force experienced by both masses.

$$F = mg = -\frac{GMm}{r^2}$$

providing for a much simpler expression for the magnitude of the gravitational field strength, g, of

$$g = \frac{GM}{r^2}$$

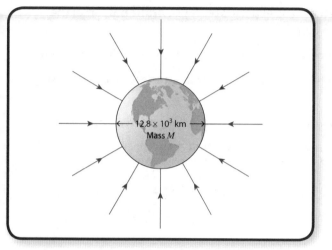

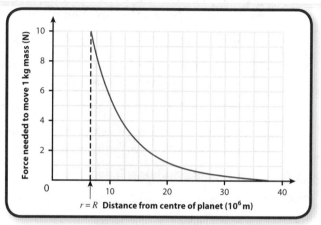

Close to the surface of the Earth, the large radius of curvature of the Earth makes the field lines look parallel and the gravitational field can be considered to be a **uniform gravitational field**, i.e. one in which the gravitational field strength has the same value at all points in the field. The gravitational field strength at or near the Earth's surface is therefore represented by a value of 9.81 N kg^{-1}. A similar analysis for the Moon reveals a gravitational field strength of 1.6 N kg^{-1}, and for the more massive Sun it is 270 N kg^{-1}.

Note that the variation of g also follows an inverse square law. As the distance from the centre increases, the force needed to move a unit mass further away decreases accordingly. If the mass is moved a small distance, Δr, further away from the planet then **work must be done** on the mass, W, and a corresponding increase in **gravitational potential energy**, E_p, is obtained. In this case

$$W = E_p = F\Delta r$$

where $F\Delta r$ is the area under the graph (shown shaded).

At a planet's surface, the field strength is given by $g_s = \frac{GM}{R^2}$, where R is the radius of the spherical planet. The general expression for the field strength can then be given in terms of the surface field as $g = g_s \left(\frac{R}{R+h}\right)^2$, where h is the height above the planetary surface.

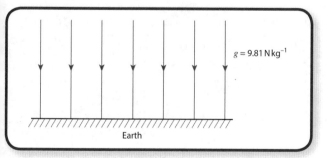

Gravitational Field Strength for Spherical Planets

As shown above, the force of gravitational attraction on the Earth must be the same as the force acting on a mass in that gravitational field, hence at a distance r from the centre of a spherical planet (of radius R)

Gravitational Field Strength and Density

The gravitational field strength can also be expressed in terms of a planet's **mean density**. For a spherical planet, $M = \frac{4}{3}\pi\rho R^3$, which leads to $g = \frac{4}{3}\pi G\rho R$ and to the fact that a planet's gravitational field strength is **directly proportional** to its mean density.

SUMMARY

- Gravitation, $F = \frac{GMm}{r^2}$, is the mutual attractive force between any two masses in the universe and is defined by Newton's Law of Gravitation
- Newton's Law of Gravitation is another example of an inverse square law
- A gravitational field is a region of space in which a mass experiences a gravitational force; the direction of the field is the direction of the force on the mass
- Gravitational field lines represent the direction of a force on a point mass in a gravitational field
- Large planetary masses have radial gravitational fields that decrease in strength with increasing distance from the centre of the mass
- Close to the surface of a planetary mass the gravitational field forms a very nearly uniform field
- Gravitational field strength is the force per unit mass acting on a small mass placed at a particular point in the gravitational field and given by $g = \frac{GM}{r^2}$
- The surface gravitational field strength for a spherical planet of radius R is $g_s = \frac{GM}{R^2}$
- For a planetary object of density ρ, the gravitational field strength at the surface is $g_s = \frac{4}{3}\pi G \rho R$

QUICK TEST

1. What is the range of the gravitational force of attraction between two masses?

2. How does the gravitational force of attraction vary with distance of separation?

3. What does a negative sign, as in Newton's Law of Gravitation, generally signify?

4. What is the constant G called and what are its units?

5. Describe a 'radial gravitational field'.

6. What is the equation that connects the gravitational field strength and G at a distance r from the centre of the planet?

7. A planet has a mass of 6.2×10^{23} kg and a radius of 3200 km. Calculate the gravitational field strength at the surface.

8. Determine the mass of the Earth given that the gravitational field strength at the surface is $9.8 \, \text{N kg}^{-1}$ and its radius is 6400 km.

9. Calculate the strength and direction of the gravitational force between the Earth (mass $M = 6.0 \times 10^{24}$ kg) and the Apollo Lunar Module (mass $m = 28\,800$ kg) at a distance from the Earth of 3.0×10^8 m.

10. Calculate the surface gravitational field strength of the Earth if its mean density is $5510 \, \text{kg m}^{-3}$ and taking the Earth's radius as 6400 km.

PRACTICE QUESTIONS

1. **a)** Define what is meant by gravitational field strength and state the SI unit. **[3 marks]**

    b) If the radius of the Earth is R, show that the gravitational field strength at a height h above the Earth is given by $g = g_s \left(\frac{R}{R+h}\right)^2$. **[3 marks]**

    c) Hence determine the gravitational field strength at a height of $h = 400\,\text{km}$. [take $R = 6400\,\text{km}$] **[1 mark]**

    d) The International Space Station orbits the Earth at a height of 400 km. Determine the weight of an astronaut on board the ISS whose mass is 70 kg. **[1 mark]**

    e) Given your answer to part **d)**, explain the notion that the astronauts on board are 'weightless'. **[1 mark]**

2. The table shows the gravitational field strength as a function of the height above the Earth's surface.

Height (km)	0	50	100	150	200	250	300	350	400	450	500
g (N kg^{-1})	9.81	9.66	9.51	9.37	9.22	9.09	8.95	8.82	8.69	8.56	8.44

    a) Plot a graph of the gravitational field strength (y-axis) against height (x-axis), starting the y-axis at $8.0\,\text{N kg}^{-1}$, and draw the best line of fit through the points. **[3 marks]**

    b) What does the graph reveal about the gravitational field of the Earth in this region of space? **[2 marks]**

    c) Mark on the graph the area that corresponds to the energy needed to move 1 kg from the surface of the Earth to a height of 400 km (the height of the International Space Station). **[2 marks]**

    d) Using this information, calculate the total energy needed to place a mass of 1200 kg at the ISS. **[4 marks]**

3. The Sun has a radius of 7.0×10^8 m and a mass of 2.0×10^{30} kg.

    a) Calculate the gravitational field strength on the surface of the Sun. **[2 marks]**

    b) Hence determine the mean density of matter within the Sun. **[3 marks]**

    c) Determine the Sun's gravitational field strength at the mean Earth–Sun distance of 1.5×10^9 m. **[2 marks]**

    The Sun towards the end of its life will become a red giant star with a mean density of only $30\,\text{kg m}^{-3}$.

    d) Calculate the radius of the future red giant stage of the Sun's evolution and comment on the fate of the Earth. **[3 marks]**

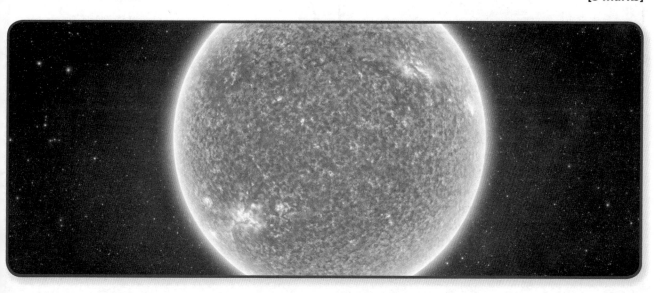

Gravitational Potential

Gravitational Potential

Every point in a gravitational field has a **gravitational potential** (V) associated with it; it is the **gravitational potential energy** that a **unit mass** would possess at that point. It therefore has units of Jkg^{-1}. Under this definition the value of the gravitational potential energy is not given by $\Delta E_p = mg\Delta h$, since this is only valid for small changes in h; for example, an object moved near the Earth's surface, where g can be considered to be constant. For **radial fields**, the expression for the gravitational potential is given by $V = -\frac{GM}{r}$, where G is the gravitational constant, M is the mass of the object (causing the gravitational field) and r is the distance from the centre of the object. Like energy, the gravitational potential is a **scalar quantity**. Gravitational potential is defined so that $V = 0$ **at infinity** and so must become more negative as a mass gets closer to the object.

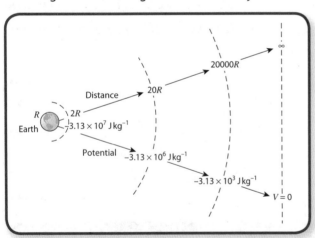

Variation of Gravitational Potential

The value of the **gravitational potential decreases** as the **distance increases** (as shown above for the Earth) where the potential is -6.3×10^7 Jkg^{-1} at the Earth's surface. Potentials have significant values even well away from the planet so that the gravitational potential due to Earth at the Moon's position is still -1.1×10^6 Jkg^{-1}. If the potential for the Earth is plotted as a function of the distance away from the centre of the Earth then a $\frac{1}{r}$ **relationship** is clearly seen. Here $M = 3 \times 10^{24}$ kg, $r = R$ (at the Earth's surface) $= 6.4 \times 10^6$ m and $G = 6.67 \times 10^{-11}$ Nm² kg⁻²,

giving a value of V at the Earth's surface of -6.3×10^7 Jkg^{-1}. This is often more conveniently expressed as -63 $MJkg^{-1}$.

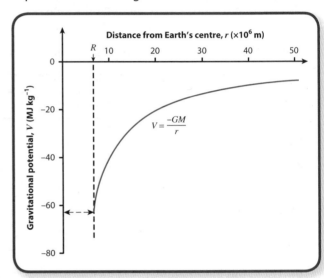

The Gradient of the Potential

The **gradient** of the gravitational potential decreases as the distance increases. This change or **gradient of the potential** gives a measure of the **gravitational field strength**, i.e.

$$g = -\frac{\Delta V}{\Delta r}$$

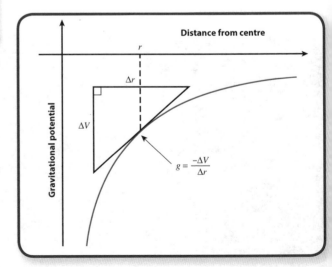

This means that g has units of $J\,kg^{-1}\,m^{-1}$, or more simply $N\,kg^{-1}$. At the Earth's surface the gradient is $9.81\,N\,kg^{-1}$ and at the height of the International Space Station (400 km above the Earth) its value is still $8.7\,N\,kg^{-1}$. At a distance of $r = 4 \times 10^7$ m (40 million km) it falls to $0.25\,N\,kg^{-1}$ and at the Moon's distance it is a mere $0.003\,N\,kg^{-1}$.

Equipotentials

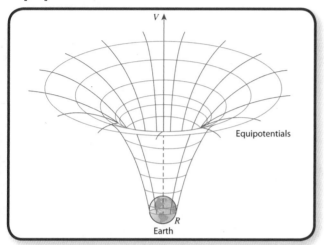

Equipotentials

Earth

The above definition of gravitational potential involves a radial gravitational field provided by a large and massive spherical planet or star. This means that all points at an equal distance above the centre of a large object of mass M must have the same gravitational potential. A line joining all points with the same potential is called an **equipotential**. For a radial field, equipotentials form **concentric circles** and the gravitational field lines are at **right angles** to these concentric equipotentials.

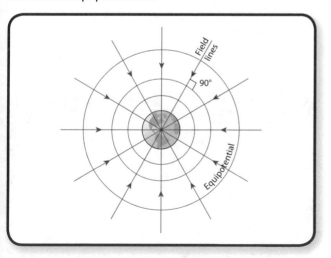

Gravitational Potential Differences

At two different distances r_1 and r_2 above a large planetary mass, an object must experience two different gravitational potentials, V_1 and V_2 respectively, i.e. there is a **gravitational potential difference** between these two positions. Moving an object from one position to another requires **work to be done** against the force of gravity (strictly the difference in gravitational field strength). This provides an alternative definition of gravitational potential: the work done against gravity when a unit mass is brought from infinity to that point. The **amount of energy** required depends on the mass of the object being moved and the gravitational potential difference that the mass moves through, i.e. energy change = mass × change in gravitational potential, or

$$\Delta W = m\Delta V = m\left(V_2 - V_1\right)$$

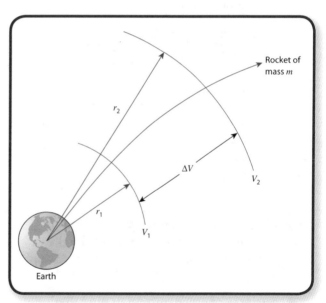

Rocket of mass m

Earth

If a small mass such as a satellite moves in a **circular orbit** about the Earth then it follows one of the equipotentials and hence there is **no change** in its gravitational potential; there is thus no change in its gravitational potential energy. Its kinetic energy therefore also remains constant as **the total energy** must be constant. For satellites in **elliptical orbits** (see later section), there must be a change in gravitational potential (as the distance from the centre continuously varies). This leads to a change in gravitational potential energy at different positions on the elliptical path. Because of the need for conservation of total energy, there must be a corresponding increase and/or decrease in the satellite's kinetic energy and hence speed as it moves around an elliptical orbit.

Launching a Satellite into Orbit

It is known that the gravitational potential at the Earth's surface is -6.3×10^7 Jkg^{-1} (call this V_1). The gravitational potential at the height that the International Space Station orbits the Earth (400 km) is -5.9×10^7 Jkg^{-1} (call this V_2). The change in gravitational potential, $\Delta V = V_2 - V_1 = \left(-5.9 \times 10^7\right) - \left(-6.3 \times 10^7\right) = 4.0 \times 10^6$ Jkg^{-1}. To place, say, a Soyuz capsule of mass 6500 kg at the ISS requires an energy of $m\Delta V = 6500 \times 4.0 \times 10^6 = 2.6 \times 10^{10}$ J or 26 GJ. This estimate of the energy requirement does not take into account factors such as the mass of the launch vehicle, the reduction in mass as fuel is burnt, or the effects of air resistance as the launch rocket travels through the Earth's atmosphere.

SUMMARY

- The **gravitational potential in a radial gravitational field** at a given point is the work done (against gravity) per unit mass in bringing a point mass from infinity to that point

- The **gravitational potential at infinity is zero**

- **Gravitational potential is inversely proportional to the distance r from the centre of a planet of mass M** that is causing the gravitational field, i.e. $V = -\frac{GM}{r}$

- Surfaces of equal potentials are called **equipotentials** and these are at right angles to the radial field lines

- Objects that **move along equipotentials** experience no change in their gravitational potential energies

- Objects that **move between potentials** experience an energy change given by the mass × change in potential

- The gradient of the potential, $\frac{\Delta V}{\Delta r}$, provides a measure of the gravitational field strength at that point

QUICK TEST

1. Why can the equation for gravitational potential energy, $\Delta E_p = mg\Delta h$, not be used to describe gravitational potential?

2. Give the expression for gravitational potential in a radial field and give its units.

3. What is the value of V at the Earth's surface and why is it negative?

4. How is the gravitational field strength defined in terms of V?

5. What does an equipotential surface represent?

6. What is the connection between an equipotential surface and a field line?

7. What is the change in gravitational potential energy when travelling along an equipotential?

8. How is the change in energy ΔE calculated for an object of mass m when going from a potential V_1 to a potential V_2?

9. Calculate the gravitational potential of a star of mass 4.7×10^{35} kg at a distance of 8.2×10^{15} m from its centre.

10. The gravitational potential at 7.0×10^7 m from the centre of a planet is 1.8×10^9 Jkg^{-1}. Determine the mass of the planet.

11. In the above question determine the gravitational field strength at this height.

12. For a satellite in a circular orbit about the Earth, why is the speed of the satellite constant?

PRACTICE QUESTIONS

In the following questions, take $G = 6.67 \times 10^{-11}\,\text{Nm}^2\,\text{kg}^{-2}$.

1. The Sun has a mass of 2.0×10^{30} kg and a mean diameter of 1.4×10^9 m.

    a) Calculate the gravitational potential of the Sun at its surface.   **[2 marks]**

    b) Using your answer to part **a)**, determine the gravitational field strength at the Sun's surface.   **[2 marks]**

    A coronal mass ejection places huge amounts of matter above the Sun's surface. In one episode, 1.6×10^{12} kg reached an altitude of 1.5×10^8 m above the Sun's surface.

    c) Calculate the gravitational potential at a height of 1.5×10^8 m and hence determine the amount of energy change required to achieve this.   **[4 marks]**

2. a) What is meant by gravitational potential?   **[2 marks]**

    b) The gravitational field strength on the surface of Mars is just 38% that of Earth's gravity. If the mass of Mars is 6.4×10^{23} kg and its mean radius is 3.4×10^3 km, show that the above statement is correct.   **[3 marks]**

    c) Calculate the gravitational potential at the Martian surface.   **[2 marks]**

    A large probe of mass 900 kg is in orbit 500 km above Mars. It then enters the Martian atmosphere, where a parachute is deployed at a height of 11 km to bring the probe safely to the surface.

    d) Calculate (i) the loss of gravitational potential energy between the orbit and the point at which the parachute is deployed and (ii) hence determine the vertical speed of the probe when the parachute is deployed.   **[6 marks]**

    e) What assumptions can be made about the gravitational field when the probe descends the final 11 km?   **[2 marks]**

3. The graph shows how gravitational potential varies with distance from the surface of an unknown planet (radius 0.8×10^6 m), and a probe has been sent to investigate its surface.

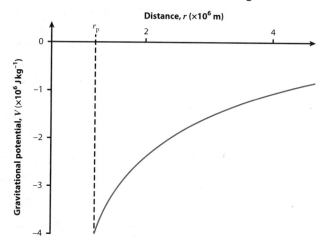

Using the graph:

    a) Estimate the gravitational field strength on the planet's surface.   **[2 marks]**

    b) Calculate the gravitational potential energy of the probe (mass 650 kg) at rest on the surface of the planet.   **[3 marks]**

    c) A section of probe (mass 120 kg) is being sent back to orbit the planet at a height of 800 km. Determine the work done in moving this part of the probe to attain the required orbit.   **[4 marks]**

Orbits of Satellites and Planets

Escape Velocity

When an object is projected vertically from the Earth with a velocity v it will reach a height that depends on v and on the gravitational field strength g. If v is too small, the object will simply return to Earth. If the value of v is increased to a velocity of about 7–8 km s^{-1}, the object will be projected into a stable **low Earth orbit** (LEO), i.e. an orbit that avoids the significant **atmospheric drag** that dominates at lower altitudes (typically < 300 km). If the object is projected at a velocity equal to or greater than a specific velocity known as the **escape velocity**, v_e, it will not return to Earth or travel in orbit but will continue to climb out of the Earth's gravitational potential well and carry on indefinitely. (In reality, satellites are not launched as projectiles but on rockets that provide continuous thrust and so the concept of escape velocity does not actually apply.) The escape velocity is determined by equating the projectile's initial kinetic energy E_k to the gain in gravitational potential energy E_p as the projectile moves from its initial position towards 'infinity', i.e. $E_k + E_p \geq 0$. This leads to

$$\frac{1}{2}mv_e^2 + mV \geq 0 \quad \text{or} \quad v_e \geq \sqrt{\frac{2GM}{R}}$$

where V is the Earth's gravitational potential. For $V = -63 \, \text{MJ kg}^{-1}$, $v_e \geq 11.1 \, \text{km s}^{-1}$.

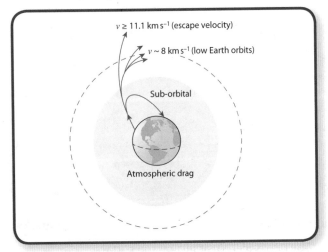

$v \geq 11.1 \, \text{km s}^{-1}$ (escape velocity)

$v \sim 8 \, \text{km s}^{-1}$ (low Earth orbits)

Sub-orbital

Atmospheric drag

Orbiting Satellites

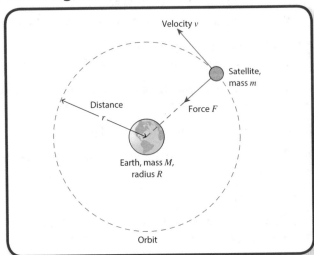

Velocity v

Satellite, mass m

Distance r

Force F

Earth, mass M, radius R

Orbit

From Newton's Law of Gravitation, the motion of a satellite of mass m orbiting a much larger planetary mass M (e.g. Earth) at a distance (centre to centre) r arises from a force of **gravitational attraction** between the two masses. For a satellite in circular orbit, this is just the **centripetal force** F that keeps the satellite on its orbit around M and is given by $\frac{GMm}{r^2}$. The gravitational field strength at a distance r is given by $g = \frac{GM}{r^2}$. At this distance r, the value of g is equal to the centripetal acceleration at that point, which is $\frac{v^2}{r}$, where v is now the orbital speed in a direction tangential to the Earth's surface. Equating these expressions gives $\frac{v^2}{r} = \frac{GM}{r^2}$ and thus $v^2 = \frac{GM}{r}$. For a mass m in circular motion at this distance, the tangential speed is given by

$$v = \frac{\text{circumference of the orbit}}{\text{time taken to complete 1 orbit}} = \frac{2\pi r}{T}$$

where T is the orbital period. Substituting for v gives $\left(\frac{2\pi r}{T}\right)^2 = \frac{GM}{r}$, which eventually gives the result

$$\frac{r^3}{T^2} = \frac{GM}{4\pi^2}$$

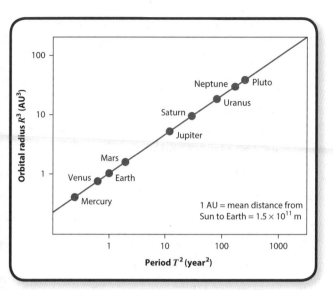

1 AU = mean distance from Sun to Earth = 1.5×10^{11} m

Notice that the mass of the object, m, does not appear in the equation. It therefore follows that for all satellites that are in orbit about a larger mass M, the cube of their orbital radius is directly proportional to the square of their orbital period, a statement that is more commonly known as **Kepler's Third Law**. For an object orbiting Earth, the further away it is the longer it takes to orbit the Earth. The International Space Station at 400 km above the Earth takes about 90 minutes to complete an orbit whereas the Moon (some 370 000 km away) takes about 28 days. Kepler's Third Law applies not just to satellites orbiting the Earth but to all moons orbiting planets and planets orbiting stars.

Satellites in Earth Orbits

In general, a **satellite** is a body that orbits a much larger body. The Earth now has a multitude of man-made satellites (and debris) that are in orbit around it. Weather satellites, communications satellites, satellites carrying telescopes and even spy satellites all orbit the Earth in very different types of orbit, both in terms of the **height** above the Earth's surface and in terms of their **orbital path** or **trajectory**. **Low Earth orbits** (LEO) of about 400 km, as used for the Hubble Space Telescope and the ISS, are designed mainly for ease of access (despite some atmospheric drag). The short orbital period also provides an opportunity to monitor movements and developments on the surface of the Earth. **Highly elliptical orbits** (HEO) provide a means of using satellites that move slowly over one half of the Earth when they are at their most distant point (**apogee**) but spend very little time on the opposite

side (**perigee**); this makes elliptical orbits useful for communication satellites. If a number of additional satellites are placed in the same elliptical orbit but are orientated differently then improved global cover is achieved. For example, three or more satellites are used in the **Global Positioning System** (GPS) that provides location and time information for civil, commercial as well as military users. **Geosynchronous orbits** are made by satellites with a period exactly equal to the Earth's rotational period on its axis of 23 hours, 56 minutes and 4 seconds (or ~24 hours). If the orbit lies in the equatorial plane and is circular, the satellite will appear to be stationary and such an orbit is referred to as a **stationary** or **geostationary orbit**. All geostationary satellites are geosynchronous but not all geosynchronous satellites are geostationary. The height above the Earth for either geostationary or geosynchronous satellites is determined using Kepler's Third Law with $T = 24$ hours (86 400 s). Substitution in the above equation gives $r = 4.2 \times 10^7$ m (42 000 km). As the mean radius of the Earth (R) is 6400 km, the height (h) of a geostationary satellite above the Earth's surface is 35 600 km.

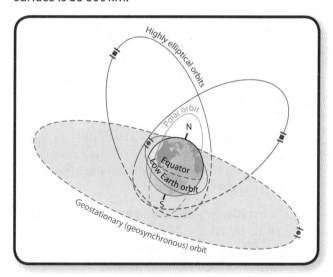

Determination of Planetary Mass

Kepler's Third Law can also be used to determine the mass of the larger object directly from measurements of an orbiting satellite provided that both the distance and period of the satellite are known. Rearranging Kepler's Third Law gives $M = \frac{4\pi^2 r^3}{GT^2} = k\frac{r^3}{T^2}$, where $k = 5.92 \times 10^{11}$ kg² m⁻² N⁻¹. An alternative approach uses the velocity of the satellite; in this case $v^2 = \frac{GM}{r} = gr$ leading to $g = \frac{GM}{r^2}$, which then gives a more simplified expression of $M = \frac{gr^2}{G}$.

For example, Oberon is one of the many moons of the gas giant Uranus. Observations reveal that it has an orbital period of 323 hours and a mean orbital radius of 5.82×10^5 km. Substitution into the above equation gives

$$M = 5.92 \times 10^{11} \times \frac{\left(5.82 \times 10^8\right)^3}{\left(323 \times 3600\right)^2} = 8.63 \times 10^{25}\,\text{kg}$$

which is in agreement with the known mass of Uranus.

SUMMARY

- The **escape velocity** is the minimum initial speed needed by a projectile to escape from the gravitational field of the Earth (or any other moon or celestial object)

- Satellites are usually placed in a **low Earth orbit** to avoid excessive atmospheric drag and for ease of access

- **Newton's Law of Gravitation** combined with the centripetal force gives **Kepler's Third Law** of planetary motion, i.e. $r^3 \propto T^2$, where r is the orbital radius and T its period

- **Kepler's Third Law** applies to any satellite that orbits a larger mass, including the solar system planets orbiting the Sun

- **Highly elliptical orbits** are used by communication satellite systems as well as by satellites within the **Global Positioning System (GPS)**

- **Geostationary orbits** and **geosynchronous orbits** both have 24 hour periods; only satellites in geostationary orbits will appear to be stationary as they lie above the equatorial plane and in a circular orbit

QUICK TEST

1. What is meant by the 'escape velocity'?

2. Give the expression that allows the escape velocity to be calculated from the gravitational potential.

3. What is the main problem with satellites orbiting at low altitudes around the Earth?

4. What keeps a satellite in a stable orbit?

5. What is the effect on an orbiting satellite if its velocity is increased?

6. State Kepler's Third Law.

7. Explain the difference between a geostationary orbit and a geosynchronous orbit.

8. Give a possible use of a satellite in a geostationary orbit.

9. What kind of orbits are used in the Global Positioning System?

10. Give the expression for the gravitational field strength at the surface of a planet of mass M and radius R.

11. The Earth orbits the Sun once a year. Determine the mass of the Sun if the mean orbital radius is 1.5×10^{11} m. [$G = 6.67 \times 10^{-11}\,\text{Nm}^2\,\text{kg}^{-2}$]

12. Calculate the speed of the International Space Station if its height above the Earth's surface is 400 km. [Earth's radius is 6400 km and mass is 6.0×10^{24} kg]

13. Calculate the mass of the Earth if the Moon's orbital period is about 28 days and its distance from the Earth is 370 000 km.

PRACTICE QUESTIONS

Take $G = 6.67 \times 10^{-11} \, \text{Nm}^2 \, \text{kg}^{-2}$.

1. The International Space Station (ISS) is in a low Earth orbit at a height of 400 km above the surface. Its mass is approximately 420 tonnes.

   a) What is meant by a low Earth orbit and give one advantage and one disadvantage of such an orbit for the ISS. **[3 marks]**

   b) Determine the orbital speed of the ISS. [Take the mass of Earth as 6.0×10^{24} kg and the radius of the Earth as 6400 km] **[2 marks]**

   c) Hence show that the magnitude of the gravitational field at this orbital radius is $8.7 \, \text{N kg}^{-1}$ and determine the centripetal force on the ISS. **[5 marks]**

   d) Using Newton's Law of Gravitation and the result from part c) above, confirm that the mass of the Earth is 6×10^{24} kg. **[3 marks]**

2. a) State Kepler's Third Law and give its equation in terms of G and M. **[2 marks]**

   The moons of Jupiter were the first to be seen through a telescope by Galileo. One of these moons, Io, is seen to orbit Jupiter once every 42 hours at a mean distance of 420 000 km.

   b) Using Kepler's Third Law and the data above, calculate the mass of Jupiter. **[2 marks]**

   c) Determine the orbital speed of Io. **[2 marks]**

   d) Another of Jupiter's moons, Ganymede, orbits the gas giant with an orbital period of 170 hours. Determine the radius of the orbit of Ganymede in km. **[3 marks]**

3. A weather satellite is being used to monitor the development of weather systems over mainland UK.

   a) What kind of orbit should this weather satellite be placed in and explain the reason for your choice. **[3 marks]**

   b) Determine the height above the Earth's surface that such a weather satellite must be placed in order to achieve this type of orbit. **[3 marks]**

   c) What would be the effect on the satellite if its speed of orbit was increased? **[2 marks]**

   d) If the satellite's height was reduced by a factor of 2, what would the new orbital period of the satellite be and how would this affect its capability of observing the fixed point on the Earth's surface. **[5 marks]**

Nuclear Size and Stability

Rutherford Scattering

In 1906 Rutherford and his colleagues used a beam of positively charged **alpha particles** (**helium nuclei**) of the **same energy** to strike a very thin piece of **gold foil** and observed the number of alpha particles at various scattering angles. The experiments were conducted in an **evacuated chamber** to avoid the alpha particles being stopped by collisions with air molecules. Although most alpha particles passed straight through the foil, approximately 1 in 2000 were scattered, and about 1 in 8000 were scattered through angles greater than 90°. Interpretation of the results provided conclusive evidence that Thomson's **plum-pudding model** (in which the positive charge was distributed throughout the atom) was incorrect. Rutherford's results showed that:

- the **positively charged nucleus is very small** (since very few alpha particles were deflected) and surrounded by the atom's orbiting electrons

- the **nucleus** contains most of the atom's mass

- an atom consists of mostly **empty space** (most alpha particles passed through undeflected)

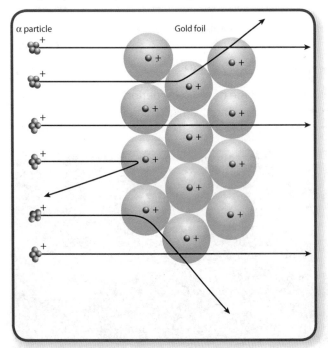

The Size of the Nucleus

Rutherford scattering provided the first real estimate for the **size of a nucleus**. An alpha particle with a charge $q_{alpha} = +2e$ (where e is the unit of electronic charge and is equal to 1.6×10^{-19} C) that is deflected almost back on itself would have reached a position extremely close to a gold nucleus ($q_{gold} = +79e$). This **closest approach** idea means that at this position all of the incoming (kinetic) energy of an alpha particle is transferred to electrical potential energy, given by Coulomb's Law,

$$E_k = \frac{q_{gold} q_{alpha}}{4\pi\varepsilon_0 r}$$

where r is the distance of closest approach for a head-on collision between an alpha particle and a gold nucleus. This distance provided Rutherford with an upper limit for the radius of a gold nucleus. With alpha particles having kinetic energies of about 5 MeV, the distance of closest approach is about 4.5×10^{-14} m or 45 fm (1 femtometre = 1×10^{-15} m). Further experiments provided values of r even smaller than this and much closer to the true nuclear radius (R), with sizes that are a factor of 10^5 smaller than an atom. More accurate values for nuclear radii have also come from **high-energy electron diffraction** measurements. Electrons accelerated through potentials in excess of 10^{11} volts

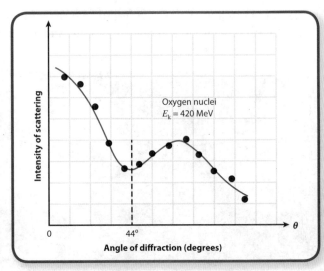

Oxygen nuclei
$E_k = 420$ MeV

44°

Intensity of scattering

Angle of diffraction (degrees)

have **de Broglie wavelengths** (given by $\lambda = \dfrac{h}{\sqrt{2meV}}$) of the order of the size of the nucleus and therefore show significant diffraction effects. According to **diffraction theory**, the first diffraction minimum is $\sin\theta_{\min} = 0.61 \times \frac{\lambda}{R}$. In such experiments, nuclear radii of the order of 2–3 fm were firmly established.

Nuclear Radii and Density

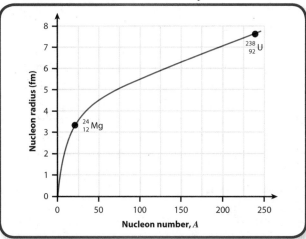

Additional and more accurate experiments to determine nuclear radii provided a means of establishing an **empirical relationship** (i.e. a relationship based on observation rather than on theory) between the nuclear radius, R, and the nucleon number, A. This relationship is shown above and is expressed by $R = r_0 A^{\frac{1}{3}}$ where r_0 represents the radius of a single nucleon and has a value of 1.2 fm. This expression for the nuclear radius can then be used to investigate the value of **nuclear density** (ρ), which is given by the nuclear mass (mass of one nucleon $\times A$) divided by the nuclear volume ($\frac{4}{3}\pi R^3$)(assuming that the nucleus is a sphere of radius R). Using $R = r_0 A^{\frac{1}{3}}$, it can be shown that $\rho \propto \frac{A}{R^3} \propto \frac{A}{A}$, which is a constant, revealing that the density of nuclear matter is independent of which particular isotope is being considered, with a value approximately equal to 2×10^{17} kgm^{-3}.

Nuclear Stability

A **nuclide** is a type of nucleus characterised by the number of protons (Z) and neutrons (N) it contains. There are over 250 nuclides that are termed stable, i.e. they have never been observed to decay. For nuclides with $Z \leq 20$, a graph of neutron number versus proton number follows an approximate straight line, i.e. the ratio $\frac{N}{Z} \approx 1$. Beyond $Z = 20$, stable nuclei have $\frac{N}{Z} > 1$ and this continues to increase for heavier nuclei as more neutrons are needed to stabilise the electrostatic repulsion between protons. The heaviest stable nuclide is bismuth-209 with 83 protons, 126 neutrons and a ratio $\frac{N}{Z} = 1.52$. There are about another 90 naturally occurring nuclides that are unstable and therefore decay through one of three mechanisms.

● Unstable nuclei above the stability line are neutron rich and gain stability by changing neutrons into protons via **beta-minus decay** such that

$$^{A}_{Z}X \rightarrow {}^{A}_{Z+1}Y + {}^{0}_{-1}\beta + {}^{0}_{0}\bar{\nu}$$

● Proton-rich nuclei change protons into neutrons via **beta-plus decay** such that

$$^{A}_{Z}X \rightarrow {}^{A}_{Z-1}Y + {}^{0}_{+1}\beta + \nu$$

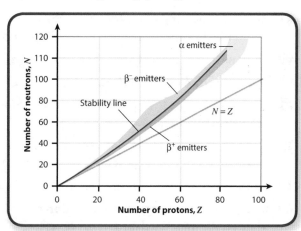

● More massive nuclei emit **alpha particles**, during **alpha decay**, changing the balance of the proton–neutron ratio in favour of the protons.

$$^{A}_{Z}X \rightarrow {}^{A-4}_{Z-2}Y + {}^{4}_{2}\alpha$$

Many unstable isotopes decay to form another isotope that may also be unstable. An unstable nucleus (**parent nucleus**) may therefore undergo several changes, creating many **daughter products** before stability is reached.

Nuclear Energy Levels

The creation of a 'daughter' nucleus after alpha or beta decay often leaves the daughter in an **excited nuclear state** (similar to excited atomic states). These

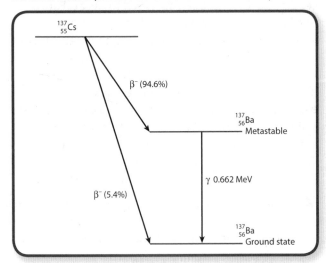

excited states are generally short-lived and, as the nucleus moves towards a lower energy state on its journey to its **ground state**, several high-energy photons in the form of **gamma rays** are emitted. On occasions, longer lived excited states can exist and these are known as **metastable states**. The half-life for metastable states varies from seconds to many years. Caesium-137 decays by beta-minus emission to a metastable state of barium (Ba-137m), which subsequently decays to the ground state by emitting intense gamma rays at 0.662 MeV.

The decay of molybdenum-99 by beta-minus emission forms a metastable state of technetium (Tc-99m), which subsequently decays to the ground state by gamma emission. Samples of Tc-99m with a half-life of 6 hours are used in **medical diagnosis** applications such as monitoring blood flow in the brain and imaging internal organs using a gamma camera.

SUMMARY

- Alpha particles are, in effect, helium nuclei and have a charge of +2e, where $e = 1.6 \times 10^{-19}$ C
- Nuclear radii (and diameters) are measured in femtometres (fm); 1 fm $= 10^{-15}$ m
- **Rutherford scattering** established the nature and structure of the atom and provided conclusive evidence that Thomson's plum-pudding model was incorrect
- The method of closest approach provided a means of establishing the size of a nucleus
- High-energy electron diffraction is an accurate technique for determining nuclear radii
- The equation for the approximate radius of a nucleus is based on experiments resulting in the empirical relationship $R = r_0 A^{1/3}$
- A graph of neutron number versus proton number is a stability graph and provides details as to those unstable nuclei that emit beta-minus, beta-plus and alpha particles
- Many unstable isotopes (parent nuclei) decay into daughter nuclei before stability is reached
- Many isotopes emit gamma radiation resulting from transitions from excited states to ground states within the nuclear energy levels
- Excited states that are longer lived are called metastable states.

QUICK TEST

1. Describe the shape of the stability line of an N–Z graph.

2. Describe the process of alpha decay with reference to an N–Z graph.

3. What metastable state is formed by decay of molybdenum-99 and give an example of one of its applications?

4. What is meant by a daughter nucleus?

5. How many neutrons and protons are there in the nuclide $^{66}_{30}$Zn and what is the value of the ratio $\frac{N}{Z}$?

6. Using the data from question 5, determine the radius of the zinc nucleus.

7. Calculate the de Broglie wavelength of electrons with an energy of 100 GeV

8. What is meant by the closest approach method?

9. Calculate the radius of the nucleus in $^{27}_{13}$Al and use this value to determine the nuclear density.

10. A metal foil has a thickness of 5.28 μm and is composed of atoms of radius 0.22 nm. Calculate the number of layers of atoms in the foil.

PRACTICE QUESTIONS

1. Alpha particles with an energy of 5.8 MeV are incident on a nickel foil target in an evacuated chamber and some are scattered back close to an angle of 180°. The mass number of nickel is 58; $\varepsilon_0 = 8.85 \times 10^{-12}$ fm^{-1}.

   a) Explain why the experiment is conducted in an evacuated chamber. **[1 mark]**

   b) Calculate the energy of the alpha particles in joules. **[2 marks]**

   c) Determine the distance of closest approach and give your answer in terms of femtometres. **[3 marks]**

   An order of magnitude calculation based on the closest approach method leads to the expression $\frac{\text{atomic radius}}{\text{nuclear radius}} \approx \frac{10^{-10}}{10^{-14}} = 10^4$.

   d) Using this expression together with the result obtained in part **c)**, estimate the size of the nickel atom and give your answer in nm. **[2 marks]**

2. The radius, R, of a nucleus with A nucleons is given by the empirical equation $R = r_0 A^{1/3}$.

   a) What is meant by an 'empirical' equation? **[1 mark]**

   b) If an $^{56}_{26}$Fe nucleus has a radius of 4.6×10^{-15} m, show that $r_0 = 1.2 \times 10^{-15}$ m. **[2 marks]**

   c) Use this information to determine the nuclear radius of $^{197}_{79}$Au. **[2 marks]**

   d) Calculate the density of a gold nucleus given that 1 u has a mass of 1.67×10^{-27} kg. **[3 marks]**

3. The metastable state of a technetium isotope $\left(^{99m}_{43}\text{Tc}\right)$ is formed by β^- emission from the molybdenum isotope $^{99}_{42}$Mo.

   a) What is meant by a metastable state? **[1 mark]**

   b) Write down the nuclear decay equation representing this process. **[1 mark]**

   c) The metastable state at 0.14 MeV decays to the ground state. What is emitted during this transition? **[2 marks]**

   d) Give a brief outline of one application where the emitted particles from technetium are used. **[2 marks]**

Nuclear Radiation

Nuclear Instability

Instability of a nucleus can arise because it has either too many protons or too many neutrons; it may also be caused by having too much energy within the nucleus itself. For example, in the case of an excess of protons, there is greater **electrostatic repulsion force** (of infinite range) than the short-range but attractive **strong nuclear force**; therefore more neutrons are needed to 'glue' such nuclei together and stable nuclides with large nuclei must have more neutrons than protons i.e. ratio $\frac{N}{Z} > 1$. A nucleus attempts to regain stability by releasing energy in the form of particles in a process called **radioactive decay**. The most common types of nuclear radiation emitted during the decay process involve alpha, beta and gamma radiation. Because these particles carry energy, they can readily knock electrons out of atoms and hence ionise them. **Ionising radiation** may therefore consist of a stream of high-energy particles (electrons, protons, alpha particles) or short-wavelength electromagnetic radiation (UV, X-rays, gamma rays). The strength of their **ionisation ability** depends largely on their charge, while the distance they travel in a material (**penetration**) and what attenuates them (**absorption, scattering**) largely depends on their energy and on the density of the material they are passing through.

Radiation	Charge	Constituent
alpha (α)	$+2e$	2 protons, 2 neutrons (i.e. a helium nucleus)
beta-minus (β⁻)	$-1e$	electron
beta-plus (β⁺)	$+1e$	positron
gamma (γ)	0	electromagnetic wave

Alpha Radiation

Alpha radiation is the least penetrating, only having a short range in air, typically 5 cm, and being stopped by a thin sheet of paper or even skin. However, it is **intensely ionising**, producing perhaps 10^4 ion-pairs per millimetre in air. Alpha radiation is only a risk inside the body since all of its energy is deposited in a small volume. As the alpha particles carries electrical charge, they show a slight deflection in a magnetic or electric field and can only be detected in a Geiger counter when very close to the tube window. The intensity of alpha radiation decreases **exponentially** with distance.

Beta Radiation

Beta-minus particles are fast-moving **electrons** emitted when a neutron decays into a proton, emitting a beta-minus particle and an antineutrino. They have a longer range than alpha particles, typically 2–3 m in air or a few mm in aluminium. Beta-minus radiation is less ionising; however, because the particles' mass is much less they are easily deflected by electric or magnetic fields. This is also true of **beta-plus** particles, i.e. **positrons**; these annihilate with electrons to produce gamma-ray photons. Outside the body, beta particles can present a health hazard although penetration of the skin is rather small. High-energy beta radiation can be detected with Geiger counters with thin end windows although this may decrease as the beta energy decreases as a result of attenuation by the window material. The intensity of beta radiation decreases **exponentially** with distance.

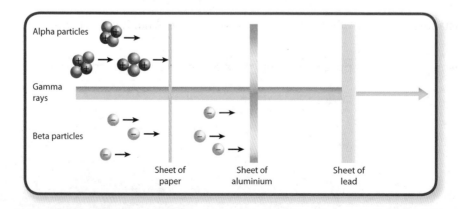

Gamma Radiation

Gamma radiation is very high frequency electromagnetic radiation emitted in all directions (**isotropic**) by the nucleus of some radionuclides. Gamma rays carry no charge and so are not deflected in electric or magnetic fields. Although they are very penetrating and can pass easily through thin sheets of metal, they are much less ionising. The amount of **shielding** needed depends on the shielding material itself and on the energy of the gamma radiation emitted. Very high energy gamma rays may require several metres of concrete shielding to provide a safe working level. The intensity of radiation obeys the **inverse square law** and is given by $I = I_0 \frac{k}{d^2}$, where d is the distance from the source. If the distance is doubled then the intensity or count rate decreases by a factor of 4. One way to maximise safety is therefore to keep well away from the source and to use long-handled tongs to manipulate the source. Often the thickness of shielding material is given in terms of a **half-value thickness**; this is the amount of shielding material that reduces the initial intensity by a factor of 2. Gamma radiation is detected using a Geiger counter although the counting efficiency of photon radiation (gamma and X-rays above 25 keV) depends on the efficiency of the interaction of the radiation with the tube walls.

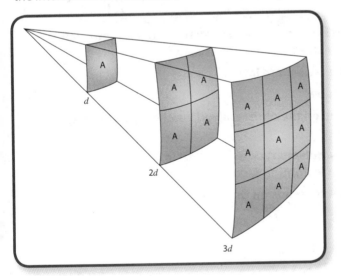

Radiation Monitoring and Identification

A simple experiment can be performed to determine the nature of the particles emitted from a radioactive source using various **absorbers** and a Geiger counter. Observing the count rate over set periods of time with various thicknesses of absorber will show what type of particle is dominating the emission. In occupations involving radiation exposure (e.g. nuclear, medical, dental and research), personal radiation dosimeters (sometimes called 'badges') are used. This includes the **thermoluminescent dosimeter** (TLD), used in the vast majority of exposure situations. TLDs work by storing energy received from ionising radiation. To determine the radiation dose received, the TLD is subsequently heated and its light output measured; the result is directly proportional to the received dose. TLDs are changed at regular intervals to monitor and record individual dose results and cumulative totals. **Neutron** and **radon dosimeters** are also used for specialised work.

Biological Effects of Radiation

Type of radiation	Weighting factor
alpha particles	20
protons	2
X-rays, gamma rays, beta particles	1

The biological effects of ionising radiation depend on the type of radiation and on the dose received. The **absorbed dose** of radiation is defined as the amount of energy absorbed per kilogram of a body, or $D = \frac{E}{m}$ in units of $J\,kg^{-1}$, called the **gray** (Gy). High doses of radiation will certainly lead to higher risks of damage.

The **equivalent dose**, however, is used to consider the effect of using different radiations, such as alpha compared with gamma, or on different parts of the body that are more sensitive to radiation damage. In radiobiology the **relative biological effectiveness** (RBE) is the ratio of biological effectiveness of one type of ionising radiation relative to that of another (given the same amount of absorbed energy). RBE is represented by the **radiation weighting factor**, W (also known as the **quality factor**). The connection therefore between absorbed dose (D) and equivalent dose (H) is $H = WD$. The unit of equivalent dose is the **Sievert** (Sv) and takes account of these other factors. For example, $1\,J\,kg^{-1}$ of gamma absorbed dose corresponds to 1 Sv of equivalent dose but, because alpha radiation is more dangerous to the body (because of its ionisation power), $1\,J\,kg^{-1}$ of alpha absorbed dose corresponds to 20 Sv of equivalent dose. Clearly such effects are not encountered for radiation sources that are external to the body; for example, alpha radiation cannot penetrate the skin's outer layers whereas gamma radiation is significantly more penetrating.

Background Radiation and Dose Limits

Background radiation occurs both naturally (~88%) and artificially (~12%) and the major sources of background radiation are shown in the diagram. The recommended maximum dose of radiation irrespective of occupation is set at 2 mSv per year except for workers in the nuclear industry where the limit is raised to 15 mSv per year. The **risk of exposure** to radiation should always be minimised and in laboratory measurements involving radioactive sources strict regulations for their use and storage should always be adhered to.

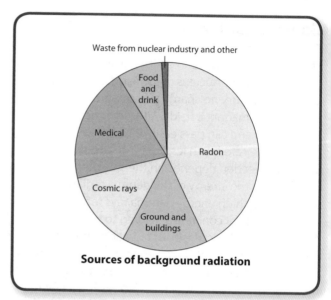

Sources of background radiation

SUMMARY

- The most common types of radiation emitted by unstable nuclei are alpha, beta and gamma radiation
- Ionising radiation is radiation of sufficiently high energy to cause the removal of electrons from atoms
- Alpha particles are helium nuclei emitted at high speed from some unstable nuclei: they are highly ionising, are easily stopped by paper and are only slightly deflected by electric and magnetic fields
- Beta particles are electrons (or positrons) emitted at high speed: they are moderately ionising, stopped by a few millimetres of aluminium and are easily deflected in electric and magnetic fields
- Gamma radiation forms part of the electromagnetic spectrum: it ionises weakly, shows considerable penetration in most materials and is not deflected in electric and magnetic fields; gamma radiation is attenuated exponentially by an absorber such as lead
- The intensity of emitted radiation obeys the inverse square law
- Ionising radiation can be detected by a Geiger tube
- The biological effects of ionising radiation depend on the dose received, on the type of radiation and on which tissues/organs are being irradiated
- Damage to biological tissue is measured by the equivalent dose ($H = WD$) in sieverts, where the dose ($D = \frac{E}{m}$) is in units of gray; W is the radiation weighting factor
- The weighting factor is a dimensionless unit that depends on the type of radiation used per unit energy deposited

QUICK TEST

1. What are the three common types of radiation emitted by unstable nuclei?
2. What is an alpha particle?
3. What is the range of beta-plus particles in air?
4. How are beta and alpha particles affected by electric and magnetic fields?

5. If a detector is moved five times further away from a radioactive gamma source, by what factor is the measured intensity diminished?

6. Give three sources of background radiation.

7. An alpha particle has an energy of 5 MeV. If 4×10^8 alpha particles are absorbed by 10 kg of body tissue, calculate the absorbed dose of radiation received.

8. For the absorbed dose in question 7, give the dose equivalent and its unit.

9. How should radioactive sources be handled safely in a school environment?

PRACTICE QUESTIONS

1. a) Explain what is meant by background radiation and give examples. **[3 marks]**

   The count rate recorded by a Geiger counter at a distance 0.1 m from a gamma ray source was 5328 counts per second. The background count rate was measured to be only 20 counts per second.

   b) Determine the count rate when the detector is moved to 0.25 m from the source. **[3 marks]**

   c) Describe an experiment that would show that the inverse square law is valid for gamma radiation. **[4 marks]**

   d) What assumptions have been made about the detection of the gamma radiation within the Geiger tube and how would this be determined from your graph? **[3 marks]**

2. A typical radioactive source used in a school experiment to determine the effects of gamma radiation had an activity of 2×10^5 particles emitted per second. The energy of the particles was 0.662 MeV.

   a) What is the energy of each of the particles in joules? **[1 mark]**

   b) Determine the total energy transfer per second from this radioactive source. **[2 marks]**

   c) The experiment lasted 30 minutes. How much energy was transferred to the surroundings in this time. **[2 marks]**

   d) If all of this energy was absorbed by 5 kg of body tissue, calculate the dose equivalent and give the correct units. **[2 marks]**

   e) If the investigation involved alpha particles, determine the new dose equivalent and explain what the effect would be on the body tissue. **[4 marks]**

3. The results of an investigation into the absorption of β^- particles from a particular radionuclide source are shown in the table. The absorption follows an exponential curve and the thickness of the aluminium sheets is given in units of $kg\,m^{-2}$.

Counts	25876	14956	6481	3092	1089	784	139	138
Time (s)	20	30	60	90	120	150	200	300
Thickness	0	0.5	2	3	4	5	6	7
Count rate (min^{-1})								
In(count rate)								

   a) Calculate the count rate per minute for each of the absorber thicknesses. **[2 marks]**

   b) Complete the table by taking the natural logarithms (ln) of the count rate. **[2 marks]**

   c) Plot a graph of ln(count rate) along the y-axis against the absorber thickness along the x-axis; extend your x-axis to include $10\,kg\,m^{-2}$. **[3 marks]**

   d) Extend your straight line to cross the x-axis. Record this value and explain what this result may suggest about beta absorption. **[2 marks]**

   e) Explain why the time period needed to be much longer for thicker absorbers. **[2 marks]**

Radioactive Decay

Radioactive Decay Rates

Radioactive isotopes (radioisotopes) have unstable nuclei and the nature of the nucleus dictates how it decays and the rate at which it decays. Radioactive decay is a **random and spontaneous process**, i.e. there is no way of predicting which nucleus will decay or when it will decay, and so only an overall rate of decay can be stated. The probability of an individual nucleus decaying per second is called the **decay constant**, λ. If 20 nuclei decay out of a total of 500 in 25 seconds then the decay constant is just $\frac{(20/500)}{25} = \frac{0.04}{25} = 0.0016\,\text{s}^{-1}$. This can be written mathematically as $\frac{\Delta N}{N \Delta t} = \lambda$. The SI unit of the decay constant is s^{-1} but min^{-1} and hr^{-1} may also be used. The decay constant is the constant of proportionality, and it is different for each radioisotope. Rearranging the equation gives $\frac{\Delta N}{\Delta t} = \lambda N$ and the ratio $\frac{\Delta N}{\Delta t}$ is called the **activity**, A, of a sample of radioactive material; it is proportional to the number of active nuclei present. Activity measures the rate of decay in all directions and has units of **becquerels**, Bq, where $1\,\text{Bq} = 1$ decay or disintegration per second.

A useful measure of the activity of a radioactive source is the time taken for the number of un-decayed atoms to reach half of its initial value, and this quantity is known as the **half-life**, $t_{1/2}$. The longer the value of the half-life, the longer the atom remains radioactive. Half-lives vary from a few milliseconds to tens of thousands of years. A longer half-life means a smaller decay constant because the probability of decay is less. Half-life and decay constant are related through the formula $t_{1/2} = \frac{\ln 2}{\lambda} \approx \frac{0.693}{\lambda}$.

The Decay Curve

The mathematical expression for the activity of a radionuclide can be expressed as $\frac{\Delta N}{\Delta n} = -\lambda N$ (the minus sign indicates a decay process). The solution to this equation is well known and given by $N = N_0 e^{-\lambda t}$. The shape of this decay curve is representative of an **exponential function** and all radionuclides decay in this way. Because the mass of a sample of a radionuclide is directly proportional to the number of nuclei (N), the mass remaining after time t is also given by a similar exponential curve with the same half-life. This is also true for both **activity** (A) and **count rate** (C) and this connection is useful when solving problems. The count rate, as recorded by a Geiger counter, only measures a small fraction of the total emissions from a source and so will always be less than the activity. The unit of count rate is also becquerels. As t increases, A, N and C all decrease and tend towards zero although the activity never reaches zero but merges into the background activity rate. Solving the above equation by taking natural logarithms gives $\ln N = \ln N_0 - \lambda t$. A plot of $\ln N$ against t (or $\ln A$ or $\ln C$ against t) will therefore give a straight line with **gradient** $-\lambda$ and **intercept** $\ln N_0$ (or $\ln A_0$ or $\ln C_0$).

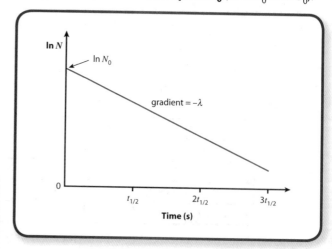

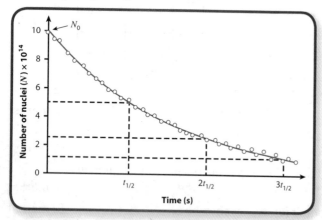

Activity and Power

A radioactive source of activity A emitting monoenergetic particles with energy E transfers a total amount of energy per second given by the product AE; this is known as the **power** of the radioactive source. If a radioactive source is contained in a sealed box then the box absorbs all of this emitted energy. For example, if a small radioactive source has an activity of $20\,MBq$ and emits alpha particles of energy $4.5\,MeV$ then the energy transferred each second is $AE = 20 \times 10^6 \times 4.5 \times 1.6 \times 10^{-13}\,Js^{-1} = 1.4 \times 10^{-5}\,W$. This power heats the container, and thermocouples are used to convert this heat to electricity using the **thermoelectric effect**. Such **radioisotope thermoelectric generators** (RTGs) are used as power sources in satellites, space probes and unmanned remote facilities.

Scientific Applications of Radioisotopes

There are numerous uses for radioisotopes, particularly in science. The choice of isotope depends on the type of application and on its half-life. **Carbon-14** is used in archaeology as a means of **dating ancient wood**, **artefacts made from wood** and **other plants** that have died. With a half-life of over 5700 years it is an ideal tool for dating wood with ages up to 10 times the half-life. The technique is based on the fact that living plants absorb carbon dioxide including carbon-14. When such plants die, no more carbon is metabolised and the amount of carbon-14 left decreases exponentially. Measuring the activity of carbon-14 enables the age of the tree or wood to be determined. Similarly, **argon-40**, with a half-life of 1.25 billion years, is particularly suited for determining the **age of igneous rocks** that contain trapped argon gas. The argon-40 arises from the decay of the radioactive isotope potassium-40 in the rock. The age the rock formed or solidified is then calculated from the ratio of potassium-40 to argon-40. Radioisotopes are used extensively in scientific research, where they are used to probe all states of matter to reveal details of the atomic and quantum structure.

Industrial Applications of Radioisotopes

There are numerous applications of radioisotopes in industry. One application uses a **beta emitter** with a long half-life to determine the precise **thickness of a metal** foil. The foil is placed on a conveyor belt and the desired thickness is monitored by a detector. The reading from the detector is used to control a set of rollers that are used to maintain a constant foil thickness. Another application includes monitoring **defects** and flaws such as cracks in underground pipes **non-destructively** and without the need to disturb or dig up the pipes. **Radioactive tracers** are also used extensively in systems where flow rate can be monitored such as in pipes, reservoirs, engine wear and the take-up of fertilisers in plants. In such processes, it is desirable to use a radioisotope with a long enough half-life to take the measurements required but also short enough to decay to a safe level soon after use.

Medical Applications of Radioactive Isotopes

Cobalt-60, caesium-137 and other high-energy gamma sources are used externally in **medical diagnosis** as well as in the **treatment of cancers**. Sophisticated devices are now available that provide a pencil beam of radiation that can be precisely targeted at the cancerous cells with a high dose of radiation while leaving the healthy cells moderately untouched with a low dose. Short bursts of gamma radiation are also used to **sterilise** medical equipment. Technetium-99m, a metastable state produced from molybdenum, is a gamma emitter with a short half-life (~6 hours) that is used as a tracer to investigate particular organs of the body. Used in conjunction with a **gamma camera**, direct images of a particular organ can be obtained; the short half-life ensures that after only a few half-lives it has decayed to an acceptable and safe level. Internal use of both **beta and alpha radionuclides (targeted alpha therapy – TAT)** can also be used to treat tumours and other cancer conditions following injection or take-up directly at the site of the cancer.

SUMMARY

- The decay constant is the probability of a particular nucleus decaying per second; it has units of s^{-1}
- The activity of a radioactive source is the rate of decay (number of disintegrations per second) and has units of becquerels (Bq)
- The half-life of a radionuclide is the time taken for half of a sample to decay; it has units of s (but other time units are also commonly used)
- The power of a radionuclide is its activity $\times$ the energy of the emitted particles (AE) in units of W.
- Radioactive decay follows an exponential law given by $N = N_0 e^{-\lambda t}$
- Carbon-14 is used in archaeology to date wood, plants and bones, and human-made artefacts; argon-40 and potassium-40 are used date rocks
- Radioactive tracers are used to determine flow rates
- Beta and gamma radionuclides have found application in determining and controlling the thickness of metals and in many applications involving non-destructive testing
- High-energy gamma sources (e.g. Cs-137 and Co-60) are used in medical applications to treat medical conditions, especially cancer, and in the sterilisation of medical equipment
- Internal use of beta and alpha radiation can directly treat tumours and other forms of cancer

QUICK TEST

1. What is meant by the term 'decay constant' and how is it related to half-life? Give its units.

2. What is meant by the term 'half-life'?

3. What type of curve describes radioactive decay?

4. Give an equation that relates activity to the decay constant and give the units for activity.

5. How are the decay constant and half-life related?

6. A radioisotope sample has a decay constant of 5.8×10^{-4} s^{-1}. Determine the half-life of this source.

7. The sample in question 6 contains 8×10^{10} atoms. How many atoms will remain after 2 hours?

8. What radionuclide is used to determine the age of dead wood and plants?

9. Give an example of the use of radionuclides in industry.

10. What type of radiation would be used to treat a tumour externally and give an example of a typical radionuclide used for this treatment?

PRACTICE QUESTIONS

1. An archaeological dig uncovered a small burial plot containing the bones of several people as well as artefacts. Small pieces of bone were extracted for carbon-14 dating.

   a) $^{14}_{6}C$ decays by beta-minus emission to form an isotope of nitrogen. Write the nuclear equation to show this decay process. **[2 marks]**

   b) The decay constant of carbon-14 is 4.0×10^{-12} s^{-1}. Determine the half-life of carbon-14 and express your answer in years. **[3 marks]**

   c) The sample of bone taken from the burial site had an activity of 0.079 Bq while a comparable sample of modern bone of exactly the same mass had an activity of 0.093 Bq. Using this information estimate the age of the bone in years to 2 s.f. **[5 marks]**

2. The table shows the results of an experiment to determine the half-life of protactinium, showing the measured count rates over a period of time.

Count rate (Bq)	7.8	7.3	6.6	6.2	5.8	5.1	4.6	4.3	4.3	4.2	3.3	3.2	2.7	3.2	2.4
Elapsed time (s)	0	10	20	30	40	50	60	70	80	90	100	110	120	130	140
Corrected count rate, C (Bq)															
ln C															

   The background count rate was measured to be 60 counts per minute. The count rate decreases exponentially according to the equation $C = C_0 e^{-\lambda t}$, where C_0 is the count rate at time $t = 0$ s.

   a) Show how this equation can be re-written to give the new equation $\ln C = -\lambda t + \ln C_0$. **[2 marks]**

   b) Complete the table by calculating the count rates corrected for the background count, and the values of $\ln C$. **[3 marks]**

   c) Plot a graph of $\ln C$ against t and draw the best line of fit. **[3 marks]**

   d) From the gradient determine the decay constant and the half-life of protactinium. **[3 marks]**

3. A small planetary probe has a back-up power supply consisting of 10 g of strontium-90, which has a half-life of 28 years. Strontium-90 emits beta particles with an energy of 0.40 MeV.

   a) Calculate the number of atoms in this sample of strontium. **[1 mark]**

   b) Hence, determine the activity of this radioisotope. **[3 marks]**

   c) Calculate the power, in watts, emitted by this source. **[2 marks]**

Nuclear Fission and Fusion

Mass Defects and Binding Energies

The rest mass of an atomic nucleus is found to be less than the sum of the rest masses of its constituent nucleons (protons and neutrons). According to Einstein's equation $E = mc^2$, this 'missing mass' or mass difference is known as the **mass defect**, and represents the energy that was released when the nucleus was formed. Conversely, the amount of energy needed to separate all of the nucleons in the nucleus is called the **binding energy** and is clearly equivalent to the mass defect. Calculations involving mass defects are usually given in terms of **atomic mass units** (u), where 1 u (sometimes symbolised as amu) is 1.67×10^{-27} kg, whereas binding energies are usually expressed in units of MeV. The binding energy per unit of mass defect gives the conversion factor of 931.3 MeV per u (or amu).

Particle	Mass (u)
neutron	1.00866
proton	1.00728
helium nucleus (alpha)	4.00151

Binding Energies per Nucleon

This is a particularly important parameter as it compares the binding energies of different nuclei directly. The **binding energy per nucleon** (i.e. the total binding energy in MeV divided by the number of nucleons) can be plotted against the nucleon number, A, as shown. The graph shows a sharp rise followed by a gradual decline with a shallow peak appearing around the **element iron** ($A_{Fe} = 50$). Elements near to iron show the **most stable nucleus arrangement** since considerably more energy is needed to remove nucleons from the nucleus. To the right of iron, the shallow decline in binding energy shows that, if a large nucleus such as uranium-235 could be split into two smaller nuclei, say rubidium and caesium (other pairs of nuclei can also be produced by splitting uranium-235), then there is a small but significant increase in the binding energy per nucleon. As a consequence, energy is released and this process is known as **nuclear fission**. In the above process, the average increase in binding energy is approximately 1.1 MeV per nucleon

and the 235 nucleons in uranium release about 260 MeV of energy during the fission process.

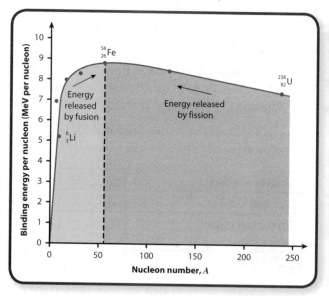

On the opposite side, nuclei of elements lighter than iron that combine together increase the binding energy per nucleon dramatically; the resulting and considerable release of energy in this process is called **nuclear fusion**. The fusion of the isotopes of water (deuterium and tritium) to form helium-4 and a neutron gives an average increase in binding energy of about 5 MeV per nucleon or about 20 MeV in total. The energy release per nucleon heavily favours nuclear fusion as an efficient energy provider.

Nuclear Fission

Nuclear fission involves splitting the nucleus into smaller fragments. Several heavy nuclei, such as uranium, thorium and plutonium, undergo both **spontaneous fission**, a form of radioactive decay, and **induced fission**, a form of nuclear reaction. The probability of spontaneous fission in, say, uranium-235 is small but fission can be induced by allowing it to absorb another neutron – a **low energy** or **thermal neutron**. The resulting isotope, uranium-236, is very unstable and it decays by fission to produce two or three fast neutrons. In nuclear reactors, it is uranium-235 that is used as the fuel that is bombarded with thermal neutrons produced in a moderator material such as graphite through inelastic collisions.

Having the correct amount of thermal neutrons allows the fission process to continue in a controlled chain reaction, with each fission reaction releasing extra neutrons that go on to induce further fission reactions. A chain reaction can only be sustained if the correct amount or mass of uranium nuclei or **'fuel'** is available, i.e. a **critical mass**. Controlling the amount of neutrons is achieved through neutron absorbers, such as boron, that act as **control rods** within a nuclear reactor. The splitting of uranium nuclei produces a substantial amount of heat and the **coolant** (e.g. water or liquid sodium) removes the heat effectively to a **heat exchanger** where steam is generated to drive the turbines that produce the electricity. The fission process also produces a significant amount of **radiation** which is absorbed by the shielding (e.g. concrete) that surrounds all nuclear power plants.

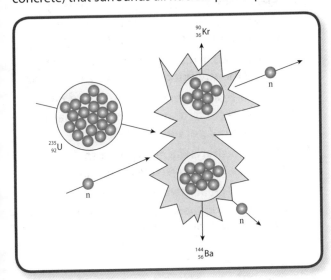

Waste Products

A major by-product of nuclear power stations are the highly active fuel rods that form part of the **high-level waste**. These components require constant cooling before eventually being reprocessed or treated. **Intermediate-level waste** comprises reactor and processing-plant components and these are solidified before being mixed with concrete and placed in steel drums and stored in mines or on the seabed. Finally, material contaminated with radioactivity, i.e. **low-level waste**, is disposed of in steel drums in concrete-lined trenches. Other by-products of nuclear reactors include the formation of **radioactive tracers** that have found application as a tool in medical diagnosis. However, all radioactive materials have to be treated

and handled with extreme care and there are very strict rules and safety procedures in place.

Nuclear Fusion

Fusion involves joining together two nuclei to create a larger nucleus, a process that takes place in our own Sun. To 'glue' two nuclei together requires a lot of energy, although the net result of this process will give rise to a substantial release of energy in the end. This means that the two nuclei must be moving at very high speeds as they must get close enough to each other to overcome the **electrostatic repulsion** and for the **strong interaction** to take effect and bind them together. There are a number of ways that light nuclei can fuse, each giving a different amount of energy released (see diagrams below). Fusion within the Sun follows a three-stage process resulting in the production of helium-4 and about 20 MeV of energy that corresponds to about 6 MeV per nucleon, considerably more than nuclear fission.

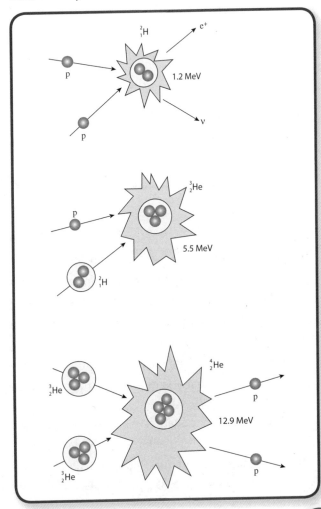

International collaborative fusion projects, such as the **Joint European Torus** (JET), provide vital information on how to produce and control fusion reactions. The JET project combines deuterium and tritium; the neutrons produced interact with a lithium blanket to produce both tritium (used in the main reaction) and helium-4. The current construction of a more substantial and larger **European fusion reactor**, ITER, should provide a working model for a nuclear fusion power plant.

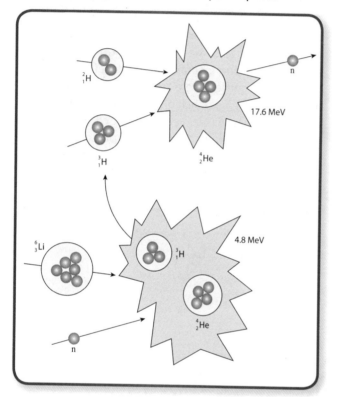

SUMMARY

- **Nuclear fission is the splitting of heavy nuclei that decay into two smaller nuclei of roughly equal mass, a few free neutrons and beta particles, releasing about 1 MeV per nucleon as energy**

- **A chain reaction is a self-sustaining fission reaction in which the neutrons released from each fission causes more fission reactions; if uncontrolled, the chain reaction avalanches to produce an explosion**

- **Nuclear reactors use fission in a controlled way to provide a steady-rate chain reaction to make energy**

- **Nuclear reactors slow down fast-moving neutrons using a moderator to provide thermal neutrons used in the fission process**

- **Control rods in nuclear reactors are used to control the amount of neutrons by absorption**

- **Nuclear fusion is the creation of a larger nucleus from two smaller nuclei, releasing about 6 MeV per nucleon of energy**

- **Nuclear fusion is the main power source of the Sun, which converts hydrogen into helium**

- **JET and ITER are two European fusion projects investigating the practical aspects of fusion as a possible future energy source**

QUICK TEST

1. What is the binding energy of a nucleus?
2. Which element has the greatest binding energy per nucleon?
3. Which reaction produces more energy per nucleon, fission or fusion?
4. In the fusion of two protons, why do they need to be moving very fast?
5. What is meant by mass defect?
6. What is a unified atomic mass unit, 'u', and what is 1 u equivalent to?
7. Write the nuclear equation for the fusion of deuterium and a proton. How much energy is released in this process?
8. Write a nuclear equation to shows the induced fission of uranium-235 into barium-144 and krypton-90.
9. Does the fission of uranium-235 always give the same fission products as shown in question **8**?
10. The fusion of deuterium (2.01355 u) and tritium (3.01550 u) produces helium-4 and a neutron, according to the reaction $_1^2H + _1^3H \rightarrow _2^4He + _0^1n$. Calculate the mass difference in (a) u and (b) MeV.

PRACTICE QUESTIONS

Take: mass of proton = 1.00728 u and mass of neutron = 1.00866 u

1. a) Define what is meant by 'binding energy' and 'mass defect' and state the relationship between these two quantities and their units. **[4 marks]**

b) Calculate the average binding energy per nucleon of an iron nucleus $^{56}_{26}$Fe given that the mass of iron-56 is 55.93494 u. **[5 marks]**

c) This is the highest value of any isotope. Why is this significant? **[1 mark]**

2. a) What is meant by induced nuclear fission? **[3 marks]**

b) The induced fission of uranium-235 produces $^{95}_{38}$Sr and $^{139}_{54}$Xe and 2 neutrons. Write down a nuclear equation to represent this reaction. **[4 marks]**

c) For the reaction to take place, thermal neutrons are required. Explain what is meant by thermal neutrons and how they are produced. **[3 marks]**

d) Describe how the above reaction can be used to generate power in a nuclear reactor plant. **[5 marks]**

3. a) Explain what is meant by the term 'nuclear fusion'. **[2 marks]**

The figure shows a graph of nuclear binding energy per nucleon as a function of nucleon number.

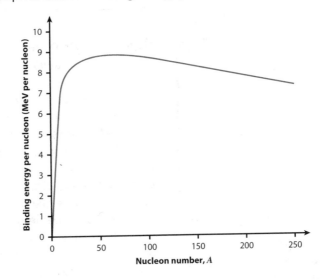

b) Using the diagram, (i) what nucleon number shows the most stable nucleus and give a value of the binding energy per nucleon (ii) in what region of the graph does nuclear fusion release energy? **[3 marks]**

c) The Sun's source of power is nuclear fusion that, during the initial stages, involves the combination of two protons to form a deuterium nucleus given by the equation

$$^{1}_{1}H + ^{1}_{1}H \rightarrow ^{2}_{1}H + ^{0}_{1}e + \nu + 1.44\,MeV$$

(i) What are the names of the other two particles that are produced in this reaction? **[1 mark]**

(ii) A deuterium nucleus collides with another proton to produce a helium-3 nucleus and a gamma-ray photon. Write an equation for this reaction. **[2 marks]**

(iii) Explain what happens to the helium-3 nuclei to produce helium-4 as the final step in the Sun's fusion process. **[3 marks]**

Telescopes

Types of telescopes

Telescopes fall into two broad types, **optical telescopes** and **non-optical telescopes**. Optical telescopes can be based either **on Earth** (terrestrial telescopes) or **in space** in orbit around the Earth (or another celestial body). Among the non-optical telescopes, radio telescopes tend to be based on Earth whereas infrared (IR), ultraviolet (UV) and X-ray telescopes tend to be placed in Earth orbit.

Telescopic observations now cover not just the **visible region** but a significant range on either side, extending to shorter **X-ray wavelengths** and longer **radio wavelengths**. As such, they provide considerably more detail and can reveal significantly more information than that obtained just optically.

Optical Telescopes

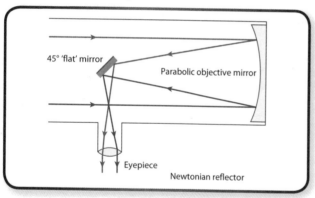

Newtonian reflector

Optical telescopes are either **reflecting telescopes** based on mirrors, or **refracting telescopes** based on lenses. The oldest refracting telescopes were based on converging lenses – a main objective lens and a smaller eye lens. The **magnifying power**, M depends on the ratio of the focal lengths of the objective (f_o) and eye lenses (f_e). There is a limit on the size of the refracting telescope because of the size and weight of the lens and associated supporting framework; while refracting telescopes can provide good images, they have largely been superseded by the lighter reflecting telescope. There are numerous different types of reflecting instruments but the two main ones are the **Newtonian reflector** and the **Cassegrain telescope**; both are based on curved mirrors that send light into a refracting eyepiece. The main advantage of a Cassegrain telescope over a Newtonian telescope is that large, heavy, complex equipment/instrumentation can be attached directly to the base of the telescope. Therefore a variety of detectors, such as cameras or spectrometers, can be used to detect and monitor the incoming radiation.

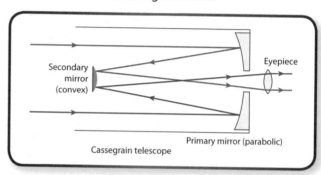

Cassegrain telescope

Resolving Power

The **resolving power** (θ) of an optical telescope is the smallest angle at which it can distinguish two distinct points. As most telescopes have a circular aperture (opening), they all suffer from diffraction and are therefore are said to be **diffraction limited**. The diffraction pattern has a central spot called an **Airy disc**. Two light sources can just be distinguished if the centre of the Airy disc from one source is at least as far away from the first minimum of the other source; this is called the **Rayleigh criterion**. If the smallest angle that can be resolved is θ in radians then $\theta \approx \frac{\lambda}{D}$, where λ is the wavelength of light in metres and D is the diameter of the objective lens or objective mirror in metres. Hence, larger diameter lenses or mirrors are needed to give better resolution and to see fine detail.

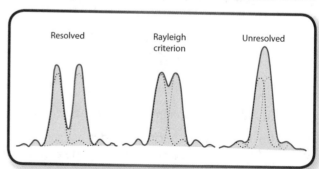

Aberrations and Limitations

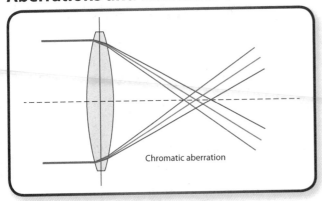
Chromatic aberration

Refracting telescopes suffer from both **chromatic** and **spherical aberration**. Chromatic aberration is due to the fact that the refractive index of glass is different for different wavelengths and this causes light to focus at different positions. This results in a blurred image. The condition is worse for poor-quality lenses.

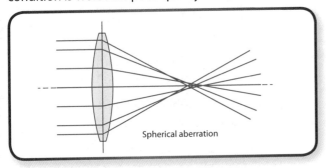
Spherical aberration

Reflecting telescopes only suffer from spherical aberration caused by the mirror not being perfectly parabolic, again producing a blurred image. The initial images from the Hubble Space Telescope suffered from this effect until the mirrors were realigned following an astronaut spacewalk. The Earth's thick **atmosphere** only allows certain wavelengths to penetrate it; other wavelengths are absorbed, and some more than others. Optically, the atmosphere lets most visible light through, together with some IR and UV. It absorbs X-rays, UV and microwaves; telescopes that utilise these wavelengths need to be placed in Earth orbit.

Radio Telescopes
Radio telescopes are similar in many ways to the objective mirror of a reflecting telescope but use a metal parabolic dish instead; the antenna is located at the focal point of the dish. Like optical devices, radio telescopes can track the movement of objects even as the Earth rotates. The **resolving power** of a radio telescope is defined as for the optical telescope, but

as the wavelength values are significantly larger than that of light there is a significant loss in resolution. However, this can be improved by linking radio telescopes together and using **radio interferometry**, which increases resolutions by at least 10^3 over their optical counterparts. Images of astronomical objects are obtained through scanning and using false colours to enhance features. Radio telescopes nevertheless also suffer from atmospheric absorption and are opaque to signals above 600 GHz and below 30 MHz.

IR, UV and X-ray Telescopes
All three of these types of telescopes use mirrors to form an image at the focal point. As IR wavelengths are much longer, **IR telescopes** are affected less by any imperfections in the mirrors but they are sensitive to heat radiation. This includes heat from the telescope itself, so careful design is required and the telescope itself has to be cooled to very low temperatures. As UV wavelengths are significantly shorter, **UV telescopes** have to use highly polished mirrors constructed to exceptionally high precision. X-ray wavelengths are much shorter than UV light and **X-ray telescopes** have to use an array of mirrors at grazing angles to focus the X-rays onto a detector, so they are often called **grazing telescopes**. In general, the **collecting power** of a telescope is the energy collected per second and this is directly proportional to its collecting area and therefore proportional to the (diameter)^2 of the lens, mirror or dish. For X-ray telescopes, the collecting power depends on the size of the aperture through which the X-rays enter the telescope and hence it is generally much lower than that of conventional telescopes.

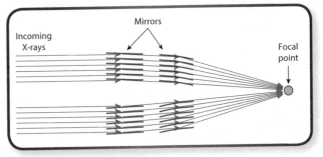

Telescope Detectors
In optical astronomy, short-time imagery of relatively bright objects can be recorded by the **eye** but for long-time exposures alternative methods are needed. Traditional astronomical methods of recording have included **photographic plate** or **film** used with sensitive

cameras, but current telescopes routinely use **charge-coupled devices** (CCDs) based on semiconductor technology that allows digital imaging and computer enhancement and analysis. When radiation enters each unique picture element (**pixel**), electrons are released; the number of electrons produced is proportional to the intensity of the incoming radiation, and this ranges from IR through visible to UV. The key advantage of CCDs is their **quantum efficiency**, which is in excess of 70% compared with photographic film (5%) and the human eye (1%). They are unsuitable for X-ray telescopes, which instead rely on wire mesh or Geiger counters. Other common detectors include **spectrometers** for analysing the emission spectra of stars and galaxies.

SUMMARY

- **Converging lenses are used in refracting telescopes to focus the light to a particular focal point**

- **Spherical aberration results from light rays not being brought to a focus after refraction or reflection**

- **Chromatic aberration results from light of different wavelengths not being brought to a focus after refraction**

- **Collecting power is a measure of how much light is collected by a telescope; it is proportional to the square of the telescope's diameter**

- **The Rayleigh criterion defines the point at which the angular separation of two sources can be resolved**

- **Strong absorption within the Earth's atmosphere prevents some forms of electromagnetic radiation from being detected by Earth-based telescopes**

- **Charge-coupled devices (CCDs) are composed of an array of semiconductor material used to detect IR, visible and UV radiation efficiently**

- **X-ray telescopes are designed using mirror reflections at glancing angles to bring the X-rays to a focal point**

QUICK TEST

1. What is the relationship between the focal lengths of the objective and eye lenses and the magnification of a telescope?

2. Name two arrangements for reflecting telescopes based on curved mirrors.

3. What do refracting telescopes suffer from, causing blurred images?

4. What is meant by the resolving power of a telescope?

5. What defines the resolving power of a telescope?

6. What devices have now effectively replaced photographic film?

7. Name two advantages of CCDs over photographic film.

8. Why is it not possible to use Earth-based UV telescopes to observe below 300 nm?

9. Why is it not possible to use an X-ray telescope on Earth?

10. Why is special shielding required in IR telescopes?

11. What is the 'collecting power' of a telescope?

PRACTICE QUESTIONS

1. **a)** Sketch a diagram that shows the essential elements of a Cassegrain telescope. **[3 marks]**

   b) Give one advantage that this telescope has over a Newtonian telescope of the same mirror diameter. **[1 mark]**

   An Earth-based Cassegrain telescope with a mirror diameter of 0.60 m collects data on a particular galaxy in 60 minutes.

   c) What is the collecting power of a telescope and how is this related to the amount of time required to collect astronomical data? **[2 marks]**

   d) How long would the Hubble Space Telescope, with a primary mirror diameter of 2.4 m, need to collect the same amount of astronomical information. **[3 marks]**

   e) Give two advantages that the Hubble Space Telescope has over Earth-based telescopes. **[2 marks]**

2. The Liverpool Telescope has a primary mirror diameter of 2.0 m and uses a charge-coupled device (CCD) to detect and record the incoming visible light of mean wavelength 510 nm.

   a) What are the advantages of using CCDs over conventional detecting devices. **[2 marks]**

   b) A telescope's resolution is based on the Rayleigh criterion. What is meant by the Rayleigh criterion and how is this related to angular resolution? **[2 marks]**

   c) Determine the angular resolution of the Liverpool Telescope in radians. **[2 marks]**

   d) Given this angular resolution, determine the smallest detail that may be seen on the surface of the Moon. [mean Earth–Moon distance $= 3.8 \times 10^8$ m] **[2 marks]**

3. The Green Bank Telescope (GBT) is the largest steerable radio telescope in the world, with a diameter of 100 m. This compares with the UK's Lovell Telescope at Jodrell Bank that has a diameter of 76 m. Both telescopes can detect radio signals with a frequency of 5 GHz.

   a) Determine the increase in collecting power of the GBT compared with the Lovell Telescope. **[2 marks]**

   b) Calculate the resolving power of the GBT. **[2 marks]**

   c) Resolving powers of radio telescopes are inferior to those of optical telescopes. Explain how resolutions of radio telescopes can be improved and state approximately what angular resolutions can be achieved. **[2 marks]**

   d) Give two disadvantages of radio telescopes when observing radio signals above 300 GHz and below 30 MHz. **[2 marks]**

Stellar Luminosity and Distance

Luminosity and Brightness

The **luminosity** (L) of a star (assuming that the star is a point source) is the total amount of energy it radiates into space per second, i.e. its power measured in Js^{-1} or W. The amount of light received from a star obeys the inverse square law. For a point source of radiation a distance R away, the observed **brightness**, b, is the amount of energy emitted per second per square metre over the surface of a sphere of radius R and given by $b = \frac{L}{4\pi R^2}$. Brightness is often called **intensity** or **radiation flux** and has units of Wm^{-2}.

Apparent Magnitude

The brightness of a star is scaled logarithmically and called **magnitude**. There are two types of magnitude that define a star's brightness – **apparent magnitude** and **absolute magnitude**. Originally, the magnitude scale was divided into six classes, with +1 representing the brightest stars and +6 those just visible to the naked eye. A magnitude +1 star has an intensity or effective brightness ~2.5 times that of a magnitude +2 star. Since the invention of the telescope, the range of magnitude now includes both large negative (very bright, e.g. Sun = −26.74) and positive values (very dim, e.g. Barnard's Star = +9.5). The **apparent magnitude**, m, of a star depends on its power output and its distance from us, and is quantified as $m = -2.5\log b$. When two stars are being compared, this expression gives

$$m_2 - m_1 = -2.5\log\left(\frac{b_2}{b_1}\right)$$

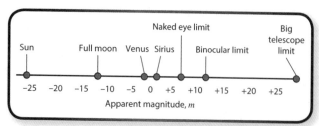

Naked eye limit

Big telescope limit

Sun   Full moon Venus Sirius   Binocular limit

−25   −20   −15   −10   −5   0   +5   +10   +15   +20   +25

Apparent magnitude, m

Stellar Distances

Distance measurements to nearby stars is found by **trigonometric parallax**, i.e. the apparent change in position every 6 months as the Earth orbits the Sun. Parallax angles can be determined to a very high degree of precision and so distances to thousands of nearby stars can be calculated accurately. Because the angles used are exceptionally small, the distance to nearby stars can be determined using the equation $d = \frac{r}{\theta}$, where d is the distance to the star, r is the radius of the Earth's orbit and θ is the angle of parallax in radians. The mean Earth–Sun distance of 1.50×10^{11} m is called the **astronomical unit** (AU); a parallax angle of just 1 second of arc, i.e. 0°0′1″ gives a mean stellar distance of 3.09×10^{16} m, which is called a **parsec** (pc). 1 pc is equivalent to 3.26 light years (the distance light would travel in 3.26 years). A star that is exactly 1 pc away (3.26 light years) has an angle of parallax of 1 arcsecond, i.e. $\left(\frac{1}{3600}\right)^\circ$.

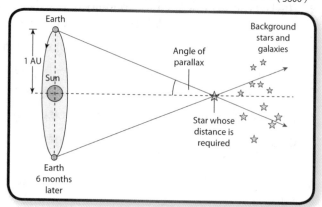

Earth

1 AU

Sun

Earth 6 months later

Angle of parallax

Star whose distance is required

Background stars and galaxies

Absolute Magnitude

Comparing the brightness of stars is more meaningful if the varying distances between stars are eliminated and a fixed distance from Earth is used. This standard distance is taken as 10 pc and the magnitude at this distance is called the **absolute magnitude**, M. As with apparent magnitudes, negative values indicate very bright stars. The relationship between the apparent and absolute magnitude scales is

$$m - M = -2.5\log\left(\frac{10}{d}\right)^2 = 5\log\left(\frac{d}{10}\right)$$

where d is the distance in pc.

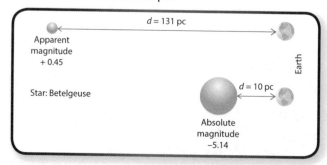

$d = 131$ pc

Apparent magnitude + 0.45

Star: Betelgeuse

$d = 10$ pc

Earth

Absolute magnitude −5.14

If the absolute magnitude of a stellar object can be determined then its distance can be found. **Cepheid variable** stars are stars that pulsate in brightness (luminosity) and this periodicity in luminosity is related directly to their maximum luminosity. Such objects can be used as **standard candles**, allowing distances to be determined accurately far beyond that attainable from stellar parallax. Astronomical objects such as **supernovae** have also been used in a similar way to push distance measurements to an even greater extent.

Stellar Luminosity

The **luminosity** (L) of a particular star or object is usually expressed in terms of our own **Sun's luminosity** ($L_\odot$). Using the relationship between luminosity and brightness gives

$$M = M_\odot - 2.5\log\left(\frac{L}{L_\odot}\right)$$

where M is the star's absolute magnitude and $M_\odot = +4.3$ is the Sun's absolute magnitude.

The luminosity of a star is related both to its size and to its temperature. The **power output** (P) of a star depends on its temperature according to **Stefan's Law**, $P = \sigma A T^4$, where σ is called Stefan's constant, A is the surface area in m^2 and T is the surface temperature in K. For a spherical star of radius r, the surface area is $4\pi r^2$ and the power radiated defines the luminosity L, i.e. $L = \sigma A T^4 = 4\pi r^2 \sigma T^4$. **Luminosity** is proportional to both r^2 and T^4. The luminosity of the Sun is $L_\odot = 3.97 \times 10^{26}$ W, and the amount of energy the Earth receives from the Sun per square metre, i.e. the intensity, is $I = \frac{L_\odot}{4\pi R_{E-S}^2} = 1400\ \text{W m}^{-2}$, where E_{E-S} is the mean Earth–Sun distance. This value is sometimes referred to as the **solar constant**.

Stellar Temperatures and Spectral Class

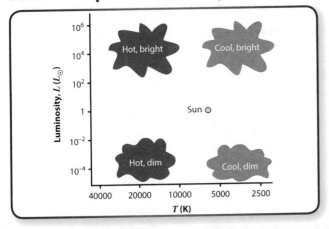

A hypothetical object that absorbs all the radiation that falls on it and reflects none is called a **black body** and the electromagnetic radiation emitted is known as **black body radiation**. Hot objects such as stars behave like black bodies and the intensity of radiation emitted at a particular wavelength is dependent only on its surface temperature. The power radiated plotted against wavelength is called a **black body curve**.

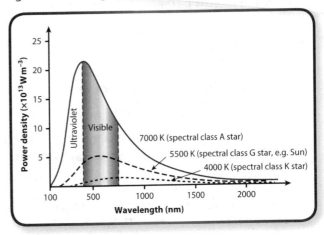

A key feature of this curve is the shift in the intensity of the peak wavelength as the temperature varies, a relationship called **Wien's Displacement Law** and given by $\lambda_{max} T = 2.9 \times 10^{-3}$ mK (units are metre kelvin). This direct connection between the intensity distribution of radiation and temperature provides a method for determining the **surface temperature** of stars. The Sun's λ_{max} value of ~500 nm indicates a surface temperature of 5800 K. The radiation detected on Earth also provides considerably more information through **stellar spectroscopy**. This is the study of starlight through both **emission** and **absorption line spectra** that allows many physical and chemical properties of stars to be inferred. In addition, the state of atoms, i.e. neutral or ionised, can also be determined and the relative strength of particular absorption lines gives the **spectral class** of a star. Seven letters are used to denote the class, from 'O' the hottest (25000–50000 K) through to 'M' the coolest (< 3500 K) via B (11000–25000 K), A (7500–11000 K), F (6000–7500 K), G (5000–6000 K) and K (3500–5000 K). As can be seen, the relationship between the temperature and the spectral class is not linear. Spectral classes are generally more complex and are further sub-divided into ten divisions from 0 to 9. The lower the numerical value, the hotter the star. Our Sun is denoted as a G2 star.

SUMMARY

- Apparent magnitude is the subjective scale for brightness of astronomical objects and is given by $m = -2.5 \log b$

- Absolute magnitude does not involve distance and allows comparisons to be made based on differences in luminosity

- Trigonometric parallax uses measurements of small angles to allow distances to nearby stars to be calculated

- The power output of a radiating object (also called the luminosity) is given by Stefan's Law, $P = \sigma A T^4$

- The intensity or radiation flux from the Sun at the Earth's surface is called the solar constant

- An object that absorbs all the radiation that falls on it and reflects none is called a black body

- The peak wavelength of a black body curve is governed by Wien's Displacement Law and is inversely proportional to the surface temperature

- Stellar spectroscopy is the study of starlight through both emission and absorption line spectra

- Spectral class or type provides a shorthand description of a star's surface temperature and is denoted by the letters O, B, A, F, G, K and M and subdivided 0–9.

QUICK TEST

1. What is meant by the luminosity (L) of a star?

2. How is luminosity related to a star's brightness (b)?

3. Barnard's Star has a brightness of 1.58×10^{-4} Wm^{-2}. Determine its apparent magnitude.

4. What distance is used to define the absolute magnitude of a star?

5. What technique is used to determine the distance to nearby stars?

6. What is the equation that connects apparent and absolute magnitude?

7. What is the name given to astronomical objects that allow their brightness to be calculated directly without knowing their distance?

8. The star Rigel has an apparent magnitude of +0.18 and lies at a distance of 773 light years from Earth. Determine its absolute magnitude.

9. How is the luminosity or power of a star related to its surface temperature?

10. What is meant by the term 'black body'?

11. State Wien's Displacement Law and give the value of the constant and its units.

12. Use the above law to determine the surface temperature of the Sun, where $\lambda_{max} = 500$ nm.

PRACTICE QUESTIONS

1. a) What is meant by a black body radiation curve and how is this related to temperature? **[3 marks]**

b) The Sun has a surface temperature of 5800 K. Use this fact to determine the peak wavelength on its black body radiation curve. **[1 mark]**

c) Calculate the Sun's luminosity, given its radius to be 7.0×10^8 m.
[Stefan's constant $= 5.7 \times 10^{-8}$ W m^{-2} K^{-4}, surface area $= 4\pi r^2$] **[3 marks]**

d) What is meant by the term 'solar constant'? **[1 mark]**

e) If the mean Earth–Sun distance is 1 AU (1.5×10^{11} m), determine the solar constant. **[3 marks]**

2. Proxima Centauri, a red dwarf star, is the nearest star to the Earth after the Sun. Its distance has been measured by trigonometric parallax.

a) What is the trigonometric parallax method? **[2 marks]**

b) The distance (d) in light years is related to the angle of parallax (α) in arcseconds by the equation $d = \frac{3.26}{\alpha}$. Use this equation to determine the distance of Proxima Centauri in light years if its parallax angle is 0.768". **[2 marks]**

c) The apparent magnitude of Proxima Centauri is +11.05. What is meant by apparent magnitude and how is this related to a star's brightness? **[2 marks]**

d) Calculate the absolute magnitude of Proxima Centauri. **[4 marks]**

e) The Sun's absolute magnitude is +4.83. Use the equation $M = M_\odot - 2.5 \log\left(\frac{L}{L_\odot}\right)$ to calculate the luminosity of Proxima Centauri in terms of the Sun's luminosity, $L_\odot$... **[3 marks]**

3. a) What is meant by the term 'standard candles' and what are they used for? **[2 marks]**

Cepheid variables are a class of star used as standard candles. Light curves from Cepheid variables are periodic and are related to their absolute magnitudes as shown in the diagram.

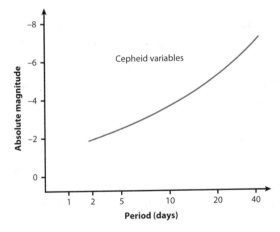

b) A certain Cepheid variable star (V1) in the direction of the Andromeda Galaxy was imaged by the Hubble Space Telescope and found to have a period of 31.4 days. Use the graph to estimate the absolute magnitude of this star. **[1 mark]**

c) V1 has an apparent (maximum) magnitude of +18.2. Determine the distance to this Cepheid variable in parsecs. **[4 marks]**

d) What conclusions can be drawn about this star in terms of its location within the universe given that the Andromeda Galaxy is 2.5 million light years away? **[2 marks]**

Stellar Evolution

The Hertzsprung–Russell Diagram

A plot of the absolute magnitude of stars (between −10 and +15) against their temperature, colour index or spectral class is known as a **Hertzsprung–Russell diagram** or **HR** for short.

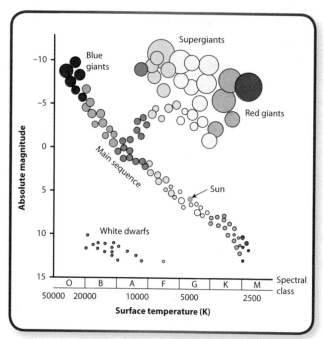

The diagram shows four distinct regions that depict common characteristics; it is an important diagram when describing the process of stellar evolution.

(i) The long diagonal band is called the **main sequence** and this is where about 90% of observable stars (including the Sun) appear. Stars in this region are stable, fusing hydrogen into helium within the star's core. When all the hydrogen in the core is converted into helium, the star evolves and moves away from the main sequence.

(ii) The **red giant** region show stars of similar mass to our Sun but that are cooler and hence greatly expanded in size. Fusion of helium occurs in the core.

(iii) High-mass stars (typically 10–100 solar masses) that are more luminous than red giants are called **supergiants**. Fusion processes within the core produce carbon and heavier elements.

(iv) Low-luminosity stars tend to be old stars of low mass but high surface temperature and therefore small, about Earth size (Stefan's Law). These stars are known as **white dwarfs** with typical densities of 10^9 kgm^{-3}.

A star on the main sequence will therefore move to different regions on an HR diagram as it evolves and the path it takes depends crucially on its mass.

Protostars

In a region of the universe where there are clouds of cold dust and hydrogen gas, gravitational attraction provides the force to condense and contract the material into denser clumps. Eventually these dense clumps contain enough mass for the core to heat up, forming a **protostar**. A protostar looks like a star but temperatures are not high enough for fusion to take place.

Stellar Evolution for Core Masses $<1.4M_\odot$

For **low-mass stars** (core mass $< 0.1M_\odot$), there is not enough heat to start nuclear fusion and the star remains a cool planet-like star of low luminosity called a **brown dwarf**. Stars with core masses between 0.1 and $0.5M_\odot$ are known as **red dwarfs**. These are relatively cool stars (<4000 K) that remain on the main sequence for perhaps 80 to 100 billion years.

Larger mass stars (core mass $\sim 1M_\odot$) mean stronger gravitational forces that produce denser and hotter cores and hence a higher rate of fusion. A star like our Sun will therefore spend about 10 billion years on the main sequence before it will leave it when most of the hydrogen has been exhausted by nuclear fusion and the outer layers will expand 'rapidly' to form a hot gas cloud called a **red giant**, with a diameter 10–100 times that of the Sun. After a further 1–2 billion years, the outer layers will have dissipated to become a **planetary nebula**, consisting of an expanding shell of ionised gas ejected from red giant stars late in their 'lives'. Fusion of helium in the core left behind eventually heats the core even more, leading to the formation of a white dwarf.

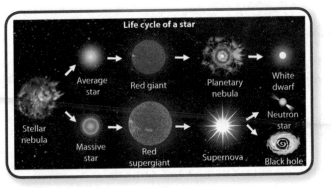

Life cycle of a star

Stellar nebula → Average star → Red giant → Planetary nebula → White dwarf

Stellar nebula → Massive star → Red supergiant → Supernova → Neutron star / Black hole

Stellar Evolution for Core Masses $>1.4M_\odot$

For stars with core masses $> 1.4M_\odot$, nuclear fusion continues, fusing helium into carbon and other heavier elements up to iron (the most stable element in terms of nuclear binding energy). These larger mass stars have significantly higher rates of fusion and a star of 15 solar masses may only spend ~10 million years on the main sequence. After this period the outer layers expand, producing **supergiants** with high luminosities.

Supernovae

The instability of a supergiant, in which the gravitational forces exceed the thermal radiation pressure, causes the star to collapse and explode catastrophically as a **supernova**. Supernova events can produce such energy as to temporarily outshine the whole galaxy, creating elements and isotopes heavier than iron that are expelled into space. The physical conditions under which a supernova event occurs, leads to changes in their absolute magnitudes that are consistent over time, commonly referred to as the **light curve**. Two types of light curves exists for supernovae, with **Type I supernovae** showing light curves that are significantly brighter than **Type II supernovae** but that fade away at a faster rate. Type II supernovae are two orders of magnitude less luminous than Type I supernovae and show a very distinct plateau in their light curve. The difference is thought to be due to two very different explosive processes, and this is reflected in their spectra. Because their luminosities can be accurately determined, Type I supernovae provide another astronomical object that can be used as a **standard candle**, pushing distance measurements to

beyond the range of 1000 Mpc (3.26 billion light years). Type I supernovae occur when a **white dwarf** star attracts material from a **companion star**, resulting in the accumulation of a **critical mass** that results in a violent and rapid collapse. The change in brightness (~billion times) is equivalent to a change in magnitude of 22–23, and the explosion leaves behind a dense, compact star called a **neutron star**. Type II supernovae occur for stars that are considerably more massive (10–100 solar masses), with the resulting implosion forming a **neutron star** or a **black hole**.

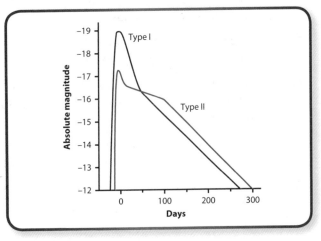

Neutron Stars and Black Holes

If the resulting star core mass after the supernova explosion is $< 3M_\odot$ then a **neutron star** is formed, with densities comparable to nuclear densities of 10^{17} kg m^{-3}. Neutron stars appear to have a rigid core of neutron-rich nuclei surrounded by an iron crust. Because of their small size and rapid rotation (perhaps 600 times per second), they are also called **pulsars**. The gravitational field strength is so high that the **escape velocity** approaches $0.8c$. Core masses $> 3M_\odot$ result in **black holes**, as the gravitational compression continues unabated. The gravitational field strength is so high that the escape velocity is c and hence not even light can escape. The distance or boundary beyond which events cannot affect an observer outside is called the **event horizon** and the size of the boundary is called the **Schwarzschild radius**, given by $R_S = \frac{2GM}{c^2}$. Details about black holes can only be inferred by the effects taking place on nearby objects. **Supermassive black holes** are to be found at the centre of galaxies.

SUMMARY

- A Herzsprung–Russell diagram is a graphical representation of the absolute magnitude of a star against spectral class, colour index or surface temperature

- A main sequence star is a stable star that balances the outward radiation pressure from nuclear fusion (hydrogen into helium) with gravitational forces

- Low-mass stars evolve into brown dwarfs

- Larger mass stars like the Sun evolve into red giants, planetary nebula and white dwarfs

- High-mass stars evolve into supergiants before imploding in a Type II supernova to form either neutron stars or black holes

- A collapsed star made of neutrons with densities comparable to nuclear densities is called a neutron star and a rapidly rotating neutron star is called a pulsar

- A collapsed star that has an escape velocity of the speed of light is a black hole; the distance from a black hole where this occurs is called the event horizon and the distance is known as the Schwarzschild radius

- Supernovae consist of two types, Type I and Type II, with very distinct light curves; Type I supernovae are more luminous but fade away faster than Type II supernovae

- Supernovae can be used as standard candles where known brightness is used to calculate galactic distances

QUICK TEST

1. What is a protostar?

2. What mechanism gives rise to the Sun's luminosity?

3. In which part of the HR diagram does the Sun appear?

4. What is a red giant?

5. What is a neutron star?

6. What is meant by the event horizon?

7. Calculate the Schwarzschild radius for a black hole of mass 5×10^{30} kg .

8. What are two key differences between a Type I and Type II supernova?

9. What name is given to rapidly rotating neutron stars?

10. Why is a black hole so named?

11. What is the critical mass (in terms of solar masses) that defines the difference between forming a neutron star or a black hole?

PRACTICE QUESTIONS

1. a) What information would be needed to plot a star's position on a Hertzsprung–Russell (HR) diagram? **[3 marks]**

b) What other property, other than temperature, could be represented on the x-axis? **[1 mark]**

The figure shows part of the HR diagram indicating the evolution of a star of mass ~$1M_\odot$.

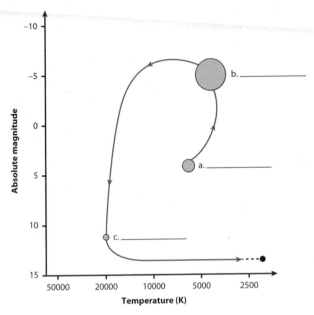

c) The star evolves into three distinct types as it moves around the HR diagram. Give the names of the type of star associated with positions a, b and c. **[3 marks]**

d) Briefly outline the evolutionary nature of such a star, indicating the four key processes that are taking place. **[4 marks]**

e) What is the final fate of the resulting star as it become colder and dimmer. **[1 mark]**

2. a) Give two main differences between Type I and Type II supernovae. **[2 marks]**

b) How are Type I supernova explosions used to measure astronomical distances? **[2 marks]**

c) Describe the result of a supernova explosion when the remnant left has a core mass greater than 3 solar masses. **[3 marks]**

d) For a core mass equal to $4M_\odot$, calculate the Schwarzschild radius in kilometres for the astronomical object described in part **c)**. [$M_\odot = 2 \times 10^{30}$ kg, $G = 6.67 \times 10^{-11}$ Nm^2 kg^{-2}, $c = 3 \times 10^8$ m s^{-1}] **[2 marks]**

e) What does the Schwarzschild radius represent? **[1 mark]**

Cosmology

Cosmology

Cosmology is the study of the nature, origin and evolution of the universe. A key principle in cosmology is known as the **cosmological principle**, which states that on a large scale the universe appears to be both **isotropic** (looks the same in all direction) and **homogeneous** (is uniform throughout). As a consequence of these observations, the universe does not appear to have a centre, nor an edge, and hence the Earth, Sun and Milky Way are in no special position within the cosmos.

An Expanding Universe

Edwin Hubble collected data on the spectra and visible images of near and distant galaxies to reveal information on galactic distances and velocities. His results showed velocity values that were extremely large and all showed them to be receding from us (the Earth); more importantly, the further away the galaxies were, the greater the velocities, culminating in an empirical relationship that is now called **Hubble's Law**, $v = H_0 d$, where H_0 is the **Hubble constant**. If v is measured in $km\,s^{-1}$ and d in Mpc then the Hubble constant is given in units of $km\,s^{-1}\,Mpc^{-1}$. Current values of the constant gives $H_0 = 68\,km\,s^{-1}\,Mpc^{-1}$ although values in the range 50–100 have also been used. As Earth is not unique within the cosmos, the recession of galaxies would be seen from any position in the universe.

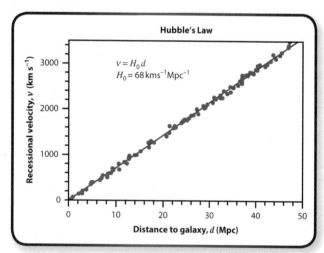

Hubble's Law

$v = H_0 d$
$H_0 = 68\,kms^{-1}Mpc^{-1}$

Recessional velocity, v (km s^{-1})

Distance to galaxy, d (Mpc)

Red Shifts

The basis for recessional velocities arises from comparing the **absorption spectra** of astronomical objects such as stars and galaxies with spectra obtained in a laboratory. The results show a distinct shift in the positions of prominent absorption lines. This shift in wavelength (frequency) is called the **Doppler shift** and is a well-known concept in classical physics. It gives the relationship between wavelength (frequency) and the relative velocity of the moving object: **blue shifted** if moving towards and **red shifted** if moving away from the observer. The change in wavelength is given by the equation $\frac{\Delta\lambda}{\lambda} = -\frac{\Delta f}{f} = \frac{v}{c}$, where $\Delta\lambda = \lambda - \lambda'$, so that for an object moving away from the observer the wavelength increases and frequency decreases. Doppler red shifts are denoted by the symbol z and the above equation can be used provided that $v < 0.1c$. For velocities in excess of $0.1c$, a **relativistic Doppler formulation** for z is required although this limits z values to less than 1. An interpretation based on the expansion of space itself gives a **cosmological red shift** that allows for much greater z values beyond 1. Current measurements indicate cosmological red shifts as high as 11.

The Hot Big Bang Model

Hubble's data suggests that the universe is expanding at a constant rate and is not static. Assuming that the universe is a **closed system** (i.e. no energy loss), it must, as a consequence, also be cooling down. On this premise, it must also be true that going back in time the universe must have been both hotter and considerably smaller so that at time zero it must have been infinitesimally small and incredibly hot. This model of the beginning of the universe is called the **Hot Big Bang model** (HBB). Rearranging Hubble's empirical equation gives $\frac{d}{v} = \frac{1}{H_0} = t$, where t is now the **age of the universe** (assuming that it has been expanding at a steady rate), i.e. the reciprocal of the Hubble constant gives a time for the age of the universe. Current values of H_0 of $68\,km\,s^{-1}\,Mpc^{-1}$ give $t = 4.6 \times 10^{17}\,s$ or **14.25 billion years**. As light has been travelling for almost all of this time, the **observable size** (radius) of the universe (assumed spherical) is therefore **14.25 billion light years**.

Cosmic Microwave Background Radiation

Theoretical models for the Hot Big Bang reveal that the universe was initially so hot that all matter was ionised (as a plasma) and opaque to electromagnetic radiation. It was only after 300 000 years, when the temperature fell below 3000 K that the universe became transparent to light which has been travelling in the expanding space ever since. The wavelength of the initial radiation should have been stretched over these 14 billion years to reveal itself as microwave radiation all around the universe. The discovery of the **cosmic microwave background radiation (CMBR)** was made (accidentally) by Penzias and Wilson in the 1960s.

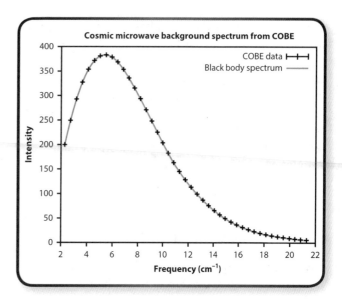

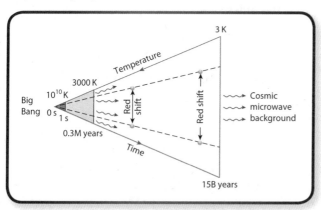

Since that initial discovery, numerous (now space-borne) probes with increasing degrees of accuracy and sensitivity have recorded the CMBR in incredible detail. It is now widely accepted that the spectrum of the CMBR shows a perfect **black body spectrum** corresponding to a temperature of 2.73 K. Such maps reveal that the universe, on a large scale, is indeed isotropic and homogeneous. However, they also reveal tiny fluctuations in the temperature (strictly energy-density) that provide the imperfections needed to explain the formation of large-scale structures such as galaxies and even larger scale structures such as the **Great Attractor**. This is a gravitational anomaly that shows the existence of a localised concentration of mass 10^4–10^5 times more massive than our own Milky Way. In addition, the HBB model also explains the **relative abundance** of hydrogen and helium in the universe observed today.

Models of the Universe

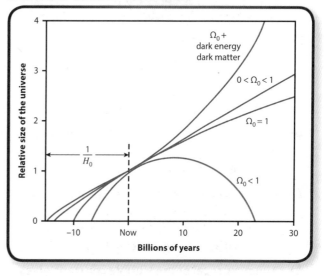

Einstein developed his general theory of relativity based on a **static (non-expanding) universe** to fit the observations at that time. Up until the late 1920s, cosmologists believed in an infinite and static universe although theoretical models included both **expanding** and **oscillating** universes. Today the rate of expansion is based on a **density parameter** Ω_0, which is defined as the ratio of the **mean density of matter** (ρ) within the universe to a **critical density** (ρ_{crit}). If $\rho < \rho_{crit}$ then $0 < \Omega_0 < 1$ and the universe will go on expanding for ever; if $\rho = \rho_{crit}$ then the expansion will eventually stop at some infinite time; and if $\rho > \rho_{crit}$ then the expansion of the universe will stop and the universe will then begin to collapse, perhaps eventually to start a new HBB. More recent observations on supernovae reveal that the rate of expansion appears to be **accelerating**. Estimates for ρ do not take account of **dark matter** or **dark energy** that has eluded detection using conventional techniques as they do not emit electromagnetic radiation. The inclusion of this not inconsiderable amount of missing mass may have profound consequences on the fate of the universe.

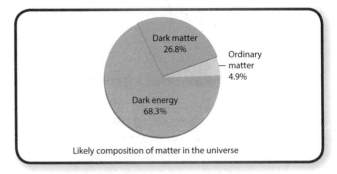

Likely composition of matter in the universe

SUMMARY

- **Cosmology is the study of the nature, origin and evolution of the universe**

- **The cosmological principle suggests that, on a very large scale, the universe is homogeneous and isotropic**

- **The shift in the absorption line spectra of astronomical objects can be associated with the classical Doppler effect; a proper description requires a relativistic formulation of the red shift parameter, z**

- **Red shifts in excess of 1 can be explained by the expansion of space and are referred to as cosmological red shifts**

- **Hubble's Law is an empirical law derived from recessional velocities of distant galaxies and is given by $v = H_0 d$, where H_0 is known as the Hubble constant**

- **The reciprocal of the Hubble constant gives a time for the age of the universe**

- **Evidence for the Hot Big Bang model comes from the cosmic microwave background radiation and the relative abundance of hydrogen and helium**

- **Models of the universe depend on a determination of the mean density of the universe**

- **Dark energy may help to explain why the universe is not only expanding but is expanding at an accelerating rate**

QUICK TEST

1. What is meant by a Doppler red shift?

2. What is the cosmological principle?

3. Give the two pieces of evidence that support the HBB model.

4. Give the empirical equation for Hubble's Law and state the units of the Hubble constant.

5. What does the reciprocal of the Hubble constant provide?

6. What is the cosmological red shift?

7. The wavelength shift of the absorption line $\lambda = 393.4\,nm$ in galaxy NGC 4889 is 8.4 nm. Determine the value of the red shift (z) of this galaxy.

8. For the above galaxy NGC 4889, calculate its recessional velocity in $km\,s^{-1}$.

9. Taking the Hubble constant to be $68\,km\,s^{-1}\,Mpc^{-1}$, calculate the age of the universe in billions of years. [$1\,pc = 3.1 \times 10^{16}\,m$]

10. Why is it so difficult to detect dark matter?

11. What do tiny fluctuations in the microwave map of the universe reveal?

PRACTICE QUESTIONS

1. The red shift of distant galaxies was shown by Edwin Hubble to be related to their distances from us by the empirical formula $v = H_0 d$.

   a) Explain the difference between 'recessional red shift' and 'cosmological red shift'? **[3 marks]**

   b) How are red shifts of distant galaxies measured? **[2 marks]**

   c) What does the parameter H_0 represent? **[2 marks]**

Galaxy	Distance (Mpc)	Velocity (km s^{-1})	H_0 (km s^{-1} Mpc^{-1})
NGC 3627	9.87	660	
NGC 2775	22.92	1470	
NGC 6764	42.31	2640	

   d) The results of distances and recessional velocities are shown for three distant galaxies. Using these data, determine a mean value of H_0. **[2 marks]**

   e) The age of the universe can be estimated from the value of $\frac{1}{H_0}$. Use the value of H_0 obtained above to estimate the age of the universe in billions of years. [1 year $= 3.2 \times 10^7$ s, 1pc $= 3.1 \times 10^{16}$ m] **[3 marks]**

2. The figure shows part of an absorption spectrum for NGC 1357 that clearly reveals a shift in its main absorption lines (calcium K and H).

   a) Determine the mean value of the shift in wavelength of the calcium K line and hence determine the value of the red shift, z, using $z = \frac{\Delta \lambda}{\lambda}$. **[3 marks]**

   b) Using the value for z, calculate the recessional velocity for this galaxy. **[2 marks]**

   c) Taking a value of H_0 as $68\,\text{km s}^{-1}\,\text{Mpc}^{-1}$, determine the mean distance to this galaxy. **[3 marks]**

   d) Suggest two reasons why this value may be inaccurate. **[2 marks]**

3. Different models of the universe are characterised by a density parameter Ω_0. This parameter is given by $\Omega_0 = \frac{\text{density of matter in the universe}}{\text{critical density}}$. The critical density (in kg m^{-3}) depends on the value of the Hubble constant and is $\rho_{\text{crit}} = \frac{3kH_0^2}{8\pi G}$, where $k = 1.04 \times 10^{-39}$ and $G = 6.7 \times 10^{-11}\,\text{Nm}^2\,\text{kg}^{-2}$.

   a) Given $H_0 = 68\,\text{km s}^{-1}\,\text{Mpc}^{-1}$, determine the value of the critical density. **[2 marks]**

   b) Explain how the universe will evolve if the density of matter in the universe was equal to this critical density. **[2 marks]**

   c) An estimate of the density of matter in the known universe is $0.4 \times 10^{-27}\,\text{kg m}^{-3}$. What does this suggest about the fate of the universe? **[2 marks]**

   d) Current experimental evidence reveals that the expansion of the universe is accelerating. What effects have not been considered so far in modelling the density of the universe? **[2 marks]**

The Physics of Vision

The Eye

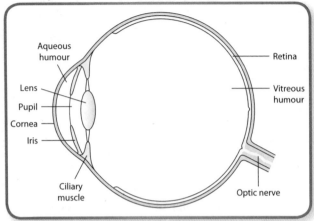

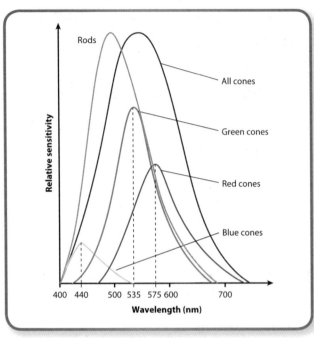

The eye's function is to provide signals that can be transmitted to the brain, which then translates these signals into images. Light enters the eye through the **cornea**, a transparent window of high refractive index that acts as a converging lens to focus images on the back of the **retina**. The amount of light entering the eye is governed by the size of the **pupil** and is controlled by muscle fibres that surround it known as the **iris**. Fine focal adjustments are performed by the **lens**, whose shape is controlled by the radial **ciliary muscles**. The **aqueous humour** and the more jelly-like **vitreous humour** provide a transparent medium that lets light through while also providing a mechanism for retaining the eye's shape. Images formed on the retina, an area that contains **light-sensitive nerve cells called rods and cones**, are then transmitted along the **optic nerve** to the brain. The arrangement of cornea, aqueous humour and lens provides the eye with a combined **refractive power** of 60 D (dioptres), which is adjustable over a limited range. In terms of focal length, f, where f (metres) $= \frac{1}{\text{power}}$ (dioptres), 60 D translates into a focal length of 0.017 m or 1.7 cm.

Sensitivity of the Eye

The retina contains over 140 million light-sensitive nerve cells. These are not uniformly distributed across the retina although they are generally about 0.003 mm apart. **Rod cells** are sensitive to low light levels but offer no colour discrimination, whereas the three types of cone cells ('red', 'green' and 'blue') are each sensitive to a different wavelength range as shown. Although the eye is far less responsive to blue light than either red or green, the brain is able to interpret the signals and weight them accordingly to form a balanced image. The eye's ability to see detail is called **visual acuity**, defined as $\frac{1}{\theta}$, where θ is the angle subtended at your eye by the smallest detail you can see. Angles are traditionally measured in minutes (1 minute is one-sixtieth of a degree), hence the unit of acuity is min^{-1}. For a human eye, the minimum resolvable angle is $\frac{2d}{f} \approx \frac{2 \times 0.003}{15} \approx 0.0004$ rad or 1.4 minutes of arc, a visual acuity of 0.72 min^{-1}. The **fovea** (sometimes called the **yellow spot**) is an area on the retina that contains no rod cells at all and is directly in the centre of field of view. In this area, the maximum resolution is improved to about 0.5 minutes of arc, corresponding to a visual acuity of 2 min^{-1}. Cone cells can react to light signals in about 50–80 ms whereas rods take 4–5 times longer. If light signals arrive faster than this then the eye cannot respond fast enough to them and they appear as a continuous stream of light known as **flicker fusion**. Eyes can detect flashing of up to 60 Hz in bright conditions but this reduces to only about 5 Hz under low-intensity conditions. Cinematography uses this **persistence of vision** to provide an illusion of a smooth and continuous picture on the screen (usually about 24 frames per second).

Short and Long Sight

There is a limit to the range of distances at which an eye can focus. The closest distance is called the near point (~25 cm) and the furthest distance is called the **far point** (at infinity). **Short-sighted (myopic)** people cannot focus on distant objects, i.e. their far point is closer than infinity. The cornea and lens are too powerful and an image is brought to focus in front of the retina. Spectacles containing a **diverging lens** or **concave lens** (with negative focal length) are used to bring the image to a sharp focus on the retina. **Long-sighted (hypermetropia)** people cannot focus on nearby objects because the cornea and lens are too weak and images are brought into focus behind the retina. This occurs if the near point is further away than normal. In these instances, a **convergent lens** (with positive focal length and hence positive power) is used to bring the image to focus on the retina. To calculate the position of a focused image or to determine the strength of a lens needed to correct for a vision defect, the **lens equation** can be used, $\frac{1}{f} = \frac{1}{u} + \frac{1}{v}$, where f is the focal length of a lens with object distance u and image distance v. When using the lens equation, the **'real is positive'** sign convention is followed, which means that a positive image distance represents a real image and a negative distance a virtual image. The **linear magnification**, m, of a lens is simply the ratio of image distance to object distance, i.e. $\frac{v}{u}$. If the distance between the lens and the retina is 20 mm then the power of the lens for someone who is short-sighted but can focus at infinity gives

$$\text{power} = \frac{1}{f} = \frac{1}{\infty} + \frac{1}{0.02} = 50\,\text{D}$$

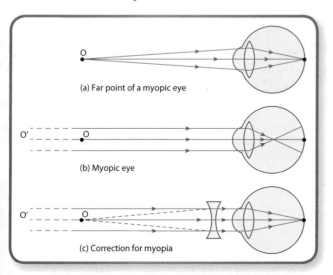

(a) Far point of a myopic eye

(b) Myopic eye

(c) Correction for myopia

However, if the far point is say only 1.2 m then the power needed to focus the object is

$$\text{power} = \frac{1}{f} = \frac{1}{1.2} + \frac{1}{0.02} = 50.8\,\text{D}$$

Hence a concave lens with a power of −0.8D is required to allow for distant objects to be brought into focus. The power required is always a negative quantity when correcting for short-sightedness, and positive when correcting for long-sightedness.

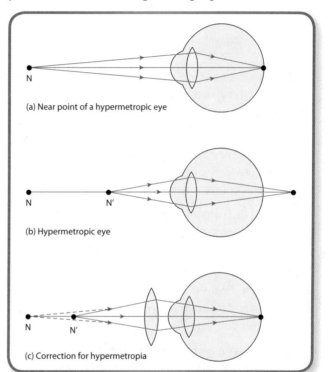

(a) Near point of a hypermetropic eye

(b) Hypermetropic eye

(c) Correction for hypermetropia

Astigmatism

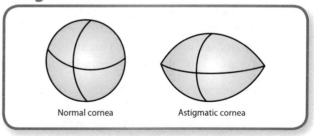

Normal cornea   Astigmatic cornea

The cornea is the transparent membrane where the majority of the light entering the eye is refracted. A cornea that does not have a spherical profile means that it has different curvatures in the horizontal and vertical directions, and hence different focal lengths in these directions. As a result, the image formed will be unevenly focused on the retina, a condition known as **astigmatism**. The condition is corrected by using a cylindrical lens. For example, a cylindrical lens can converge the horizontal light before entering the eye while leaving the light in the vertical plane unaffected. This is achieved by altering the angle between the vertical axis of the lens and the horizontal. As such, any prescription for the correction of astigmatism will have two power values and an angle value for each eye.

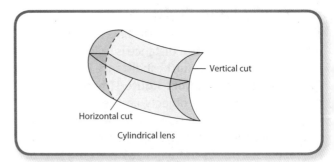

Vertical cut

Horizontal cut

Cylindrical lens

SUMMARY

- The **cornea** is a transparent window of high refractive index that acts as a converging lens to focus images on the back of the **retina**

- Fine focal adjustments are performed by the **lens**, whose shape is controlled by the radial **ciliary muscles**

- Signals from the light-sensitive **rods** and **cones** are carried along the **optic nerve** to the brain, where images are formed

- The eye's ability to see detail is called **visual acuity**, defined as $\frac{1}{\theta}$, where θ is the angle subtended at your eye by the smallest detail you can see

- The **fovea** (sometimes called the **yellow spot**) is an area on the retina that contains no rod cells resulting in a small region of enhanced visual acuity

- **Short-sighted** people cannot focus on distant objects and suffer from **myopia**; **long-sighted** people cannot focus on nearby objects and suffer from **hypermetropia**

- In people with **astigmatism**, the cornea has different curvatures in the horizontal and vertical directions and the image formed on the retina is unevenly focused

QUICK TEST

1. What is the main role of the cornea?

2. What do the ciliary muscles control?

3. What is the retina composed of and what is its main function?

4. What is the difference between rod and cone cells?

5. What is meant by the term 'visual acuity'?

6. What is the fovea and where is it positioned?

7. What is meant by long-sightedness and how is it rectified?

8. What is meant by 'persistence of vision'?

9. What is astigmatism?

10. What type of lens is used to correct for astigmatism?

11. What is the connection between the power of a lens and the focal length of a lens?

12. If the power of an unaccommodated eye is 60 D, calculate the image distance when the eye focuses on infinity.

PRACTICE QUESTIONS

1. a) What is meant by hypermetropia?   [2 marks]

    b) In a human eye the distance between the lens and the retina is 20 mm. If a person's near point is 75 cm, determine the power of the lens needed to bring an object into focus.   [2 marks]

    c) What would be the power of a lens needed to bring an object into focus at 50 mm?   [2 marks]

    d) Hence determine the power of the lens required to correct the vision.   [1 mark]

2. The first figure below shows the far point that can be seen in focus at the retina. The second figure shows a more distant object that results in a blurred image on the retina.

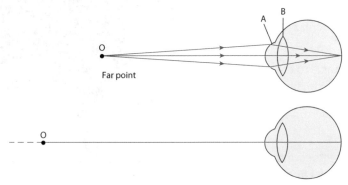

O
Far point

O

    a) Complete the light ray diagram in the second figure by drawing two more light rays to show how the blurred image is produced.   [2 marks]

    b) What is the name given to this type of eye defect?   [1 mark]

    c) The refractive power of the eye is provided by the two components labelled A and B in the first figure. What are these two components?   [2 marks]

    d) If the minimum refracting power of these two components is 52 D and the far point is 50 cm, determine the image distance between the lens and the retina.   [3 marks]

    e) Hence calculate the power of the correcting lens needed to bring objects at infinity into focus at the retina. What type of correction lens is needed?   [4 marks]

3. Following a routine eye test, a person is informed that they suffer from astigmatism.

    a) What is the main cause of astigmatism?   [1 mark]

    b) A standard eye test showed the effects of astigmatism. State the effect seen in this test that indicates astigmatism.   [1 mark]

    c) What type of lens is used to correct for this type of eye defect?   [1 mark]

    d) Give two quantities that are needed in order for a lens to be manufactured that corrects for this defect.   [2 marks]

The Physics of the Ear

The Structure of the Ear

The ear has a unique structure that can be divided into three key sections:

- the **outer ear** consisting of the pinna and auditory canal
- the **middle ear** consisting of the ossicles and Eustachian tube
- the **inner ear** with its semicircular canals, cochlea and auditory nerve.

The essential function of the ear is to collect sound energy and convert this into electrical energy that can be analysed by the brain.

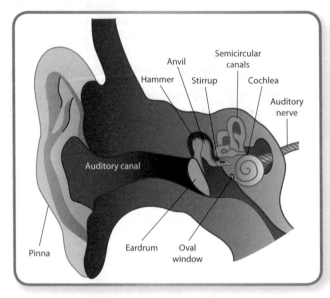

How the Ear functions

The **pinna** or external ear collects sound signals and channels them into the **auditory canal**. Because the cross-sectional area of the canal is smaller than the pinna, the intensity of the sound (i.e. energy per second per unit area) increases. Sound is simply the variation of air pressure and this causes the **tympanic membrane** (often called the **eardrum**) to vibrate in sympathy with the sound waves. The tympanic membrane separates the outer ear from the middle ear. The vibrations of the tympanic membrane are passed on to the **malleus** (hammer), the **incus** (anvil) and finally the **stapes** (stirrup). These three tiny bones are collectively known as the **ossicles** that act as a lever magnifying the sound signal; they also dampen any reflected signals from the inner ear. The middle ear contains air at atmospheric pressure due to the **Eustachian tube** that connects to the throat and the pressure is maintained by yawning and swallowing. The amplification is a result of the difference in area between the tympanic membrane and the area of the **oval window**. The area of the oval window is about one 20th of that of the tympanic membrane so that the overall effect is to increase the pressure acting on the fluid in the middle ear by a factor of about 25. The oval window transmits these vibrations to the fluid in the inner ear called the **perilymph** as pressure waves, and then on to the **basilar membrane** in the **cochlea**.

Conversion to Electrical Pulses

Different regions of the basilar membrane have different natural frequencies that range from 20 Hz (low pitch) to 20 kHz (high pitch). A signal received by the inner ear causes pressure waves in the fluid of the cochlea, making the membrane vibrate and resonate with a particular frequency. This causes a large increase in amplitude in that region and this is picked up by fine **hair cells** attached to the membrane. These signals are then sent as nerve cell electrical impulses along the **auditory nerve** to the brain where they are processed and interpreted as sound. How **loud** we perceive a sound depends on the frequency and on the intensity of sound waves. **Intensity** is measured in watts per square metre ($W\,m^{-2}$) and the **threshold of hearing** is defined as the lowest intensity that a normal human ear can detect; it is about $1 \times 10^{-12}\,W\,m^{-2}$ at a frequency of 1 kHz. The human ear can detect and respond to a considerable range of intensities, with sounds of frequencies around 3 kHz being perceived as the loudest. The highest intensity that a normal human ear can detect without severe discomfort is about $100\,W\,m^{-2}$; this is often referred to as the **threshold of pain**. Generally, sound intensities above $1\,W\,m^{-2}$ will cause some degree of discomfort.

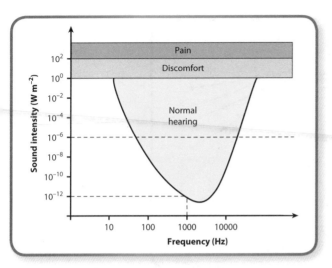

Loudness and Intensity

The **loudness** of a sound is a subjective term and is difficult to measure. However, the loudness (L) that we experience is proportional to the logarithm of the intensity rather than to the intensity itself (it also depends on its frequency), and given by $L \propto \log\left(\frac{\text{new intensity}}{\text{initial intensity}}\right)$. This logarithmic response means that the ear has an enormous **dynamic range** of a ratio of intensities of about 10^{14}. Because the ear has a logarithmic response to intensity, a logarithmic scale is used to measure **sound intensity**. Such measurements are made relative to a standard **threshold of hearing** intensity, I_0, where $I_0 = 10^{-12}\,\text{W m}^{-2}$. This logarithmic scale is called the **decibel scale** of sound intensity, where $I\,(\text{dB}) = 10\log\left(\frac{I}{I_0}\right)$.

This means that the threshold of hearing (i.e. the minimum intensity of sound that can be heard by a normal ear at a frequency of 1 kHz) takes the value 0 decibels (0 dB). A sound that has 10 times the intensity of the threshold value has a value of 10 dB whereas a sound 100 times more intense has a level of 20 dB. A quiet room may have a sound level of 40 dB whereas a washing machine may be 70 dB and a plane taking off may be in excess of 120 dB. A 'safe' level would be in the region of 90 dB (corresponding to $I_0 = 10^{-3}\,\text{W m}^{-2}$).

Equal Loudness Curves

Equal loudness curves show sound intensity levels that are required to produce the same perception of loudness at different frequencies (although it is important to note that the intensity of a sound wave

is independent of frequency – it is only the human perception of loudness that produces these equal loudness curves). A 1 kHz source, placed next to a source of unknown loudness, is adjusted until it sounds as loud as the unknown source. If the standard source is measured to be 70 dB then the unknown source has a loudness of 70 **phons** (the phon being the unit of loudness). Repeating this process over the range of frequencies generates a family of phon curves as shown.

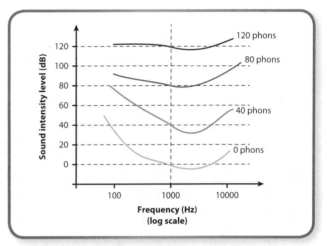

Audiograms and Hearing Defects

Hearing defects or hearing problems may arise from damage to the hair cells in the cochlea or damage to the auditory nerve, known collectively as **sensorineural deafness**, or due to infections and blockages, perhaps in the middle ear, called **conductive hearing loss**. They may also be due to damage from long-term exposure to loud noises, referred to as **progressive deafness**. Hearing damage and the degree of deafness can be assessed using an **audiometer**, and a plot of the hearing level or threshold level (in dB) against frequency is known as an **audiogram**. For example, age-related hearing loss affects high-frequency sounds more than low-frequency sounds, whereas damage through excessive noise show a loss in a frequency band around 4 kHz. Monitoring sound levels in the environment is usually undertaken with sound meters that have been modified to take account of the response of the human ear. The weighted sound intensity levels are expressed on a **dBA scale** where sounds of the same intensity level have the same loudness for the 'average' human ear.

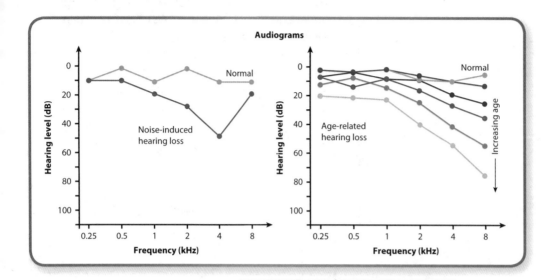

Audiograms

SUMMARY

- The outer ear consists of the pinna and auditory canal, the middle ear consists of the ossicles and Eustachian tube, and the inner ear has the semicircular canals, cochlea and auditory nerve

- Sound is simply the variation of air pressure that causes the tympanic membrane (the eardrum) to vibrate

- Different regions of the basilar membrane have different natural frequencies that range from 20 Hz (low pitch) to 20 000 Hz or 20 kHz (high pitch)

- The perceived loudness of sound depends on the frequency and on the intensity of the sound waves

- Loudness, L, is proportional to the logarithm of the fractional change in intensity according to $L \propto \log\left(\frac{\text{new intensity}}{\text{initial intensity}}\right)$ and hence the ear has an enormous dynamic response range of the order of about 10^{14}

- The intensity of sound in decibels (dB) is given by sound intensity level (dB) $= 10\log\left(\frac{I}{I_0}\right)$, where I_0 is the threshold of hearing

- Equal loudness curves show the sound intensity levels required to produce the same perception of loudness at different frequencies

- Hearing damage and the degree of deafness can be assessed through an audiogram

QUICK TEST

1. What is the function of the ossicles?

2. What is the function of the oval window?

3. What is the frequency range of a normal healthy ear?

4. What does perceived loudness depend upon?

5. Define what is meant by the 'threshold of hearing'.

6. If the sound intensity at a disco is $1 \times 10^{-3}\,\mathrm{W\,m^{-2}}$, calculate the sound intensity level in dB.

7. What is the threshold of pain in terms of the dB scale? Give an example of what may cause severe discomfort.

8. What is an audiogram?

9. What is a phon?

10. What is meant by the dBA scale and what is it used for?

11. What is meant by age-related hearing loss?

PRACTICE QUESTIONS

1. **a)** What is meant by the intensity of sound, and what are its units?   **[2 marks]**

    b) Give a reason why sounds of equal intensity are not necessarily of equal loudness.   **[1 mark]**

    The sound intensity level in dB is given by $10\log\left(\frac{I}{I_0}\right)$, where $I_0 = 1 \times 10^{-12}\,\mathrm{W\,m^{-2}}$.

    c) What does I_0 represent and what is its value in dB?   **[2 marks]**

    d) At a music concert the sound intensity level measured near one of the large speakers was 110 dB. Determine the intensity of the sound at this point.   **[3 marks]**

2. **a)** The diagram shows the key components of the ear. Name the parts labelled A, B, C and D. **[4 marks]**

    b) Explain the function of the tympanic membrane.   **[1 mark]**

    c) The inner ear is filled with fluid called perilymph. Describe the function of this fluid with reference to the basilar membrane.   **[1 mark]**

    d) Describe the path of sound waves through the inner ear, from vibrations in the oval window to nerve impulses in the auditory nerve.   **[4 marks]**

3. **a)** What is a phon?   **[2 marks]**

    b) Describe how curves of equal loudness are generated.   **[3 marks]**

    c) Hearing problems can be diagnosed using an audiogram. Describe the nature of an audiogram.   **[1 mark]**

    d) The figure shows a person suffering from a hearing problem. Explain with reference to the figure what type of hearing problem is shown.   **[3 marks]**

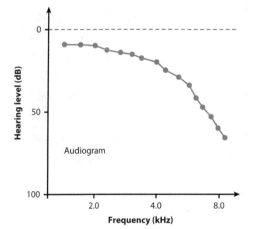

The Heart and Biological Measurements

The Heart

The hardest working muscle within the human body is the **heart** and the purpose of the heart is to pump blood from the lungs to the rest of the body (the left half of the heart) and to pump blood from the body back to the lungs (the right half of the heart). The heart has four chambers, **two atria** and **two ventricles**, that are connected by one-way valves. Deoxygenated blood returning from the body enters the right atrium through the **vena cavae** and is pumped into the right ventricle. When the right ventricle contracts, it forces blood through the **pulmonary arteries** to the lungs. Oxygenated blood from the lungs enters the left atrium along the **pulmonary veins** and from here it is pumped into the left ventricle. Contraction of the left ventricle sends blood into the **aorta** for distribution around the body. On average, the left ventricle pumps about 70–100 ml of blood every beat, allowing the heart to pump between 5 and 20 litres of blood every minute, depending on the heart rate.

Electrical Activity in the Heart

The four main heart chambers contract in sequence and this sequence is controlled by electrical signals generated by the **sino-atrial node**. This effectively acts as a pacemaker that sends electrical signals from the right atrium to the left atrium, causing them to contract. The size, polarity and duration of these signals are crucial to the way the heart maintains a steady rhythmic function. The way the potentials change in the cardiac muscle is similar to nerve and other muscle fibres and is called the **action potential**, although for cardiac muscles changes in potential travel more slowly and hence lasts for much longer (see section opposite on **Action Potentials**). A change in potential in one part of the nerve initiates a new (action) potential on the opposite side of the membrane and this propagates through the nerve fibre in milliseconds. On reaching the muscle cells, the action potential travels much more slowly, initiating the contraction. The size of these potentials can be measured by placing electrodes on the skin and, in the case of the heart, the response obtained is called an **electrocardiogram** or **ECG**.

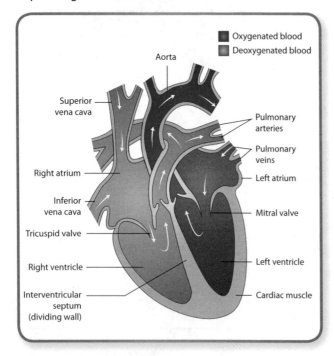

Oxygenated blood
Deoxygenated blood

Aorta
Superior vena cava
Pulmonary arteries
Pulmonary veins
Right atrium
Left atrium
Inferior vena cava
Mitral valve
Tricuspid valve
Right ventricle
Left ventricle
Interventricular septum (dividing wall)
Cardiac muscle

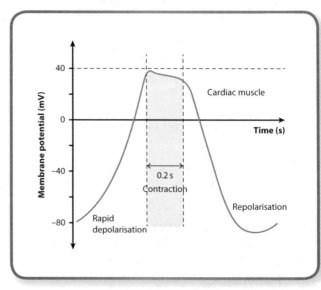

ECG

An **ECG** is a plot of the small but measurable potential on the skin as a function of time that allows the condition of the heart to be monitored. A normal ECG contains three key parts: a P wave, a QRS wave and a T wave. The **P wave** corresponds to the depolarisation and contraction of the atria followed just 0.2 s later by the **QRS wave**, displaying the depolarisation and contraction of the ventricles (the repolarisation and relaxation of the atria is masked by the size of the QRS wave). Finally, the **T wave** shows the repolarisation and relaxation of the ventricles, and the sequence is then repeated. Good electrical contact with the skin is essential for accurate readings to be obtained and dead skin and hair is removed and a gel applied to the electrodes. Other precautions include screening all electrical equipment to eliminate unwanted electrical interferences.

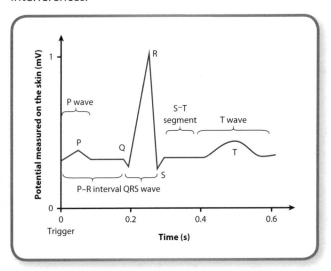

Action Potentials

Electrical signals are transmitted through the body along **nerve fibres**. These signals are in the form of a **changing potential difference**, known as an **action potential**, which is generated by the movement of ions across a cell membrane. Although water will readily diffuse across a cell membrane, the passage of ions, particularly potassium (K^+) and sodium (Na^+) ions, is more difficult; this barrier to movement is usually referred to as **permeability**. The imbalance between the permeability of sodium and potassium ions across a cell membrane is what gives rise to the action potential. Proteins within the cell allow potassium ions into the cell and sodium ions to leave the cell, setting up a **concentration gradient**. Cells therefore have a high potassium concentration and low sodium concentration compared with the surrounding fluid. This concentration gradient causes potassium ions to leave the cell until an equilibrium state is reached between the concentration gradient and the potential gradient, and the cell is said to be **polarised**. At this point in time, the potential within the cells is −70 mV compared with its surroundings (the **resting potential**). When a nerve impulse is received, part of the cell membrane becomes more permeable to sodium ions and an influx of sodium ions occurs over a period of about 1 ms. This is sufficient for the cell to become positively charged to +35 mV (a process called **depolarisation**) before the cell responds, allowing potassium ions to leave to restore the cell voltage to −70 mV once again (in a process called **repolarisation**). The propagation of an impulse along nerve fibres can reach $100\,m\,s^{-1}$ until they reach a muscle cell, where the action potential travels at a much reduced rate causing the muscle to react. Although nerve fibres are only a few microns in diameter, they may be up to a metre in length in some parts of the body.

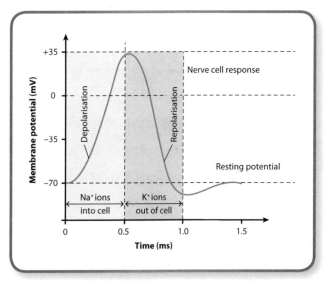

SUMMARY

- The **heart** pumps blood from the lungs to the rest of the body (the left half of the heart) and pumps blood from the body back to the lungs (the right half of the heart)

- The heart has four chambers, **two atria** and **two ventricles**, that are connected by one-way valves

- **Deoxygenated** blood returning from the body enters the right atrium through the **vena cavae** and is pumped into the **right ventricle**; when the right ventricle contracts, it forces blood through the **pulmonary arteries** to the lungs

- **Oxygenated** blood from the lungs enters the left atrium along the **pulmonary veins** and is pumped from the **left atrium** into the **left ventricle**; contraction of the left ventricle sends blood into the **aorta** for distribution

- The four heart chambers contract in sequence and this is controlled by electrical signals (**action potentials**) generated by the **sino-atrial node**

- The size of heart potentials and the way they respond can be obtained from an **electrocardiogram** or **ECG**

- A **normal ECG** contains three key parts: a **P wave**, a **QRS wave** and a **T wave**

- Electrical signals are transmitted through the body along **nerve fibres**; these signals are in the form of a **changing potential difference**, known as an **action potential**, which is generated by the movement of ions across a cell membrane

QUICK TEST

1. What are the four main chambers of the heart called?

2. Oxygenated blood enters which chamber and along which vessel?

3. What controls the electrical signals to the heart?

4. What are these electrical signals more commonly referred to as?

5. What procedure is used to look at the electrical signals generated by the heart?

6. Give two precautions that are taken when performing the above procedure to ensure accurate readings?

7. What does a QRS wave represent?

8. What allows an action potential to be generated in a nerve cell?

9. What is the range in potential difference set up in a nerve cell?

10. What is the main difference between the action potentials in nerve cells and in the cardiac muscle?

PRACTICE QUESTIONS

1. Figure 1 shows part of a normal electrocardiogram (ECG) obtained at the surface of the skin from a patient.

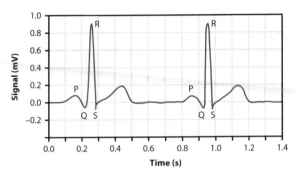

Time (s)

a) What do the P wave and the QRS wave correspond to? **[4 marks]**

b) One wave on the ECG has not been labelled. Label this wave correctly and explain its function. **[3 marks]**

c) What is the amplitude of the main pulse? **[1 mark]**

d) From the trace, determine the period for the heart beat and calculate the pulse rate per minute. **[3 marks]**

e) Give an example of a difference that would appear in the ECG trace if this person started to exercise. **[1 mark]**

2. a) What is meant by the term 'action potential'? **[2 marks]**

b) How is the action potential generated? **[1 mark]**

c) Sketch a graph to show the action potential in a nerve cell. On your graph:

   (i) add suitable scales to both the x- and y-axes to represent a nerve cell's response **[4 marks]**

   (ii) label your graph to indicate the three key modes involved in an action potential. **[3 marks]**

3. The figure shows the basic structure or the heart.

a) Label the structures A, B, C, D and E. **[5 marks]**

b) On your diagram shade the side of the heart that receives oxygenated blood. **[1 mark]**

c) Explain the function of the sino-atrial node. **[3 marks]**

d) Give one difference between the action potential of a nerve cell and the action potential of a cardiac muscle. **[1 mark]**

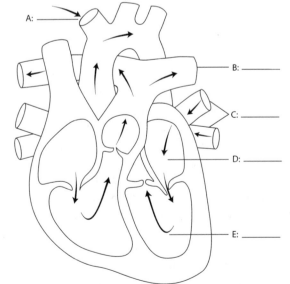

Medical Imaging with Non-ionising Radiation

Magnetic Resonance Imaging

Magnetic resonance imaging (MRI) is a non-invasive imaging technique that is used to diagnose and treat medical conditions. MRI uses a powerful (superconducting) magnet to produce a uniform magnetic field into which the patient is placed. Body tissue contains water and water contains hydrogen nuclei, i.e. protons, that spin; **spinning protons** create their own small magnetic field. The strong external magnetic field produced by the superconducting magnet aligns all of the spinning protons in the same direction. A short pulse of **radio frequency radiation** is then directed at the patient and this disturbs the orientation of the protons as they **absorb** the radiation. When the pulse stops, the protons return to their original state (a process called **relaxation**) and in doing so emit a radio frequency signal, called the **MRI signal**, before another pulse is sent.

The strength of the emitted radio frequency signal depends on the proton density and all of the resulting signals received are collected and computer-analysed to reconstruct a detailed image of a section through the patient's body. In this way, images of organs, soft tissue, bone and other internal structures can be readily built-up. Different organs can be analysed in more detail by altering the time between pulses so that rapidly repeating pulses are used to look at large molecules such as fat, whereas delayed pulses enhance the response to fluids such as blood. High-quality 2D image slices, particularly of soft tissue such as found in the brain, can be obtained to produce a full 3D picture. Any part of the body can be as scanned with an MRI scanner and there are no known side effects. However, scanners are very expensive to construct and run, and the production of high-quality images can often take a long time. They are not suited to detailed studies of bone and cannot be used on patients that have metal implants including pacemakers.

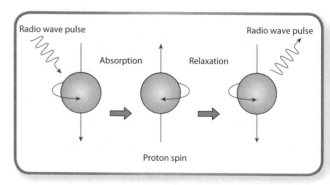

Radio wave pulse — Radio wave pulse

Absorption — Relaxation

Proton spin

Ultrasound Imaging

Ultrasound waves are sound waves in excess of 20 kHz (the upper limit of human hearing). For medical applications, they are usually in the range 1–15 MHz. They are produced by **piezoelectric transducers** that convert electrical signals into pressure waves and vice versa; an alternating potential difference deforms the crystal that resonates at the same frequency. Deformation also produces an alternating potential difference which means that the same transducer can act as a detector. Modern devices use **lead zirconate titanate** (PZT) crystals. When ultrasound waves meet a boundary, some are reflected and it is these waves that are used to create an image. The amount of reflection depends on the **specific acoustic impedance**, Z, of the material it is travelling through (given by $Z = \rho c$, where ρ is the density and c the velocity of sound in the material) and the acoustic impedance of the medium it is about to enter. Acoustic impedance has units of $kg\,m^{-2}\,s^{-1}$.

Material	c (ms^{-1})	ρ (kgm^{-3})	Z (kgm^{-2}s^{-1} ×10^6)
fat	1450	920	1.38
muscle	1580	1080	1.70
bone	3500	1500	6.48
water	1450	1000	1.50
air	330	1.3	0.0004

If the **relative impedance** at the boundary between these two materials is large then most of the energy in the wave is reflected. The fraction of the wave intensity that is reflected is given by a **reflection coefficient**, α, which can be expressed through the equation

$$\alpha = \frac{I_R}{I_I} = \left(\frac{Z_2 - Z_1}{Z_2 + Z_1} \right)^2$$

where I_R and I_I are the intensities of the reflected and incident waves in $W\,m^{-2}$, and Z_1 and Z_2 are the specific acoustic impedances of materials 1 and 2 in $kg\,m^{-2}\,s^{-1}$. The intensity (I) of the ultrasound wave is reduced **exponentially** due to scattering and absorption so that $I = I_0 e^{-\mu x}$, where I_0 is the original intensity on entering the material of thickness x and μ is the **intensity attenuation coefficient** for that material in units of m^{-1}; this attenuation coefficient is also proportional to the frequency of the sound wave. The absorption of ultrasound causes a slight heating effect in the body.

Two types of scans are now readily available with ultrasound: **A-scans** (amplitude scans) and **B-scans** (brightness scans), which produce linear and 2D images, respectively. Such scans are used for observing the developing foetus and provide information on gestational age and/or abnormalities. **Echocardiograms** provide real-time ultrasound images of the heart, and 3D scans are also being developed for foetal investigations. The advantages of ultrasound include there being no known hazards and that the devices are cheap to produce and are readily portable. They also provide real-time images and are particularly good when observing soft tissue; however, the resolution is poor compared with other non-invasive techniques.

Endoscopy

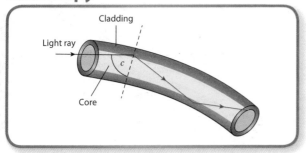

Cladding

Light ray

c

Core

An **endoscope** is a versatile medical instrument used by surgeons to examine inside the body without recourse to larger surgical procedures. The endoscope is based on the use of tens of thousands of **optical fibres** (extremely fine strands of flexible glass or plastic) in which light is **critically reflected** at the boundary between the core and the cladding. The cladding has a slightly lower refractive index than the core itself, increasing the critical angle and using **total internal reflection** to transmit light signals along each of the fibres. The critical angle, c, for light rays travelling along the fibre can be determined using the equation $\sin c = \frac{n_{cladding}}{n_{core}}$, where $n_{cladding}$ and n_{core} are the refractive indices of the cladding and core, respectively. Typical values for the refractive indices of core and cladding give critical angles around 70°. The cladding is also used to protect each individual fibre from touching and from damage. The illumination light is carried along and through thousands of fine optical fibres packed together into an **incoherent bundle**, while the returning image light is carried along a similar set of optical fibres packed into a **coherent bundle**. The coherency of the optical fibres ensures that each of the fibres has the same spatial position at both ends of the bundle, allowing an accurate and detailed image to be seen. The action end of the fibre (the **distal end**) carries water, light and suction, and possibly also a cutting tool that allows biopsies to be carried out (called an anthroscope). Endoscopes are also used to examine the upper digestive tract (gastroscopy) or the colon (colonoscopy). A more rigid form of the endoscope called the laparoscope is used to perform key-hole surgery where a scalpel is attached at the distal end.

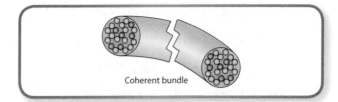

Coherent bundle

SUMMARY

- Magnetic resonance imaging (MRI) is a non-invasive imaging technique that uses a powerful superconducting magnet to align spinning protons

- Pulses of radio frequency radiation are used to disturb the orientation of the protons through absorption; when the pulse stops, the protons return to their original state in a process called relaxation and emit an MRI signal

- The strength of the MRI signal is proportional to the proton density and both 2D and 3D images are reconstructed from these signals

- Ultrasound waves (sound waves in excess of 20 kHz) are produced by piezoelectric transducers that convert electrical signals into pressure waves

- The specific acoustic impedance, Z, of a material depends on its density and the speed of sound in it ($Z = \rho c$)

- Ultrasound images are formed when there is a significant difference in the specific acoustic impedance at the boundary between two materials; the strength of the reflected signal is characterised by the reflection coefficient, α

- Ultrasound A-scans (amplitude scans) provide linear images whereas B-scans (brightness scans) produce 2D images

- Endoscopes are versatile medical instruments that are based on bundles of optical fibres

QUICK TEST

1. What do the letters 'MRI' mean?

2. What is the MRI process based upon?

3. Give one advantage and one disadvantage of MRI scanning.

4. What is ultrasound and how is it produced?

5. What is specific acoustic impedance?

6. What is needed to obtain a good ultrasound image?

7. Calculate the fraction of intensity reflected when ultrasound waves pass from air to soft tissue. [$Z_{air} = 0.4 \times 10^3\,\text{kg m}^{-2}\,\text{s}^{-1}$, $Z_{tissue} = 1630 \times 10^3\,\text{kg m}^{-2}\,\text{s}^{-1}$]

8. What are endoscopes based upon for creating images?

9. What is the purpose of the cladding?

10. What is the critical angle if the refractive index of the cladding is 1.54 and the refractive index of the optical fibre is 1.58?

PRACTICE QUESTIONS

1. Ultrasound is used to observe the development of a foetus.

    a) Explain what ultrasound is and how it is produced.   **[3 marks]**

    b) What is the basic method behind imaging with ultrasound.   **[4 marks]**

    c) The reflection coefficient (the ratio of the reflected intensity to the incident intensity) is given by

$$\alpha = \frac{I_R}{I_I} = \left(\frac{Z_{muscle} - Z_{bone}}{Z_{muscle} + Z_{bone}} \right)^2$$

Using the data given, calculate the proportion of the intensity that is reflected at the bone–muscle boundary.
[$Z_{bone} = 6.5 \times 10^6 \, kg\,m^{-2}\,s^{-1}$, $Z_{muscle} = 1.7 \times 10^6 \, kg\,m^{-2}\,s^{-1}$]   **[3 marks]**

    d) Give two advantages of using ultrasound for foetal scanning.   **[2 marks]**

2. The figure shows part of a single optical fibre with a core refractive index of 1.55 surrounded by cladding with a refractive index of 1.40

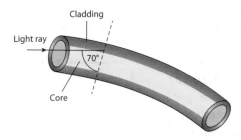

    a) Calculate the critical angle, c, for the boundary between the fibre and the cladding.   **[2 marks]**

    b) The figure shows a light ray entering the optical fibre. Show how the path of light travels along the fibre.   **[2 marks]**

    c) In an endoscope two bundles of optical fibres are used. Name these two types of bundles and explain the purpose of them.   **[6 marks]**

    d) Describe the effect of increasing the refractive index of the cladding material while retaining the same core fibre.   **[2 marks]**

3. Another imaging technique that is used in medical diagnosis is MRI scanning.

    a) Briefly outline how an MRI scanner is used to create images.   **[1 mark]**

    b) How is the contrast enhanced on an image produced by an MRI scanner?   **[1 mark]**

    c) Give two advantages of MRI compared with other imaging techniques.   **[2 marks]**

Imaging with Ionising Radiation

The Production of X-rays

X-rays are produced when high-energy charged particles such as electrons (charge e) are brought to rest. In an X-ray machine, electrons are emitted from a hot cathode through the process of **thermionic emission**. These free electrons are accelerated across a large potential difference, the **tube voltage** (V), before impinging on a heavy metal anode (often tungsten). These high-energy electrons decelerate extremely rapidly within the target, where their kinetic energy is converted into electromagnetic energy. If an electron loses all of its energy, $E = eV$, in one collision with a target atom then the photon emitted will have an energy $E = hf$ or a **wavelength** given by $\lambda = \frac{c}{f} = \frac{hc}{E} = \frac{hc}{eV}$. The resulting radiation emitted has two distinct features: firstly, a continuous but large background radiation called **bremsstrahlung** (or braking radiation), and secondly, several sharp line features (line spectra) that are specific of the target atom and are known as **characteristic X-ray photons**. The latter are emitted at precise energies, with the two features superimposed on one another. The efficiency for X-ray production is generally poor with ~1% conversion and the rest of the energy being converted into heat. This heat is extracted by several methods that depend on the size of the X-ray device but water cooling, rotating anodes and copper blocks are all used as a means to conduct the heat away efficiently.

electrons interacting with inner shell (level) atomic electrons in the target. The interaction is sufficient to ionise these inner core electrons and the vacancies or holes left behind are filled by outer shell electrons in the target atom. It is the **transitions** from **higher to lower energy levels** that result in the emission of high-energy photons in the X-ray region. The precise energy of these characteristic lines is determined by the energy difference between the levels involved. The **intensity** of the X-rays emitted can be increased by **increasing the current** applied to the cathode filament. **Increasing the tube voltage** only increases the energy of the emitted photons, with the characteristic X-ray lines of the anode material becoming more prominent, as shown in the diagram.

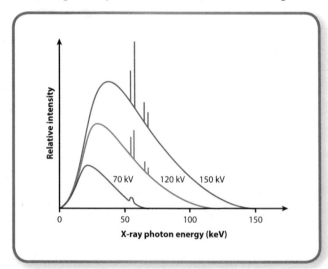

Radiography

X-rays are used extensively in many areas to provide 2D images on a photographic film (an '**X-ray**'). These 'shadow' pictures simply represent the attenuation of the X-rays as they pass through the material and onto the film. The contrast in attenuation between bone and soft tissue has allowed X-rays to become a routine tool in diagnosing bone damage and fractures. However, X-ray images do not carry any information about depth. Because X-rays are highly **ionising**, they often provide a substantial dose of radiation to a patient. Medical personnel (**radiographers**) ensure that sufficient detail is obtained while minimising exposure time and hence dose. Procedures include:

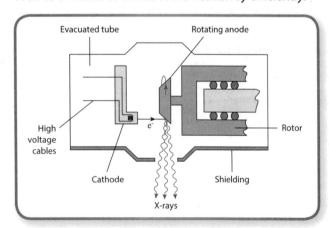

X-ray Spectra

The bremsstrahlung radiation forms a strong and intense background, and superimposed on this is the emission line spectrum. This arises from the incoming

- placing the X-ray window away from the patient but the photographic plate or film as close to the patient as possible
- placing shielding materials between the photographic plate or film and the patient to reduce the scattering of X-rays that affects contrast (this is known as 'fogging')
- ensuring that the patient remains as immobile as possible to avoid the 'blurring' of the final image
- intensifying screens that can be used in some instances to provide a faster photographic image that helps reduce exposure time and hence dose to the patient.

X-ray Absorption

When X-rays pass through matter they are absorbed and scattered. The intensity of the X-ray beam decreases, i.e. it is **attenuated**, and this decrease can be modelled as an **exponential decay** that depends on the thickness of material and on the nature of the material itself. The **intensity** is given by $I = I_0 e^{-\mu x}$, where I_0 is the initial source intensity, x is the distance or thickness and μ represents the overall **attenuation coefficient** of the material or materials. Attenuation coefficients tend to include both **absorption** (photoelectric effect, pair production) and **scattering** (Compton scattering) processes that are a function of both the atomic number of the materials involved and the incident energy. A useful measure of attenuation is the thickness needed to reduce the initial intensity by a factor of 2 and this is referred to as the **half-value thickness**, $x_{1/2}$.

X-ray images will show good contrast and therefore detail if the materials the X-ray beam passes through comprise of very different (contrasting) atomic numbers. A more useful measure of the absorption of radiation that takes account of density variations within materials is called the **mass attenuation coefficient**, μ_m, and given by $\frac{\mu}{\rho}$. It is this contrast between materials such as **soft tissue** and **bone** that allows bone fractures to be imaged. In tissues that have similar atomic numbers or attenuation coefficients, such as normal tissue and a tumour, an artificial contrast medium can be introduced. An X-ray of the digestive tract often involves a 'barium meal'; barium is an ideal **image contrast enhancer** as it has a large atomic number and it is readily absorbed by tissue, providing sufficient contrast for an X-ray image of the internal organs. It is also possible to follow the movements as the barium passes through, say, the digestive tract by taking a series of low-dose X-ray images over a period of time.

Energy (keV)	Mass attenuation coefficient, $\frac{\mu}{\rho}$ ($m^2\,kg^{-1} \times 10^{-3}$)		
	Bone	Muscle	Water
50	0.424	0.226	0.227
100	0.186	0.169	0.171
500	0.092	0.096	0.097
1000	0.066	0.070	0.071

Fluoroscopy

A continuous stream of X-rays (as opposed to a pulsed X-ray beam used in radiography) that have passed through the patient can be used to obtain real-time moving images using a technique known as **fluoroscopy**. The transmitted X-ray photons are sent into an image intensifier where the X-ray energies are transformed into electrons. These electrons are subsequently accelerated towards a fluorescent viewing screen and, with adequate focusing, an enhancement of the order of 5000 is possible. The slow decay response of the screen allows the image to be visible for several minutes and therefore viewed in real time. The output can also be recorded on video camera or on a **charge-coupled device** (CCD) that allows digital recording for computer enhancement and processing. Because a continuous stream of radiation is used, patients are exposed to higher absorbed doses than with an ordinary radiograph.

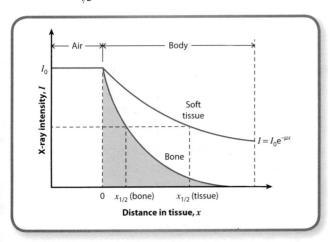

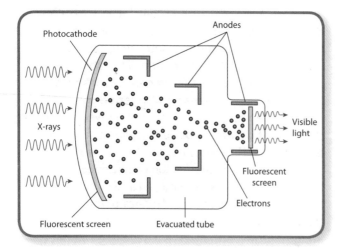

Photocathode / Anodes / X-rays / Visible light / Fluorescent screen / Electrons / Fluorescent screen / Evacuated tube

Computed Tomography

Computed tomography (CT) is a method that uses X-rays to obtain 2D images of slices through a body or object. Modern CT scanners use a **focused monochromatic** (single wavelength or energy) X-ray beam that is emitted in a fan shape towards the patient. An array of **digital photon detectors** records the transmitted intensity at each position on the other side of the patient before the X-ray beam is rotated to

the next position and a similar set of results recorded. An image is then built-up by **high-speed computer processing** of the recorded data and often a complete scan can be recorded within 5 minutes. However, CT cameras are relatively expensive (but still cheaper than MRI scanners) and they can give a higher dose of radiation to the patient. Nonetheless, they do provide very detailed images with spatial resolutions of ~1 mm and they can detect density differences of typically less than 1%.

SUMMARY

- **X-rays** are produced by thermionic emission of electrons from a cathode that are then accelerated into a metal target (the anode); the process of deceleration converts a small amount of this energy into electromagnetic radiation

- The anode emits a continuous spectrum, called bremsstrahlung, and a line spectrum that has energies that are characteristic of the metal target

- The X-ray beam intensity can be adjusted by increasing the tube voltage or by altering the current to the filament

- The intensity of the X-ray beam is attenuated when it passes through matter following an exponential decay

- The half-value thickness is the amount of matter required to reduce the intensity to half its original value

- The attenuation of X-rays depends on the mass attenuation coefficient, which itself depends on the atomic number of the material and on the X-ray energy

- Computed tomography scanning uses X-rays to produce a 2D slice through an object or body; it requires considerable computer processing

- Fluoroscopy provides an efficient method for transforming X-rays into electrons and subsequently light that can be used to make observations of organs as they function

QUICK TEST

1. What is 'bremsstrahlung'?

2. How are the characteristic spectral lines produced in an X-ray device?

3. What is an advantage of a rotating anode X-ray machine?

4. In an X-ray device, electrons are accelerated through a potential difference of 90.0 kV. Calculate the maximum energy of the emitted photons in (a) joules (b) eV.

5. What is the wavelength of the X-rays in the above question (assume no energy losses)?

6. What is meant by half-value thickness?

7. What does 'CT' mean and give a major disadvantage of these machines.

8. Explain what a barium meal is used for.

9. Give one advantage of fluoroscopy.

PRACTICE QUESTIONS

1. An efficient method of producing X-rays is to use a rotating anode X-ray tube.

    a) Explain why the anode is rotated. **[2 marks]**

    b) Describe a typical spectrum of the radiation that is produced by a rotating anode device. **[4 marks]**

    c) Describe how an X-ray image of a bone fracture is produced. **[3 marks]**

    d) What is meant by the term 'half-value thickness' **[1 mark]**

    e) The linear attenuation coefficient (μ) of bone at 50 keV is 0.57 cm^{-1}. Use the equation $I = I_0 e^{-\mu x}$ to determine the half-value thickness for bone. **[4 marks]**

2. The diagram shows a fluoroscopic image intensifier with key components labelled A to G.

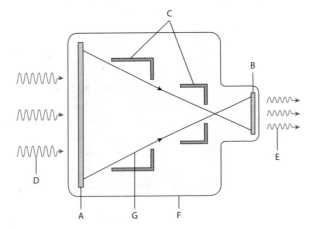

    a) Name the key components shown in the diagram. **[5 marks]**

    b) Explain the purpose of the key components A, C and B for producing an image. **[5 marks]**

    c) Give one medical application for which an image intensifier could be used and explain why it would be useful in this particular application. **[2 marks]**

3. An X-ray tube accelerates electrons through a potential difference of 75 kV before hitting the target anode.

    a) Calculate the kinetic energy, in joules, of an electron as it reaches the anode, giving your answer to 2 s.f. **[3 marks]**

    b) The electron gives up all of its kinetic energy to emit an X-ray photon. Calculate the wavelength of the photon emitted. **[2 marks]**

    c) X-ray photons can be used in a CT scanner. Describe briefly how a CT scanner produces an image. **[4 marks]**

    d) Give the main advantage of a CT scanner over other medical imaging techniques. **[1 mark]**

Answers

Day 1

Circular Motion

QUICK TEST (page 6)

1. radians
2. at right angles to the centre of rotation in the direction of rotation
3. $\omega = \frac{\theta}{t}$; $\mathrm{rad\,s^{-1}}$
4. $v = r\omega$
5. frequency
6. $T = \frac{1}{f}$; $\omega = \frac{2\pi}{T} = 2\pi f$
7. $f = 0.017\,\mathrm{Hz}$; $\omega = 0.105\,\mathrm{rad\,s^{-1}}$
8. $1.5 \times 10^{-5}\,\mathrm{m\,s^{-1}}$
9. tension in the string
10. $F = \frac{mv^2}{r} = mr\omega^2$; directed towards the centre of the circle
11. The object would fly off tangentially to the circle with a speed v.
12. gravitational force
13. $15\,000\,\mathrm{N}$
14. $12.1\,\mathrm{m\,s^{-1}}$

PRACTICE QUESTIONS (page 7)

1. a) period $T = \frac{1}{f} = \frac{1}{1.1 \times 10^4} = 90.6 \times 10^{-6} = 91 \times 10^{-6}\,\mathrm{s} = 91\,\mu\mathrm{s}$ **[1 mark]**

   b) angular velocity $\omega = 2\pi f = \frac{2\pi}{T}$

   $\omega = \frac{2\pi}{91 \times 10^{-6}} = 6.9 \times 10^4\,\mathrm{rad\,s^{-1}}$ **[1 mark]**

   c) $v = r\omega = \frac{\text{circumference}}{2\pi} \times \omega$ **[1 mark]**

   $v = \frac{27 \times 10^3}{2\pi} \times 6.9 \times 10^4$ **[1 mark]**

   $v = 2.97 \times 10^8\,\mathrm{m\,s^{-1}} = 0.99c$ **[1 mark]**

   d) $m_\mathrm{p} = 3.94 \times 10^{-23}\,\mathrm{kg}$

   centripetal force $F = m\omega^2 r$ **[1 mark]**

   $F = 3.94 \times 10^{-23} \times (6.9 \times 10^4)^2 \times \frac{27 \times 10^3}{2\pi}$ **[1 mark]**

   $F = 8.1 \times 10^{-10}\,\mathrm{N}$ **[1 mark]**

2. a) $h = 400\,\mathrm{km}$, $v = 7.68\,\mathrm{km\,s^{-1}}$

   $v = r\omega \rightarrow \omega = \frac{v}{r} = \frac{7.68 \times 10^3}{(6400 + 400) \times 10^3}$ **[1 mark]**

   $\omega = 1.13 \times 10^{-3}\,\mathrm{rad\,s^{-1}}$ **[1 mark]**

   b) $T = \frac{1}{f}$ and $\omega = 2\pi f$ $\therefore T = \frac{2\pi}{\omega}$ **[1 mark]**

   $T = \frac{2\pi}{1.13 \times 10^{-3}} = 5560\,\mathrm{s} \approx 92.7\,\mathrm{min} \approx 1.54\,\mathrm{hr}$ **[1 mark]**

   no. of orbits/day $= \frac{24}{1.54} = 15.5\,\text{orbits} \approx 16\,\text{orbits}$ **[1 mark]**

   c) $a = \omega^2 r = (1.13 \times 10^{-3})^2 \times 6800 \times 10^3$ **[1 mark]**

   $a = 8.68\,\mathrm{m\,s^{-2}}$ **[1 mark]**

   $g \approx 9.81 \left(\frac{6400}{6800}\right)^2 = 8.69\,\mathrm{m\,s^{-2}}$ **[1 mark]**; this value is only about 11% different than that on the surface of the Earth **[1 mark]**

3. $r = 3\,\mathrm{km} = 3000\,\mathrm{m}$, $v = 215\,\mathrm{m\,s^{-1}}$

   a) **Top of loop:**

   $R_\mathrm{T} + mg = \frac{mv^2}{r}$ **[1 mark]**

   $R_\mathrm{T} = \frac{mv^2}{r} - mg = mg\left(\frac{v^2}{gr} - 1\right)$ **[1 mark]**

   $R_\mathrm{T} = mg\left(\frac{215^2}{9.81 \times 3000} - 1\right) = 0.57mg$ **[1 mark]**

   b) **Bottom of loop:**

   $R_\mathrm{B} - mg = \frac{mv^2}{r}$ **[1 mark]**

   $R_\mathrm{B} = \frac{mv^2}{r} + mg = mg\left(\frac{v^2}{gr} + 1\right)$ **[1 mark]**

   $R_\mathrm{B} = mg\left(\frac{215^2}{9.81 \times 3000} + 1\right) = 2.57mg$ **[1 mark]**

   c) At the bottom of the loop, the contact force is larger than the weight (feels 'heavier') **[1 mark]**
   At the top of the loop, the contact force is less than the weight (feels 'lighter') **[1 mark]**

   d) When $R_\mathrm{T} = 0$, $\frac{mv^2}{r} = mg$ **[1 mark]**

   $\therefore v = \sqrt{rg} = \sqrt{3000 \times 9.81}$ **[1 mark]**

   $v = 171.6 = 172 \approx 170\,\mathrm{m\,s^{-1}}$ **[1 mark]**

   e) This is the minimum speed required just to make the loop **[1 mark]** and is the position when the pilot is momentarily 'weightless'. **[1 mark]** Any slower and the pilot would begin to fall out of their seat. **[1 mark]**

Simple Harmonic Motion

QUICK TEST (page 10)

1. the motion of an object such that its force or acceleration is proportional to its displacement from a fixed point and is always directed towards that point
2. The restoring force is the force that pulls or pushes the object back towards the midpoint or equilibrium position
3. $a = -\omega^2 x$ or $a = -\frac{kx}{m}$
4. the rate of change of angle, measured in radians per second, and given by $\omega = 2\pi f$
5. $T = \frac{1}{f}$
6. $0.45\,\mathrm{Hz}$; $-0.49\,\mathrm{m\,s^{-2}}$
7. amplitude $= 0.16\,\mathrm{m}$ or $16\,\mathrm{cm}$; $f = 4\,\mathrm{Hz}$ and $T = \frac{1}{4} = 0.25\,\mathrm{s}$
8. (a) $0.16\,\mathrm{m}$; (b) $0\,\mathrm{m}$
9. (a) $\pm 0.79\,\mathrm{m\,s^{-1}}$; (b) $-24.7\,\mathrm{m\,s^{-2}}$
10. (a) $0\,\mathrm{J}$; (b) $0.029\,\mathrm{J}$
11. (a) $0.029\,\mathrm{J}$; (b) $0\,\mathrm{J}$; (c) $0.018\,\mathrm{J}$

PRACTICE QUESTIONS (page 11)

1. a)

[3 marks: 1 mark for a sinusoidal curve, 1 mark for time scale to 24 hours, 1 mark for showing amplitude = 3 m]

   b) $T = 12\,\text{hours} = 43200\,\mathrm{s}$

   $\omega = 2\pi f = \frac{2\pi}{T} = \frac{2\pi}{43200} = 1.45 \times 10^{-4}\,\mathrm{s^{-1}}$ **[1 mark]**

c) Ship requires 4 m depth, $x = 1$ m and $A = 3$ m
use $x = A \sin \omega t$

$1 = 3 \sin(\omega t)$ **[1 mark]**

$\omega t = \sin^{-1}\left(\frac{1}{3}\right)$

$\omega t = 0.3398$

$t = \frac{0.3398}{0.000145} = 2344$ s **[1 mark]**

$t = 0.65$ hours ($\equiv 39$ minutes)

Ship can enter harbour after 00:39 (39 minutes after midnight) **[1 mark]**

d) velocity $v = \omega \sqrt{A^2 - x^2}$

$v = 0.000145\sqrt{3^2 - 1^2}$ **[1 mark]**

$v = 4.10 \times 10^{-4}$ ms^{-1} **[1 mark]**

$v = 1.48$ m per hour ≈ 1.5 m per hour **[1 mark]**

2. a) Simple harmonic motion is the motion of an object whose acceleration (or force) is directly proportional to its displacement **[1 mark]** (from a fixed point or equilibrium position) and is always directed towards that point or equilibrium position **[1 mark]**

b) $f = 440$ Hz, $A = 0.62$ mm $= 0.00062$ m $\left(6.2 \times 10^{-4}$ m$\right)$
At $t = 0$, $A = 0$, hence **[1 mark]**

$x = 0.000062 \sin(880\pi t)$ [accept $6.2 \times 10^{-4} \sin\{2\pi(440)t\}$] **[1 mark]**

c) (i) maximum velocity $v_{\max} = \pm \omega A$

$\omega = 2\pi f$ and $A = 6.2 \times 10^{-4}$ m **[1 mark]**

$\therefore v_{\max} = \pm 2\pi(440)\left(6.2 \times 10^{-4}\right)$

$= \pm 1.71$ ms^{-1} **[1 mark]**

(ii) maximum acceleration $a_{\max} = -\omega^2 A$

$\omega = 2\pi f$ and $A = 6.2 \times 10^{-4}$ m

$\therefore a_{\max} = -(2\pi \times 440)^2\left(6.2 \times 10^{-4}\right)$ **[1 mark]**

$= -4739$ ms$^{-2} \approx -4700$ ms^{-2} **[1 mark]**

d) mechanical energy = total energy

$= \frac{1}{2}m\omega^2 A^2$

$= \frac{1}{2}(0.0136) \times (2\pi \times 440)^2 \times \left(6.2 \times 10^{-4}\right)^2$ **[1 mark]**

$= 0.0199 \approx 0.02$ J **[1 mark]**

e) The tuning fork is freely vibrating **[1 mark]**

3. a) total energy = maximum kinetic energy = 1.4 J **[1 mark]**

b) $E_{k,\max} = \frac{1}{2}mv_{\max}^2$ **[1 mark]**

$\therefore v_{\max} = \sqrt{\frac{2E_{k,\max}}{m}} = \sqrt{\frac{2 \times 1.4}{0.85}}$ **[1 mark]**

$v_{\max} = 1.81$ ms$^{-1} \approx 1.8$ ms^{-1} **[1 mark]**

c) $E_p = \frac{1}{2}kA^2$ where $A = 4$ cm $= 0.04$ m

$E_p = 1.4$ J or using $E_T = E_k + E_p$, $\therefore E_p = 1.4$ J **[1 mark]**

$k = \frac{2E_p}{A^2} = \frac{2 \times 1.4}{(0.04)^2} = 1750$ Nm^{-1} **[1 mark]**

hence $\omega^2 = \frac{k}{m} = \frac{1750}{0.04}$

$\therefore \omega = 209.2$ s$^{-1} \approx 210$ s^{-1} **[1 mark]**

$T = \frac{2\pi}{\omega} = 0.03$ s **[1 mark]**

Simple Harmonic Oscillators

QUICK TEST (page 14)

1. a system that undergoes simple harmonic motion
2. because it predicts the behaviour of the movement of atoms/ions about their mean position
3. the amplitude of the oscillation
4. the simple pendulum, as T^2 can be plotted as a function of l
5. (a) 1.42 s (b) 2.0 s
6. $T \propto \frac{1}{g}$ so, as g is less on the Moon, $\frac{1}{g}$ is greater, and thus T is longer.
7. 36.8 Nm^{-1}
8. 0.57 s
9. 0.50 ms^{-1}
10. 0.36 ms^{-1}
11. 4.7×10^{13} Hz

PRACTICE QUESTIONS (page 15)

1. a) $k = 40$ Nm^{-1}, $A = 5$ mm $= 0.005$ m, $m = 0.1$ kg

$F = mg = k\Delta L$ $\therefore \Delta L = \frac{mg}{k}$ **[1 mark]**

$\Delta L = \frac{0.1 \times 9.81}{40} = 0.0245$ m ≈ 0.025 m (2.45 cm or 2.5 cm) **[1 mark]**

b) $T = 2\pi\sqrt{\frac{m}{k}} = 2\pi\sqrt{\frac{0.1}{40}}$ **[1 mark]**

$T = 0.3142$ s ≈ 0.31 s **[1 mark]**

and $f = \frac{1}{T} = 3.18$ Hz ≈ 3.2 Hz **[1 mark]**

c) (i) $v_{\max} = \pm 2\pi f A$

$v_{\max} = \pm 2\pi \times 3.18 \times 0.005 = \pm 0.10$ ms^{-1} **[1 mark]**

(ii) $a_{\max} = -(2\pi f)^2 A = -(2\pi \times 3.18)^2 \times 0.005$

$= -2.0$ ms^{-2} **[1 mark]**

d) when extended by 2 mm, $\Delta L = 0.002$ m

net force $= k\Delta L = 40 \times 0.002$ m $= 0.08$ N **[1 mark]**

2. a) because interatomic forces act in a similar way to the forces exerted by springs **[1 mark]**

b) $T = 2\pi\sqrt{\frac{m}{2k}} = 2\pi\sqrt{\frac{1.2 \times 10^{-25}}{2 \times 220}}$ **[1 mark]**

$T = 1.04 \times 10^{-13}$ s **[1 mark]**

$\therefore f = \frac{1}{T} = 9.64 \times 10^{12}$ Hz $\approx 9.6 \times 10^{12}$ Hz **[1 mark]**

c) $A = 1.1 \times 10^{-11}$ m

(i) $E_{total} = E_{k,\max} = \frac{1}{2}mv_{\max}^2 = \frac{1}{2}m(2\pi f A)^2 = \frac{1}{2}m4\pi^2 f^2 A^2$

$= 2m\pi^2 f^2 A^2$ **[1 mark]**

$= 2 \times 1.2 \times 10^{-25} \times \pi^2 \times \left(9.64 \times 10^{12}\right)^2 \times \left(1.1 \times 10^{-11}\right)^2$ **[1 mark]**

$= 2.66 \times 10^{-20}$ J $\approx 2.7 \times 10^{-20}$ **[1 mark]**

(ii) $\therefore v_{\max} = \sqrt{\frac{2 \times E_{total}}{m}} = \sqrt{\frac{2 \times 2.66 \times 10^{-20}}{1.2 \times 10^{-25}}}$ **[1 mark]**

$v_{\max} = 666$ ms$^{-1} \approx 670$ ms^{-1} **[1 mark]**

3. a) Simple harmonic motion is the motion of an object that is acted upon by a restoring force **[1 mark]** whose magnitude is proportional to the displacement of the object from its equilibrium position **[1 mark]** and whose direction is always towards the equilibrium position. **[1 mark]**

   b) 10 oscillations in 16.8 s gives 1 oscillation in $1.68\,\text{s} = T$ **[1 mark]**

   c) $T = 2\pi\sqrt{\frac{l}{g}} \rightarrow l = \frac{gT^2}{4\pi^2}$ **[1 mark]**

   $l = \frac{9.81 \times (1.68)^2}{4\pi^2} = 0.70\,\text{m}$ **[1 mark]**

   d) $E_p = mgh = 0.15 \times 9.81 \times 0.015 = 0.022\,\text{J}$ **[1 mark]**

   $E_p \rightarrow E_k = \frac{1}{2}mv^2 \quad \therefore v_{max} = \sqrt{\frac{2E_k}{m}} = \sqrt{\frac{2E_p}{m}}$ **[1 mark]**

   $\therefore v_{max} = \sqrt{\frac{2 \times 0.022}{0.15}} = 0.54\,\text{m s}^{-1}$ **[1 mark]**

Forced Oscillations and Resonance
QUICK TEST (page 18)

1. when a system oscillates without a periodic force being applied

2. In free vibrations the total energy of the system stays the same over time; forced vibrations occur when there is an external driving force acting on the system

3. 90° or $\frac{\pi}{2}$

4. when the amplitude of the oscillation becomes zero in the shortest amount of time without any overshoot

5. Resonance occurs when the driving frequency is the same as the natural frequency of an object

6. Any two from mechanical, acoustic, quantum, classical, electrical

7. a force that acts on an oscillating system and causes it to lose energy to its surroundings, reducing the amplitude of the oscillations

8. car suspension systems

9. The mass–spring system will exhibit damped oscillations. The nature of the damping will depend on the size (area) of the sheet.

10. Systems that take much longer to return to their equilibrium position than a critically damped system; for example, heavy doors that open quickly and close slowly

PRACTICE QUESTIONS (page 19)

1. a) light damping: the amplitude of oscillation decreases only slowly over time **[1 mark]**
   heavy damping: the amplitude decreases significantly and comes to rest after undergoing some oscillation **[1 mark]**
   critical damping: the amplitude reduces to zero in the shortest possible time without undergoing any oscillation **[1 mark]**

   b) $A = 8.6\,\text{m}, k = 200\,\text{N m}^{-1}, m = 65\,\text{kg}$

   $T = 2\pi = 2\pi\sqrt{\frac{65}{200}} = 3.58\,\text{s} \approx 3.6\,\text{s}$ **[1 mark]**

   $f = \frac{1}{T} = 0.28\,\text{Hz}$ **[1 mark]**

   c) $v_{max} = \pm 2\pi fA = \pm 2\pi \times 0.28 \times 8.6 = 15.1\,\text{m s}^{-1} \approx 15\,\text{m s}^{-1}$ **[1 mark]**

   $a_{max} = -(2\pi f)^2 A = -26.6\,\text{m s}^{-2} \approx -27\,\text{m s}^{-2}$ **[1 mark]**

   d) for equilibrium, $F = mg = k\Delta L$

   $\therefore \Delta L = \frac{mg}{k}$ **[1 mark]** $= \frac{65 \times 9.81}{200} = 3.19\,\text{m} \approx 3.2\,\text{m}$ **[1 mark]**

   $\therefore$ equilibrium position below bridge $= 13.2\,\text{m} \approx 13\,\text{m}$ **[1 mark]**

   e) The bungee jumper experiences damped simple harmonic motion **[1 mark]**. This means that the amplitude of the oscillations reduces over a shorter period of time **[1 mark]** caused by energy losses such as air resistance **[1 mark]**.

2. a) resonance **[1 mark]**

   b) The driving frequency **[1 mark]** must be equal to the natural frequency of the system **[1 mark]**

   c) $\lambda = 2.7\,\mu\text{m} = 2.7 \times 10^{-6}\,\text{m}$

   $f = \frac{c}{\lambda} = \frac{3.0 \times 10^8}{2.7 \times 10^{-6}} = 1.11 \times 10^{14}\,\text{Hz} \approx 1.1 \times 10^{14}\,\text{Hz}$ **[1 mark]**

   d) $m = 2.0 \times 10^{-26}\,\text{kg}$

   at resonance, $f = \frac{1}{2\pi}\sqrt{\frac{k}{m}}$ **[1 mark]**

   $\therefore k = (2\pi f)^2 m$

   $= (2\pi \times 1.11 \times 10^{14})^2 \times 2.0 \times 10^{-26}$ **[1 mark]**

   $= 9747\,\text{N m}^{-1} \approx 9700\,\text{N m}^{-1}$ **[1 mark]**

Day 2

Thermal Energy
QUICK TEST (page 22)

1. the amount of heat needed to raise the temperature of a mass of 1 kg by 1 K

2. $\text{J kg}^{-1}\,\text{K}^{-1}$

3. $c = \frac{\Delta Q}{m\Delta T}$, where ΔQ is the energy required, m is the mass of material and ΔT is the change in temperature

4. when all parts of a system have the same temperature and there is no net heat flow

5. 252 kJ

6. the thermal energy required to change the state of a material without a change in temperature; there are two types: latent heat of fusion when a material melts and latent heat of vaporisation when a material turns to vapour

7. $\Delta Q = mL$

8. 167 kJ

9. 0.03 kg

PRACTICE QUESTIONS (page 23)

1. a) The specific heat capacity is the amount of heat required to raise the temperature of 1 kg of a material by 1K [accept 1°C] **[2 marks]**

b) $m_p = 0.25\,\text{kg}, \quad c_p = 910\,\text{Jkg}^{-1}\text{K}^{-1}$

$\Delta T = 100 - 22 = 78°\text{C or } 78\,\text{K}$ **[1 mark]**

$\Delta Q = mc\Delta T = 0.25 \times 910 \times 78$ **[1 mark]**

$= 17.75 \times 10^3\,\text{J} = 17.8\,\text{kJ} \approx 18\,\text{kJ}$ **[1 mark]**

c) $m_w = 1.75\,\text{kg}, \quad c_w = 4200\,\text{Jkg}^{-1}\text{K}^{-1}, \quad \Delta T = 78\,\text{K}$

$\Delta Q = mc\Delta T = 1.75 \times 4200 \times 78$ **[1 mark]**

$= 573.3 \times 10^3\,\text{J} \approx 573\,\text{kJ} \approx 570\,\text{kJ}$ **[1 mark]**

d) $\Delta Q = 2.5\,\text{kW} = 2.5 \times 10^3\,\text{W} = 2.5 \times 10^3\,\text{Js}^{-1}.$ **[1 mark]**

$\Delta Q_{\text{total}} = 17.8\,\text{kJ} + 573\,\text{kJ} = 590.8\,\text{kJ}$ **[1 mark]**

$\therefore t = \frac{590.8 \times 10^3}{2.5 \times 10^3}$ **[1 mark]**

$t = 236.32\,\text{s} \approx 236\,\text{s} \approx 3.9\,\text{minutes}$ **[1 mark]**

e) There is no heat transfer to the surroundings **[1 mark]**

2. a) Specific latent heat is the heat transferred to 1 kg of a material when changing state (solid → liquid or liquid → vapour) **[1 mark]** without change in temperature **[1 mark]**

b) ice cubes from −8°C to 0°C

$\Delta Q = mc\Delta T = 40 \times 10^{-3} \times 2200 \times 8$ **[1 mark]**

$= 704\,\text{J} \approx 700\,\text{J} = 0.7\,\text{kJ}$ **[1 mark]**

c) ice → water at 0°C

$\Delta Q = mL_f = 40 \times 10^{-3} \times 334 \times 10^3$ **[1 mark]**

$= 13360\,\text{J} \approx 13\,\text{kJ}$ **[1 mark]**

d) The energy needed to raise the melted water from 0°C to T is

$\Delta Q = mc\Delta T = 40 \times 10^{-3} \times 4200 \times T$

$= 168T\,\text{J}$ **[1 mark]**

The energy released in cooling the water from 23°C to T is

$\Delta Q = 250 \times 10^{-3} \times 4200 \times (23 - T)$ **[1 mark]**

$= 1050(23 - T)$ **[1 mark]**

Hence,

$168T + 704 + 13360 = 1050(23 - T)$ **[1 mark]**

$168T + 1050T = 1050(23) - 704 - 13360$

$1218T = 10086$ **[1 mark]**

$\therefore T = 8.3 \approx 8°\text{C}$ **[1 mark]**

3. a)

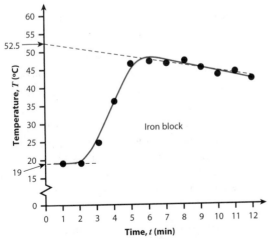

[2 marks: 1 mark for each line drawn]

b) $\Delta T = 52.5 - 19.0 \approx 33.5°\text{C}\,(\pm 1°\text{C}) = 33.5\,\text{K}\,(\pm 1\text{K})$ **[2 marks]**

c) $V = 12.0\,\text{V}, \quad I = 4.0\,\text{A}, \quad t = 5\,\text{min} = 300\,\text{s}$

$\Delta Q = VIt = 12 \times 4 \times 300$ **[1 mark]**

$= 14\,400\,\text{J or } 14\,\text{kJ}$ **[1 mark]**

d) $m = 0.954\,\text{kg}$

$\Delta Q = mc\Delta T$

$\therefore c = \frac{\Delta Q}{m\Delta T} = \frac{14\,400}{0.954 \times 33.5}$ **[1 mark]**

$c = 450.6\,\text{Jkg}^{-1}\text{K}^{-1} \approx 451\,\text{Jkg}^{-1}\text{K}^{-1}$ **[1 mark]**

e) **[any two from]** heater does not heat the metal block uniformly; lack of insulation or poor insulation results in heat losses; temperature recorded at only one specific location in the block; poor thermal contact between block and thermometer **[2 marks]**

Ideal Gases

QUICK TEST (page 26)

1. An ideal gas is one in which all collisions between molecules/atoms are elastic, there are no intermolecular attractive forces, and it obeys the gas laws

2. 295 K

3. $\frac{V}{T}$ = constant at constant pressure; volume, $V\,(\text{m}^3)$ plotted against absolute temperature, $T\,(\text{K})$

4. $1.5 \times 10^6\,\text{Pa}$

5. 360 K

6. $n = \frac{N}{N_A}$

7. 28 g or 0.028 kg

8. $pV = nRT$

9. at high temperatures or low pressures

10. 0.014 moles

11. 8.6×10^{21} molecules

12. $1.05 \times 10^4\,\text{Pa}$

PRACTICE QUESTIONS (page 27)

1. a) An ideal gas is a gas that is modelled by ignoring the potential energy components carried by intermolecular forces **[1 mark]**

or

a gas that obeys the gas laws (Boyle's, Charles' and pressure law) **[1 mark]**

b) $V = 0.1\,\text{m}^3, \quad T = 25°\text{C} = 298\,\text{K}, \quad p = 2.4 \times 10^5\,\text{Pa}$

$pV = nRT$

$n = \frac{pV}{RT} = \frac{2.4 \times 10^5 \times 0.1}{8.31 \times 298}$ **[1 mark]**

$n = 9.69\,\text{moles} \approx 9.7\,\text{moles}$ **[1 mark]**

c) $n = \frac{N}{N_A} \rightarrow N = nN_A$

$N = 9.69 \times 6.02 \times 10^{23}$

$N = 5.83 \times 10^{24}$ molecules $\approx 5.8 \times 10^{24}$ molecules **[1 mark]**

d) using $\frac{p}{T}$ = constant $\rightarrow \frac{p_1}{T_1} = \frac{p_2}{T_2}$ at constant volume **[1 mark]**

$\therefore p_2 = p_1 \frac{T_2}{T_1} = 2.4 \times 10^5 \times \frac{265}{298}$ **[1 mark]**

$p_2 = 2.13 \times 10^5\,\text{Pa} \approx 2.1 \times 10^5\,\text{Pa}$ **[1 mark]**

e) isothermal charge **[1 mark]**

2. a) p is pressure in Pa or $N m^{-2}$

V is volume in m^3

n is the number of moles

T is the temperature in K

R is the molar gas constant $= 8.31 J K^{-1} mol^{-1}$

[3 marks: −1 mark for each error]

b) Charles' Law states that $\frac{V}{T} = $ constant or $V \propto T$ or $V = kT$ **[1 mark]**. This is only true if T is measured in kelvin as $V = 0$ when $T = 0 K$, i.e. absolute zero. This is not the case when temperature is in °C **[1 mark]**.

c) $p = 220 kPa, \quad T = 290 K, \quad V = 1.2 \times 10^{-2} m^3$

$pV = nRT$

$n = \frac{pV}{RT} = \frac{220 \times 10^3 \times 1.2 \times 10^{-2}}{8.31 \times 290}$ **[1 mark]**

$n = 1.095$ moles ≈ 1.1 moles **[1 mark]**

d) $M_m = 2.9 \times 10^{-2} kg$

(i) mass of air $= 1.1 \times 2.9 \times 10^{-2} kg = 0.032 kg$ **[1 mark]**

(ii) $\rho = \frac{\text{mass of air}}{\text{volume of air}} = \frac{0.032}{1.2 \times 10^{-2}}$ **[1 mark]** $= 2.66 \approx 2.7 kg m^{-3}$
[1 mark]

3. a) sea level: $p = 1.0 \times 10^5 Pa, \quad T = 300 K$

Everest: $p = 2.1 \times 10^4 Pa, \quad T = 270 K$

$V = 1 m^3$

(i) sea level: $pV = nRT \rightarrow n = \frac{pV}{RT}$

$n = \frac{1.0 \times 10^5 \times 1}{8.31 \times 300} = 40.1$ moles ≈ 40 moles **[1 mark]**

(ii) Everest summit:

$n = \frac{2.1 \times 10^4 \times 1}{8.31 \times 270} = 9.36 \approx 9.4$ moles **[1 mark]**

b) $n = \frac{N}{N_A} \rightarrow N = n N_A$

$N = 40.1 \times 6.02 \times 10^{23}$

$N = 2.41 \times 10^{25}$ molecules $\approx 2.4 \times 10^{25}$ molecules
[1 mark]

c) number of molecules of oxygen at sea level

$= 2.41 \times 10^{25} \times 0.22$

$= 5.31 \times 10^{24}$ molecules $\approx 5.3 \times 10^{24}$ molecules **[1 mark]**

at Everest summit:

$N = 9.36 \times 6.02 \times 10^{23} \times 0.22$

$= 1.24 \times 10^{24}$ molecules $\approx 1.2 \times 10^{24}$ molecules
[1 mark]

percentage difference $= \frac{5.31 - 1.24}{5.31} \times 100$

$= 76.6 \approx 77\%$ **[1 mark]**

The Kinetic Theory of Gases
QUICK TEST (page 30)

1. the visible but erratic and random motion of particles that result from collisions with smaller unseen molecules

2. any three from: large number of molecules; molecules move rapidly and randomly; motion follows Newton's laws; collisions between particles or walls are perfectly elastic; no attractive forces between particles; time for collisions is negligible compared with time between collisions.

3. $2mv$

4. the square root of the mean squared speed gives a true measure of the mean speed of molecules in a gas

5. $pV = \frac{1}{3} Nm \overline{c^2}$

6. the temperature also increases

7. (a) $335 m s^{-1}$ (b) $343 m s^{-1}$

8. none or no change

9. $490 m s^{-1}$

10. $1800 m s^{-1}$

PRACTICE QUESTIONS (page 31)

1. a) $pV = \frac{1}{3} Nmc_{rms}^2$

p is pressure; V is volume; N is the number of molecules; m is the mass of a molecule; c_{rms}^2 is the mean square speed [not mean speed squared!] **[3 marks: −1 mark for each error]**

b) Only the kinetic energy components are considered **[1 mark]** so potential energy contributions via intermolecular forces are ignored **[1 mark]**

c) [any two from] collisions are elastic; volume of molecules is negligible; Newton's laws of motion are valid; large number of molecules; all molecules are identical; collision times are small compared with time between collisions **[2 marks: 1 mark for each point made]**

d) Boyle's law states that, at constant temperature,

$pV = $ constant **[1 mark]**

If temperature is constant then c_{rms}^2 is also constant **[1 mark]**; as N and n are also constants then Boyle's Law is valid **[1 mark]**

2. a) An elastic collision means there is no loss of kinetic energy, or that kinetic energy is conserved **[1 mark]**

b) Molecules travel at a velocity u and a distance $2L$ between collisions **[1 mark]**, hence $t = \frac{\text{distance}}{\text{velocity}} = \frac{2L}{u}$ **[1 mark]**

c) change in momentum $\Delta(mv) = $ final momentum − initial momentum **[1 mark]**

As momentum is a vector, $\Delta(mv) = mu - (-mu) = 2mu$ **[1 mark]**

As the collision is elastic, $mu = mv$ **[1 mark]**

d) force $= $ rate of change of momentum per molecule **[1 mark]**

$F = \frac{\Delta(mv)}{\Delta t} = \frac{2mu}{2L} \times u = \frac{mu^2}{L}$ **[1 mark]**

and for N molecules, $F = \frac{Nmu^2}{L}$ **[1 mark]**

e) pressure $= \frac{\text{force}}{\text{area}} = \frac{Nmu^2}{L} \times \frac{1}{L^2} = \frac{Nmu^2}{L^3}$ **[1 mark]**

$\therefore p = \frac{Nmu^2}{V} \rightarrow pV = Nmu^2$ **[1 mark]**

f) In three dimensions, $u^2 = u_x^2 + u_y^2 + u_z^2$ **[1 mark]**

and since $\overline{u_x^2} = \overline{u_y^2} = \overline{u_z^2} \rightarrow c_{rms}^2 = 3u^2$ **[1 mark]**

Hence $pV = \frac{1}{3} Nmc_{rms}^2$

i.e. velocity can be written as a sum of its vector components **[1 mark]** and there is no preferred direction, motion is random **[1 mark]**

3. a) $p = 1.4 \times 10^5 Pa, \quad V = 0.06 m^3$

$N = 1.4 \times 10^{25}$ molecules, $\quad c_{rms} = 392 m s^{-1}$

$pV = \frac{1}{3} Nmc_{rms}^2$

$\therefore m = \frac{3pV}{Nc_{rms}^2} = \frac{3 \times 1.4 \times 10^5 \times 0.06}{1.4 \times 10^{25} \times (392)^2}$ **[1 mark]**

$m = 1.17 \times 10^{-26} kg \approx 1.2 \times 10^{-26} kg$ **[1 mark]**

b) $p = \frac{1}{3}\rho c_{rms}^2$ **[1 mark]**

$\therefore \rho = \frac{3p}{c_{rms}^2} = \frac{3 \times 1.4 \times 10^5}{(392)^2}$ **[1 mark]**

$\rho = 2.73\,\text{kg}\,\text{m}^{-3} \approx 2.7\,\text{kg}\,\text{m}^{-3}$ **[1 mark]**

c) If p is constant but ρ increases by a factor of 2 then c_{rms}^2 decreases by a factor of 2 **[1 mark]** and c_{rms} decreases by a factor of $\sqrt{2}$ **[1 mark]**

d) If $p \gg 0$ then either density of gas or temperature (molecular speed) is very high **[1 mark]** and distance between gas molecules is small **[1 mark]**. Intermolecular forces are then significant **[1 mark]** and the kinetic model is no longer valid **[1 mark]**

Energy and Temperature

QUICK TEST (page 34)

1. The shape become sharper as the spread of speeds becomes more restricted, and the peak speed moves towards a lower value

2. $pV = \frac{1}{3}Nmc_{rms}^2$

3. zero

4. Boyle's Law

5. $U = \frac{3}{2}NkT$

6. $5.65 \times 10^{-21}\,\text{J}$

7. $1840\,\text{m}\,\text{s}^{-1}$

8. $480\,\text{m}\,\text{s}^{-1}$

9. $4.5\,\text{kJ}$

PRACTICE QUESTIONS (page 35)

1. $M_m = 0.028\,\text{kg}$, $n = 1\,\text{mol}$

   a) $T = 295\,\text{K}$

   use $\frac{1}{2}mc_{rms}^2 = \frac{3}{2}kT$

   $\therefore c_{rms}^2 = \frac{3kT}{m}$ **[1 mark]**

   $m = \frac{M_m}{N_A} = \frac{2.8 \times 10^{-2}}{6.02 \times 10^{23}} = 4.65 \times 10^{-26}\,\text{kg}$ **[1 mark]**

   $\therefore c_{rms}^2 = \frac{3 \times 1.38 \times 10^{-23} \times 295}{4.65 \times 10^{-26}}$

   $= 2.63 \times 10^5\,\text{m}^2\,\text{s}^{-2}$ **[1 mark]**

   $\therefore c_{rms} = 512\,\text{m}\,\text{s}^{-1} \approx 510\,\text{m}\,\text{s}^{-1}$ **[1 mark]**

   b) Gas molecules move at different speeds because they have different amounts of energy **[1 mark]**, because they constantly collide and transfer energy **[1 mark]**

   c) $\overline{E_k} = \frac{1}{2}mc_{rms}^2 = \frac{1}{2} \times 4.65 \times 10^{-26} \times 2.63 \times 10^5$ **[1 mark]**

   $\overline{E_k} = 6.1 \times 10^{-21}\,\text{J}$ **[1 mark]**

   d) $T \propto c_{rms}^2$ so if T increases from 295 to 365 K, the factor is 1.237 **[1 mark]** and hence c_{rms}^2 also increases by 1.237

   $\therefore c_{rms}$ increases by $\sqrt{1.237} = 1.112 \rightarrow 567\,\text{m}\,\text{s}^{-1} \approx 570\,\text{m}\,\text{s}^{-1}$

   [1 mark]

   e) A greater temperature gives a flatter and broader speed distribution **[1 mark]**

2. $T_1 = 298\,\text{K}$, $V_1 = 0.06\,\text{m}^3$, $p_1 = 1.0 \times 10^5\,\text{Pa}$

   a) at 15 km: $p_2 = 1.4 \times 10^4\,\text{Pa}$, $T_2 = 217\,\text{K}$

   $\frac{p_1 V_1}{T_1} = \frac{p_2 V_2}{T_2}$ **[1 mark]**

   $V_2 = \frac{p_1 V_1 \times T_2}{p_2 \times T_1} = \frac{1.0 \times 10^5 \times 0.06 \times 217}{1.4 \times 10^4 \times 298}$ **[1 mark]**

   $= 0.312\,\text{m}^3 \approx 0.31\,\text{m}^3$ **[1 mark]**

b) $\overline{E_k} = \frac{3}{2}kT = \frac{3}{2} \times 1.38 \times 10^{-23} \times 217$ **[1 mark]**

$= 4.49 \times 10^{-21}\,\text{J} \approx 4.5 \times 10^{-21}\,\text{J}$ **[1 mark]**

c) $\overline{E_k} = \frac{1}{2}mc_{rms}^2$

$\therefore c_{rms}^2 = \frac{2\overline{E_k}}{m} = \frac{2\overline{E_k}}{M_m} \times N_A$ **[1 mark]** where $M_m = 0.004\,\text{kg}$

$= \frac{2 \times 4.49 \times 10^{-24} \times 6.02 \times 10^{23}}{0.004}$

$= 1.35 \times 10^6\,\text{m}^2\,\text{s}^{-2}$ **[1 mark]**

$\therefore c_{rms} = 1160\,\text{m}\,\text{s}^{-1} \approx 1200\,\text{m}\,\text{s}^{-1}$ **[1 mark]**

d) $p = \frac{1}{3}\rho c_{rms}^2 \quad \therefore \rho = \frac{3p}{c_{rms}^2}$ **[1 mark]**

$\therefore \rho = \frac{3 \times 1.4 \times 10^4}{1.35 \times 10^6} = 0.031 \approx 0.03\,\text{kg}\,\text{m}^{-3}$ **[1 mark]**

3. **a)**

Speed, c (m s^{-1})	280	300	320	340	360	380	400
Number of molecules	5	17	23	25	14	9	7
c^2 (km^2 s^{-2})	0.0784	0.0900	0.1024	0.1156	0.1296	0.1444	0.1600

[2 marks: –1 for each error or omission]

b) $c_{rms}^2 =$

$\frac{(0.0784 \times 5) + (0.0900 \times 17) + (0.1024 \times 23) + (0.1156 \times 25) + (0.1296 \times 14) + (0.1444 \times 9) + (0.1600 \times 7)}{100}$

[1 mark]

$= 0.1140\,\text{km}^2\,\text{s}^{-2}$ **[1 mark]**

$\therefore c_{rms} = 0.338\,\text{km}\,\text{s}^{-1} \approx 0.34\,\text{km}\,\text{s}^{-1}$ [or $338\,\text{m}\,\text{s}^{-1} \approx 340\,\text{m}\,\text{s}^{-1}$]

[1 mark]

c) $M_m = 0.0202\,\text{kg}$

$\overline{E_k} = \frac{1}{2}mc_{rms}^2$

$= \frac{1}{2} \times \frac{M_m}{N_A} \times c_{rms}^2$ **[1 mark]**

$= \frac{1}{2} \times \frac{0.0202}{6.02 \times 10^{23}} \times 0.1139$ **[1 mark]**

$= 1.91 \times 10^{-21}\,\text{J} \approx 1.9 \times 10^{-21}\,\text{J}$ **[1 mark]**

d) $\overline{E_k} = \frac{3}{2}kT \rightarrow T = \frac{2\overline{E_k}}{3R}$ **[1 mark]**

$\therefore T = \frac{2 \times 1.91 \times 10^{-21}}{3 \times 1.38 \times 10^{-23}} = 92.3\,\text{K}$ **[1 mark]**

$= -180.7\,°\text{C} \approx -181\,°\text{C}$ **[1 mark]**

Day 3

Electric Fields

QUICK TEST (page 38)

1. The force between two point charges separated by a distance r is given by $F = \frac{Qq}{4\pi\varepsilon_0 r^2}$

2. the permittivity of free space; F m^{-1}

3. yes, provided the distance between them is the distance between their centres

4. 0.86 N

5. a field in which the electric field strength is constant

6. Potential difference, $V = \frac{\text{work done}}{\text{charge}} = \frac{\text{force} \times \text{distance}}{\text{charge}}$; hence in terms of units: $V\text{m}^{-1} = \frac{N \times m}{m \times C} = NC^{-1}$

7. 2.4×10^{-3} N; downward

8. Electrical potential at a point is the work done per unit positive charge in moving a point charge from infinity to that point

9. $V = \frac{Q}{4\pi\varepsilon_0 r}$; units are volts or joules per coulomb (J C^{-1})

PRACTICE QUESTIONS (page 39)

1. a) The work done against the electric field in moving a charge from a lower potential to a higher potential defines the potential difference **[1 mark]**; work done $\Delta W = \Delta V Q$ **[1 mark]**

b) $V = \frac{Q}{4\pi\varepsilon_0 r}$

V is the potential (V) **[1 mark]**

Q is the charge producing the field (C) **[1 mark]**

ε_0 is the permittivity of free space (F m^{-1}) **[1 mark]**

r is the distance from the point to the centre of the charge (m) **[1 mark]**

c)

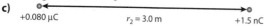
+0.080 μC $r_2 = 3.0$ m   +1.5 nC

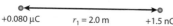
+0.080 μC $r_1 = 2.0$ m   +1.5 nC

(i) $\Delta V = \frac{Q}{4\pi\varepsilon_0}\left(\frac{1}{r_1} - \frac{1}{r_2}\right)$ **[1 mark]**

$= \frac{0.08 \times 10^{-6}}{4\pi \times 8.85 \times 10^{-12}}\left(\frac{1}{2} - \frac{1}{3}\right)$ **[1 mark]**

$= 119.9 \approx 120$ V **[1 mark]**

(ii) $\Delta W = \Delta V Q$

$= 119.9 \times 1.5 \times 10^{-9}$ **[1 mark]**

$= 1.798 \times 10^{-7} \approx 180 \times 10^{-9}$ J $= 180$ nJ **[1 mark]**

2. a) $E = \frac{V}{d} = \frac{1200}{50 \times 10^{-3}} = 24\,000$ **[1 mark]**

$E = 2.4 \times 10^4$ V m^{-1} or 24 kV m^{-1} **[1 mark]**

b) $F = ma$

$\therefore a = \frac{F}{m} = \frac{Eq}{m}$ **[1 mark]**

$a = \frac{2.4 \times 10^4 \times 1.6 \times 10^{-19}}{9.1 \times 10^{-31}}$ **[1 mark]**

$a = 4.2 \times 10^{15}$ m s^{-2} **[1 mark]**

c) $s = ut + \frac{1}{2}at^2 \to \frac{1}{2}at^2$

$= \frac{1}{2} \times 4.22 \times 10^{15} \times \left(2.4 \times 10^{-9}\right)^2$ **[1 mark]**

$= 0.0122$ m ≈ 12 mm **[1 mark]**

3. a) (i) The electric field outside a sphere is the same as that from a point charge **[1 mark]**, so that electrical potential looks like that from a point charge **[1 mark]**

(ii) The electric field inside the sphere is zero **[1 mark]**; therefore $\Delta V = 0$ and hence V is a constant and equal to the value outside the sphere **[1 mark]**

b)

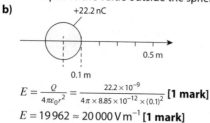
+22.2 nC

0.5 m

0.1 m

$E = \frac{Q}{4\pi\varepsilon_0 r^2} = \frac{22.2 \times 10^{-9}}{4\pi \times 8.85 \times 10^{-12} \times (0.1)^2}$ **[1 mark]**

$E = 19\,962 \approx 20\,000$ V m^{-1} **[1 mark]**

when $r = 0.5$ m, $E \propto \frac{1}{r^2} = \frac{19662}{25}$ **[1 mark]**

$= 798 \approx 800$ V m^{-1} **[1 mark]**

c) $V = \frac{Q}{4\pi\varepsilon_0 r} = \frac{22.2 \times 10^{-9}}{4\pi \times 8.85 \times 10^{-12} \times 0.1}$ **[1 mark]**

$V = 1996$ V ≈ 2000 V **[1 mark]**

when $r = 0.5$ m, $V \propto \frac{1}{r} = \frac{1996}{5}$ **[1 mark]**

$= 399.2$ V ≈ 400 V **[1 mark]**

Capacitors
QUICK TEST (page 42)

1. capacitance (C), potential difference (V), current (A) and charge (Q)

2. 133 μF

3. 600 μF

4. $E = \frac{1}{2}QV$

5. 9.7×10^{-4} μF or 970 μF

6. the relative permittivity of an insulating material

7. $E = \frac{1}{2}CV^2$

8. 6.9×10^{-3} F or 6.9 mF

9. $\tau = RC = \frac{Q}{V} \times \frac{V}{I} \to \frac{\text{coulombs}}{\text{amperes}} = \frac{\text{amperes} \times \text{seconds}}{\text{amperes}} = \text{seconds}$

10. 28 s

11. 0.144 J

PRACTICE QUESTIONS (page 43)

1. a) $\tau = RC = 3.3 \times 10^3 \times 0.68 \times 10^{-6}$ **[1 mark]**

$= 2.24 \times 10^{-3}$ s ≈ 2.2 ms **[1 mark]**

b) $V = IR \to I = \frac{V}{R} = \frac{12}{3.3 \times 10^3}$ **[1 mark]**

$I = 3.64 \times 10^{-3}$ A ≈ 3.6 mA **[1 mark]**

As $t \gg \tau$ then $I \to 0$ **[1 mark]**

c) $Q = CV = 0.68 \times 10^{-6} \times 12$ **[1 mark]**

$Q = 8.16 \times 10^{-6} \approx 8.2 \times 10^{-6}$ C or 8.2 μC **[1 mark]**

d) $E = \frac{1}{2}CV^2 = \frac{1}{2} \times 0.68 \times 10^{-6} \times (12)^2$ **[1 mark]**

$= 4.896 \times 10^{-5} \approx 4.9 \times 10^{-5}$ J or 49 μJ **[1 mark]**

2. $t = 2.0$ ms $= 2.0 \times 10^{-3}$ s $C = 33$ μF $= 33 \times 10^{-6}$ F

$P = 2.5$ kW $= 2.5 \times 10^3$ J s^{-1}

a) $P = \frac{E}{t} \to E = Pt = 2.5 \times 10^3 \times 2.0 \times 10^{-3}$ **[1 mark]**

$E = 5.0$ J **[1 mark]**

b) $E = \frac{1}{2}CV^2 \to V = \sqrt{\frac{2E}{C}} = \sqrt{\frac{2 \times 5.0}{33 \times 10^{-6}}}$ **[1 mark]**

$V = 550$ V **[1 mark]**

c) $Q = CV = 33 \times 10^{-6} \times 550$ **[1 mark]**

$= 0.018$ C $= 18$ mC **[1 mark]**

d) mean current, $I = \frac{Q}{t} = \frac{0.018}{2.0 \times 10^{-3}}$ **[1 mark]**

$= 9.08$ A ≈ 9.1 A **[1 mark]**

3. a) The time constant is the time interval during which the charging (or discharging) current for a capacitor in series with a resistor **[1 mark]** falls to $\frac{1}{e}$ of its initial value; **[1 mark]** the larger the time constant, the slower the charging (or discharging) process **[1 mark]**

b) (i) Charging

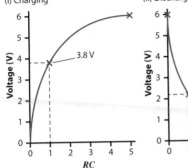

(ii) Discharging

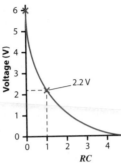

Axes labelled **[1 mark]**, correct curves drawn **[1 mark]** and values at $1RC$ labelled correctly on both graphs (±0.1 V) **[2 marks]**

c) $\tau = RC = 5.6 \times 10^3 \times 47 \times 10^{-6}$

$\quad = 0.2632 \approx 0.26$ s **[1 mark]**

$E = \frac{1}{2}CV_t^2$ where $V_t = V_0\left(1 - e^{-t/RC}\right)$

$V_t = 6\left(1 - 0.0224\right)$ **[1 mark]**

$\quad = 5.87$ V **[1 mark]**

$\therefore E = \frac{1}{2} \times 47 \times 10^{-6} \times \left(5.87\right)^2$ **[1 mark]**

$E = 8.097 \times 10^{-4}$ J **[1 mark]**

$E \approx 8.1 \times 10^{-4}$ J or 8×10^{-4} J or 0.8 mJ **[1 mark]**

Magnetic Fields
QUICK TEST (page 46)

1. represents the strength of a magnetic field
2. Hall probe
3. represents the magnetic flux density (B) in a conducting wire carrying a current (I) as a function of distance (r) from the wire; μ_0 is the permeability of free space (air)
4. 13 μT
5. direction of the force
6. $n = 1500\,\text{m}^{-1}$; $B = 2.6 \times 10^{-3}$ T
7. $F = BIl$
8. 0.016 N
9. moves in a circular path; $r = \frac{mv}{Be}$
10. a device used to identify different isotopes and measure relative abundances; velocity v and magnetic field B are constant

PRACTICE QUESTIONS (page 47)

1. a) $F = Bqv$, and the centripetal force $F = \frac{mv^2}{r}$

$\therefore \frac{mv^2}{r} = Bqv$ **[1 mark]**

$r = \frac{mv^2}{Bqv}$

$r = \frac{mv}{Bq}$ **[1 mark]**

b) Using Fleming's Left-Hand Rule, the direction of the force is always 90° to the particle's circular path and therefore always directed towards the centre of this circle **[1 mark]**

c) $r = \frac{mv}{Bq} = \frac{9.1 \times 10^{-31} \times 5.0 \times 10^6}{2.2 \times 10^{-4} \times 1.6 \times 10^{-19}}$ **[1 mark]**

$r = 0.129$ m ≈ 0.13 m **[1 mark]**

d) The positron would circulate in the opposite direction to that of the electron **[1 mark]**

2. a)

Current (A)	−2.0	−1.5	−1.0	−0.5	0	0.5	1.0	1.5	2.0
Change in mass (g)	1.49	1.14	0.78	0.41	0.00	−0.42	−0.81	−1.18	−1.57
Force (N)	0.0146	0.0111	0.0076	0.0040	0.0000	−0.0041	−0.0079	−0.0116	−0.0154

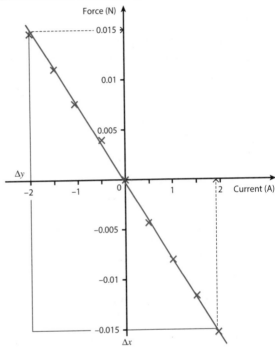

Table completed showing correct force values at least to 3 decimal places, **[1 mark]** graph plotted correctly, **[2 marks]** and line of best fit drawn **[1 mark]**

b) gradient of line $= \frac{\Delta y}{\Delta x} = \frac{0.030}{3.9}$ **[1 mark]**

$\quad = 0.0077\,\text{N A}^{-1} \approx 0.008 \pm 0.001\,\text{N A}^{-1}$ **[1 mark]**

c) $F = BIl = Bl \times I$

gradient represents Bl **[1 mark]**

d) $l = 50\,\text{mm} = 0.05\,\text{m}$

$Bl = 0.0077$ **[1 mark]**

$B = \frac{0.0077}{0.05}$

$B = 0.15$ T **[1 mark]**

Electromagnetism
QUICK TEST (page 50)

1. magnetic flux density; tesla
2. the product of the magnetic flux density and the area through which the magnetic flux passes

3. weber
4. defined when an object, e.g. a coil, passes through a magnetic field and is said to 'cut' through the lines of magnetic flux
5. 0.084 Wb
6. The magnitude of the emf induced (in volts) is equal to the rate of change of the magnetic flux linkage, i.e. $\varepsilon = \frac{\Delta(N\Phi)}{\Delta t}$
7. The direction of the induced emf opposes the change in flux that is producing it
8. 0.58 weber-turns
9. zero
10. 9×10^{-3} V

PRACTICE QUESTIONS (page 51)

1. a) Magnetic flux density is a measure of the strength of a magnetic field **[1 mark]** with units of tesla; **[1 mark]** magnetic flux is the product of the magnetic flux density and the area normal to the field through which the field is passing, **[1 mark]** and it has units of weber (Wb) **[1 mark]**

   b) $A = 18 \, \text{cm}^2 = 18 \times 10^{-4} \, \text{m}^2, \quad B = 2 \times 10^{-3} \, \text{T}$

   $\Phi = BA = 2 \times 10^{-3} \times 18 \times 10^{-4}$ **[1 mark]**

   $= 3.6 \times 10^{-6}$ Wb **[1 mark]**

   c) $N = 500$

   $N\Phi = BAN = 3.6 \times 10^{-6} \times 500$ **[1 mark]**

   $N\Phi = 1.8 \times 10^{-3}$ weber-turns **[1 mark]**

   d) $\Delta B = 2.0 \times 10^{-3} - 1.2 \times 10^{-3}$

   $= 8.0 \times 10^{-4}$ T **[1 mark]**

   $\varepsilon = N \frac{\Delta\Phi}{\Delta t} = NA \frac{\Delta B}{\Delta t}$

   $\varepsilon = \frac{500 \times 18 \times 10^{-4} \times 8 \times 10^{-4}}{2.0}$ **[1 mark]**

   $\varepsilon = 3.6 \times 10^{-4}$ V or 0.36 mV **[1 mark]**

2. a) Faraday's Law states that the induced emf (ε) is proportional to the rate of change of magnetic flux linkage ($N\Phi$); **[1 mark]** $\varepsilon = -\frac{\Delta(N\Phi)}{\Delta t}$, **[1 mark]** where t is the time

   b) $v = 630 \, \text{km per hour} = \frac{630 \times 10^3}{3600} \, \text{m s}^{-1}, \quad l = 34 \, \text{m}$

   Area $A = \frac{630 \times 10^3}{3600} \times 34$ **[1 mark]**

   $= 5950 \, \text{m}^2 \approx 6000 \, \text{m}^2$ **[1 mark]**

   c) $\varepsilon = \frac{\Delta(N\Phi)}{\Delta t}$ with $N = 1$ and $\Delta\Phi = BA$ and $\Delta t = 1$ **[1 mark]**

   $\varepsilon = BA = 5 \times 10^{-5} \times 5950$ **[1 mark]**

   $= 0.298 \approx 0.3$ V **[1 mark]**

   d) The direction of the emf is determined using Fleming's right-hand rule **[1 mark]**

3. a) Magnetic flux linkage or flux linkage is the product of the magnetic flux passing through a coil and the number of turns on the coil, **[1 mark]** i.e. $N\Phi$ with units of weber or weber-turns **[1 mark]**

b) $N = 3000, \quad A = 1.2 \, \text{cm}^2 = 1.2 \times 10^{-4} \, \text{m}^2,$
$\Delta t = 0.20 \, \text{s}, \quad \varepsilon = 0.45 \, \text{V}$

$\varepsilon = N\frac{\Delta\Phi}{\Delta t} \rightarrow \Delta\Phi = \frac{\varepsilon\Delta t}{N}$ **[1 mark]**

and $\Delta\Phi = B\Delta A$

$\therefore B\Delta A = \frac{\varepsilon\Delta t}{N} \rightarrow B = \frac{\Delta t}{N\Delta A}$ **[1 mark]**

$B = \frac{0.45 \times 0.2}{3000 \times 1.2 \times 10^{-4}}$ **[1 mark]**

$= 0.25$ T **[1 mark]**

A.C. Generators and Transformers

QUICK TEST (page 54)

1. sinusoidally
2. $I_{\text{rms}} = \frac{I_0}{\sqrt{2}}$
3. 325 V
4. 90° out of phase
5. 0.75 V
6. An alternating current flows in the primary coil and this produces an alternating magnetic field in the soft iron core; the magnetic flux linkage of the secondary coil constantly changes and so an alternating voltage is induced across it
7. 60
8. creation of eddy currents; laminated core

PRACTICE QUESTIONS (page 55)

1. a) A solid soft iron core can generate large eddy currents because the paths they follow within the iron core have very low resistance; **[1 mark]** these large currents can cause the soft iron core to become very hot; **[1 mark]** the effect can be significantly reduced by laminating the core with layers of insulators **[1 mark]**

   b) $V_{\text{p}} = 12 \, \text{V}, \quad N_{\text{p}} = 250, \quad V_{\text{s}} = 132 \, \text{V}$

   $\frac{V_{\text{p}}}{V_{\text{s}}} = \frac{N_{\text{p}}}{N_{\text{s}}} \rightarrow N_{\text{s}} = N_{\text{p}} \frac{V_{\text{s}}}{V_{\text{p}}} = 250 \times \frac{132}{12}$ **[1 mark]**

   $N_{\text{s}} = 2750$ or 2800 turns **[1 mark]**

   c) $I_{\text{p}} = 1.65 \, \text{A}$

   $\frac{N_{\text{p}}}{N_{\text{s}}} = \frac{I_{\text{s}}}{I_{\text{p}}} \rightarrow I_{\text{s}} = I_{\text{p}} \times \frac{N_{\text{p}}}{N_{\text{s}}}$

   $I_{\text{s}} = 1.65 \times \frac{12}{132}$ **[1 mark]** $= 0.15 \, \text{A}$ **[1 mark]**

   d) for 100% efficiency, power $= I_{\text{s}}V_{\text{s}} = I_{\text{p}}V_{\text{p}}$

   $= 0.15 \times 132 = 19.8 \, \text{W}$ **[1 mark]**

   $\therefore$ efficiency $\eta = \frac{18}{19.8} \times 100 = 91\%$ **[1 mark]**

   e) resistance in the coils **[1 mark]**

2. a) $N\Phi = BAN \cos\theta$ **[1 mark]**

   b) $\omega = 2\pi f = 30\pi \, \text{rad s}^{-1}$ and $\theta = \omega t$

   (i) max value of Φ when $\cos\omega t = \pm 1$ **[1 mark]**

   $\therefore \Phi = BAN \cos\omega t = BAN$ **[1 mark]**

   $= 0.05 \times 6 \times 10^{-4} \times 1000$

   $\Phi = 0.03$ Wb **[1 mark]**

(ii) max value of ε when $\sin \omega t = \pm 1$ **[1 mark]**

$$\varepsilon = BAN\omega \sin \omega t = BAN\omega \text{ [1 mark]}$$

$$= 0.03 \times 30\pi$$

$$= 2.8\,\text{V} \approx 3\,\text{V} \text{ [1 mark]}$$

c)

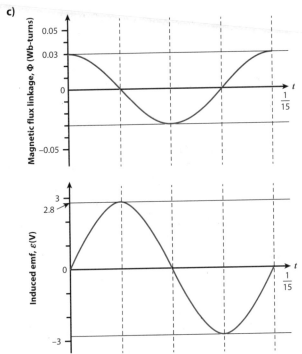

[5 marks: 2 marks for correct max Φ and ε, 2 marks for correct sinusoidal slope and 1 mark for emf 90° out of phase with Φ]

Day 4

Gravitational Fields
QUICK TEST (page 58)

1. infinite
2. inverse square law
3. indicates an attractive force
4. the gravitational constant; $N\,m^2\,kg^{-2}$
5. a field around a massive planetary object that decreases with increasing distance from the centre of the planet (according to the inverse square law)
6. $g = \dfrac{GM}{r^2}$
7. $4.0\,N\,kg^{-1}$
8. $6.0 \times 10^{24}\,\text{kg}$
9. 123 N or 120 N towards Earth
10. $9.85\,N\,kg^{-1}$

PRACTICE QUESTIONS (page 59)

1. a) Gravitational field strength, g, is the force per unit mass **[1 mark]** acting on a small mass placed at a particular point in the gravitational field **[1 mark]**; units are $N\,kg^{-1}$ **[1 mark]**

b) $g_s = \dfrac{GM}{R^2}$ and $g = \dfrac{GM}{r^2} = \dfrac{GM}{(R+h)^2}$ **[1 mark]**

$\therefore GM = g_s R^2$ **[1 mark]** hence $g = \dfrac{g_s R^2}{(R+h)^2} = g_s \left(\dfrac{R}{R+h}\right)^2$ **[1 mark]**

c) $R = 6400\,\text{km}, \quad h = 400\,\text{km}$

$\therefore g = 9.81\left(\frac{6400}{6800}\right)^2 = 8.69\,N\,kg^{-1} \approx 8.7\,N\,kg^{-1}$ **[1 mark]**

d) $m = 70\,\text{kg}$

weight $= mg = 70 \times 8.69 = 608.3\,N \approx 610\,N$ **[1 mark]**

e) Astronauts appear 'weightless' as everything on the ISS and the ISS itself are falling with an acceleration of $8.69\,m\,s^{-1}$ **[1 mark]**

2. a)

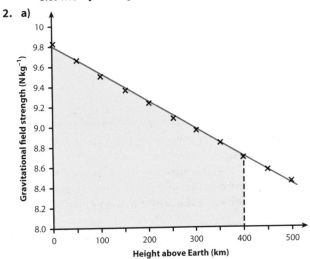

[3 marks: 1 mark for axes drawn and labelled correctly; 1 mark for points plotted correctly; 1 mark for line of best fit]

b) In this region of space just above the Earth, the gravitational field strength is proportional to the height, i.e. it is a straight line or behaves as a linear function **[2 marks]**

c) [2 marks: 1 mark for a line drawn at $h = 400\,\text{km}$ and 1 mark for the area between $h = 0\,\text{km}$ and $h = 400\,\text{km}$ shown shaded]

d) area under graph = area of trapezium

$= \frac{1}{2}(8.69 + 9.81) \times 400 \times 10^3$ **[1 mark]**

$= 3.7 \times 10^6 = 3.7\,MJ\,kg^{-1}$ **[1 mark]**

[or area calculation via rectangle and triangle]

Hence if $m = 1200\,\text{kg}$:

energy required $= 3.7 \times 10^6 \times 1200$ **[1 mark]**

$= 4.4 \times 10^9\,\text{J}$ or $4.4\,\text{GJ}$ **[1 mark]**

3. a) $R = 7.0 \times 10^8$ m, $\quad M = 2.0 \times 10^{30}$ kg

$g_s = \frac{GM}{R^2} = \frac{6.67 \times 10^{-11} \times 2 \times 10^{30}}{\left(7 \times 10^8\right)^2}$ **[1 mark]**

$g_s = 272\,\text{Nkg}^{-1} \approx 270\,\text{Nkg}^{-1}$ **[1 mark]**

b) $g_s = \frac{4}{3}\pi G \rho R \rightarrow \rho = \frac{3g_s}{4\pi GR}$ **[1 mark]**

$\rho = \frac{3 \times 272}{4\pi \times 6.67 \times 10^{-11} \times 7 \times 10^8}$ **[1 mark]**

$\quad = 1392\,\text{kgm}^{-3} \approx 1400\,\text{kgm}^{-3}$ **[1 mark]**

c) when $r = 1.5 \times 10^9$ m

$g = \frac{GM}{r^2} = \frac{6.67 \times 10^{-11} \times 2 \times 10^{30}}{\left(1.5 \times 10^9\right)^2}$ **[1 mark]**

$g = 59.3\,\text{Nkg}^{-1} \approx 60\,\text{Nkg}^{-1}$ **[1 mark]**

d) $\rho = 30\,\text{kgm}^{-3}$

$\therefore R = \frac{3g_s}{4\pi G\rho} = \frac{3 \times 272}{4\pi \times 6.67 \times 10^{-11} \times 30}$ **[1 mark]**

$R = 3.2 \times 10^{10}$ m $= 32 \times 10^9$ m **[1 mark]**

This is $21\times$ the current Earth–Sun distance, the Earth will be 'swallowed up' by the sun's expansion **[1 mark]**

Gravitational Potential
QUICK TEST (page 62)

1. because the value for 'g' is not constant for large changes in h; the Earth's field is a radial field and so for only small changes of h (or r) can the field be considered uniform

2. $V = -\frac{GM}{R}$; Jkg^{-1}

3. $-63\,\text{MJkg}^{-1}$; the potential is defined as zero at infinity and therefore becomes increasingly negative as it approaches Earth; work needs to be done in moving a mass away from the Earth

4. It is the gradient of a $V - r$ graph at the point r, i.e. $g = -\frac{\Delta V}{\Delta r}$

5. lines along which a mass experiences no change in gravitational potential

6. They are always perpendicular

7. zero

8. $\Delta E = m\left(V_2 - V_1\right)$

9. $-3.8 \times 10^9\,\text{Jkg}^{-1}$

10. 1.9×10^{27} kg

11. $g = 25.7\,\text{Nkg}^{-1}$

12. The satellite moves along an equipotential and there is thus no change in potential energy; as total energy is conserved, there is no change in kinetic energy, so speed remains constant

PRACTICE QUESTIONS (page 63)

1. a) $M = 2 \times 10^{30}$ kg, $\quad r = 0.7 \times 10^9$ m

$V = -\frac{GM}{R} = -\frac{6.67 \times 10^{-11} \times 2 \times 10^{30}}{0.7 \times 10^9}$ **[1 mark]**

$\quad = -1.91 \times 10^{11}\,\text{Jkg}^{-1}$ **[1 mark]**

b) at the surface, $g = \frac{V}{R} = \frac{1.91 \times 10^{11}}{0.7 \times 10^9}$ **[1 mark]**

$g = 272.9\,\text{Nkg}^{-1} \approx 270\,\text{Nkg}^{-1}$ **[1 mark]**

c) $M = 1.6 \times 10^{12}$ kg, $\quad h = 1.5 \times 10^8$ m above surface

$V_r = -\frac{GM}{r} = -\frac{6.67 \times 10^{-11} \times 2 \times 10^{30}}{0.7 \times 10^9 + 1.5 \times 10^8}$ **[1 mark]**

$\quad = -1.57 \times 10^{11}\,\text{Jkg}^{-1}$ **[1 mark]**

$\therefore \Delta V = V_r - V = \left(-1.57 \times 10^{11}\right) - \left(-1.91 \times 10^{11}\right)$

$\quad = 0.34 \times 10^{11}\,\text{Jkg}^{-1}$ **[1 mark]**

$\therefore \Delta E = m\Delta V = 1.6 \times 10^{12} \times 0.34 \times 10^{11}\,\text{J}$

$\quad = 5.4 \times 10^{22}\,\text{J}$ **[1 mark]**

2. a) Gravitational potential is the amount of work done against gravity **[1 mark]** when bringing a unit mass from infinity to that point **[1 mark]**

b) $M = 6.4 \times 10^{23}$ kg, $\quad R = 3.4 \times 10^3$ km

$g_M = \frac{GM}{R^2} = \frac{6.67 \times 10^{-11} \times 6.4 \times 10^{23}}{\left(3.4 \times 10^6\right)^2}$ **[1 mark]**

$g_M = 3.7\,\text{Nkg}^{-1}$ **[1 mark]**

Compared with g_E of $9.8\,\text{N kg}^{-1}$: $\frac{3.7}{9.8} \times 100 = 37.8\% \approx 38\%$

[1 mark]

c) $V = -\frac{GM}{R} = -\frac{6.67 \times 10^{-11} \times 6.4 \times 10^{23}}{3.4 \times 10^6}$ **[1 mark]**

$\quad = -1.26 \times 10^7\,\text{Jkg}^{-1} \approx -1.3 \times 10^7\,\text{Jkg}^{-1}$ or $-13\,\text{MJkg}^{-1}$

[1 mark]

d) (i) height $h = 500\,\text{km} \rightarrow r = \left(3.4 \times 10^6\right) + \left(500 \times 10^3\right)$

$r = 3.9 \times 10^6$ m **[1 mark]**

$V_h = -\frac{GM}{r} = -\frac{6.67 \times 10^{-11} \times 6.4 \times 10^{23}}{3.9 \times 10^6}$

$V_h = -10.95\,\text{MJkg}^{-1}$ **[1 mark]**

$\therefore \Delta E = m\Delta V = 900 \times \left(-10.95 \times 10^6\right) - \left(-12.6 \times 10^6\right)$

$\Delta E = 1.5 \times 10^9$ J **[1 mark]**

(ii) This energy is turned into kinetic energy,

$\frac{1}{2}mv^2 = 1.5 \times 10^9$ J **[1 mark]**

$\therefore v = \sqrt{\frac{2 \times 1.5 \times 10^9}{900}}$ **[1 mark]** $= 1826\,\text{ms}^{-1} \approx 1800\,\text{ms}^{-1}$

[1 mark]

e) The gravitational field is a uniform field **[1 mark]** with field strength of $3.7\,\text{N kg}^{-1}$ **[1 mark]**

3. a) Triangle drawn: $g = \frac{\Delta V}{\Delta r} = \frac{4 \times 10^6}{1.2 \times 10^6} = 3.3\,\text{Nkg}^{-1}$

[2 marks: 1 mark for largest correct triangle, 1 mark for correct answer]

b) $V_s = -4 \times 10^6\,\text{Jkg}^{-1}$ **[1 mark]**

$E_P = mV_s = 650 \times \left(-4 \times 10^6\right)$ **[1 mark]**

$\quad = -2.6 \times 10^9\,\text{J}$ **[1 mark]**

c) height $= 800\,\text{km}$ above surface $\rightarrow$

$r = \left(0.8 \times 10^6\right) + \left(800 \times 10^3\right)$

$r = 1.6 \times 10^6$ m **[1 mark]**

at $r = 1.6 \times 10^6\,\text{m} \rightarrow V_h = -2.4 \times 10^6\,\text{Jkg}^{-1}$ **[1 mark]**

[accept -2.3×10^6 to -2.5×10^6]

$\therefore \Delta E_p = m\Delta V$

$\quad = 120 \times \left(-2.4 + 4\right) \times 10^6$ **[1 mark]**

$\quad = 190 \times 10^6\,\text{J} = 190\,\text{MJ}$ **[1 mark]**

Orbits of Satellites and Planets
QUICK TEST (page 66)

1. the initial vertical velocity that a projectile needs in order to escape from the gravitational potential well

2. $v = \sqrt{2V}$

3. atmospheric drag
4. the gravitational force of attraction
5. A velocity increase tends to lead to a higher orbit
6. The cube of the orbital radius is directly proportional to the square of the orbital period, or $r^3 \propto T^2$
7. Both have orbital periods of 24 hours; geostationary orbits lie directly above the equator whereas a geosynchronous orbit may not
8. weather/spy satellite
9. highly elliptical orbits
10. $g = \frac{GM}{R^2}$
11. 2.0×10^{30} kg
12. $7700 \, \text{m s}^{-1}$
13. 5.1×10^{24} kg

PRACTICE QUESTIONS (page 67)

1. a) A low Earth orbit is an orbit more than 300 km above the Earth and so avoiding significant atmospheric drag [1 mark]

    Advantage: ease of access to the ISS [1 mark]

    Disadvantage: still experiences atmospheric drag so requires energy to maintain orbit [1 mark]

   b) $v = \sqrt{\frac{GM}{r}} = \sqrt{\frac{6.67 \times 10^{-11} \times 6.0 \times 10^{27}}{(6400 + 400) \times 10^3}}$ [1 mark]

    $= 7672 \, \text{m s}^{-1} \approx 7700 \, \text{m s}^{-1}$ [1 mark]

   c) centripetal acceleration $a = \frac{v^2}{r}$ [1 mark]

    $\therefore a = \frac{(7672)^2}{(6400 + 400) \times 10^3}$ [1 mark]

    $= 8.65 \, \text{N kg}^{-1} \approx 8.7 \, \text{N kg}^{-1}$ [1 mark]

    hence, $F = ma = 42\,000 \times 8.7$ [1 mark]

    $F = 3.6 \times 10^6$ N [1 mark]

   d) $F = \frac{GMm}{r^2} \rightarrow M = \frac{Fr^2}{Gm}$ [1 mark]

    $M = \frac{3.6 \times 10^6 \times (6800 \times 10^3)^2}{6.67 \times 10^{-11} \times 420\,000}$ [1 mark]

    $= 6 \times 10^{24}$ kg [1 mark]

2. a) The square of the orbital period T is directly proportional to the cube of the orbital radius r [1 mark], i.e. $\frac{r^3}{T^2} = \frac{GM}{4\pi^2}$ [1 mark]

   b) $r = 420\,000 \, \text{km}, \quad T = 42 \, \text{hours}$

    $M = \frac{r\pi^2 r^3}{GT^2} = \frac{4\pi^2 (420\,000 \times 10^3)^3}{6.67 \times 10^{-11} \times (42 \times 3600)^2}$ [1 mark]

    $= 1.9 \times 10^{27}$ kg [1 mark]

   c) orbital speed $v = \sqrt{\frac{GM}{r}} = \sqrt{\frac{6.67 \times 10^{-11} \times 1.9 \times 10^{27}}{420\,000 \times 10^3}}$ [1 mark]

    $v = 17\,378 \, \text{m s}^{-1} \approx 17 \, \text{km s}^{-1}$ [1 mark]

   d) $T = 170 \, \text{hours}$

    $r^3 = \frac{GMT^2}{4\pi^2} = \frac{6.67 \times 10^{-11} \times 1.90 \times 10^{27} \times (170 \times 3600)^2}{4\pi^2}$ [1 mark]

    $r^3 = 1.20 \times 10^{27} \rightarrow r = 1.1 \times 10^9$ m [1 mark]

    $\therefore r = 1.1 \times 10^6$ km [1 mark]

3. a) Weather satellites may be placed in a geosynchronous/polar orbit [1 mark]; for observing the UK, a geosynchronous orbit is necessary [1 mark]; these orbits are 24 hours to match the Earth's rotation [1 mark]

   b) $T = 1 \, \text{day} = 24 \, \text{hours} = 86\,400 \, \text{s}$

    using Kepler's Third Law, $\frac{r^3}{T^2} = \frac{GM}{4\pi^2}$:

    $r^3 = \frac{GMT^2}{4\pi^2} = \frac{6.67 \times 10^{-11} \times 6.0 \times 10^{24} \times (86\,400)^2}{4\pi^2}$ [1 mark]

    $r^3 = 7.6 \times 10^{22} \, \text{m}^3 \quad \therefore r = 4.2 \times 10^7$ m [1 mark]

    $r = 42\,000 \, \text{km}$

    so, height above Earth $= 42\,000 - 6400 = 35\,600 \, \text{km}$ [1 mark]

   c) $v = \frac{2\pi r}{T}$ so if v increases either r increases [1 mark] or T decreases [1 mark]

   d) height decreased by factor of $2 \rightarrow$ new height $= 17\,800 \, \text{km} \rightarrow$ new $r = 24\,200 \, \text{km}$ [1 mark]

    $T^2 = \frac{4\pi^2 r^3}{GM} = \frac{4\pi^2 \times (24\,200 \times 10^3)^3}{6.67 \times 10^{-11} \times 6.0 \times 10^{24}}$ [1 mark]

    $T^2 = 1.4 \times 10^9 \rightarrow T = 37\,390 \, \text{s}$

    $\therefore T = 10.4 \, \text{hours}$ [1 mark]

    Satellite no longer in geosynchronous orbit due to shorter orbital period [1 mark]; renders satellite impossible to observe the same fixed point over the UK [1 mark]

Day 5

Nuclear Size and Stability

QUICK TEST (page 70)

1. It's an increasing curve extending from the origin to values of N and Z about 120 and 80, respectively
2. Alpha decay involves the decrease in nucleon number of 4 and decrease of 2 in the atomic number; occurs in heavy nuclei usually with more than 82 protons, moving the nucleus towards a more stable region
3. forms technetium-99m; medical diagnosis, e.g. blood flow/internal organ imaging
4. the product of the decay of a radioactive 'parent' nucleus
5. 30 protons (Z); $66 - 30 = 36$ neutrons (N); ratio $\frac{N}{Z} = 1.2$
6. 4.8×10^{-15} m or 4.8 fm
7. 3.9×10^{-15} m or 3.9 fm
8. When the kinetic energy of an alpha particle becomes zero at the point of closest approach to the nucleus which is then equal to the electrical potential energy between the two charges
9. 3.6×10^{-15} m or 3.6 fm; $2.3 \times 10^{17} \, \text{kg m}^{-3}$
10. 12 000 layers

PRACTICE QUESTIONS (page 71)

1. a) Alpha particles collide easily with air molecules and are scattered/deflected/lose kinetic energy before reaching the target [1 mark]

   b) $E_\alpha = 5.8 \, \text{MeV} = 5.8 \times 1.6 \times 10^{-13}$ J [1 mark]

    $E_\alpha = 9.3 \times 10^{-13}$ J [1 mark]

   c) $9.3 \times 10^{-13} = \frac{q_\alpha q_{\text{nickel}}}{4\pi\varepsilon_0 r}$ [1 mark]

    $r = \frac{(2e)(58e)}{4\pi\varepsilon_0 (9.3 \times 10^{-13})} = 2.87 \times 10^{-14}$ m [1 mark]

    $= 29$ fm [1 mark]

d) atomic radius = nuclear radius $\times 10^4$

$$= 29 \times 10^{-15} \times 10^4 = 29 \times 10^{-11}\,\text{m} \text{ [1 mark]}$$
$$= 0.29\,\text{nm or } 290\,\text{pm} \text{ [1 mark]}$$

2. a) an equation that is derived or obtained directly by experiment rather than from theory **[1 mark]**

b) $R = 4.6 \times 10^{-15}$ m

$$r_0 = \frac{R}{A^{1/3}} = \frac{4.6 \times 10^{-15}}{(56)^{1/3}} \text{ [1 mark]}$$
$$= 1.202 \times 10^{-15}\,\text{m} \approx 1.2 \times 10^{-15}\,\text{m} \text{ [1 mark]}$$

c) $A = 197$, $\therefore R_{\text{gold}} = 1.2 \times 10^{-15} \times (197)^{1/3}$ **[1 mark]**

$R_{\text{gold}} = 6.98 \times 10^{-15}\,\text{m} \approx 7.0 \times 10^{-15}\,\text{m}$ **[1 mark]**

d) mass of gold $= 197\,\text{u} = 197 \times 1.67 \times 10^{-27}$ kg **[1 mark]**

volume of gold $= \frac{4}{3}\pi R^3$

density of gold $\rho = \frac{M}{V} = \frac{197 \times 1.67 \times 10^{-27}}{\frac{4}{3}\pi \times (7.0 \times 10^{-15})^3}$ **[1 mark]**

$\rho = 2.289 \times 10^{17}\,\text{kg m}^{-3} \approx 2.3 \times 10^{17}\,\text{kg m}^{-3}$ **[1 mark]**

3. a) an excited state of a nucleus that has an appreciable half-life **[1 mark]**

b) $^{99}_{42}\text{Mo} \rightarrow {}^{99m}_{43}\text{Tc} + {}^{0}_{-1}\beta + (\bar{v})$ **[1 mark]**

c) A gamma ray photon **[1 mark]** of energy 0.14 MeV is emitted **[1 mark]**

d) Samples of Tc-99m in used in medical diagnosis **[1 mark]** for monitoring blood flow in the brain or imaging internal organs using a gamma camera **[1 mark]**

Nuclear Radiation
QUICK TEST (page 74)

1. alpha, beta and gamma radiation
2. a helium nucleus; 2 protons and 2 neutrons
3. essentially zero due to annihilation with electrons
4. Beta particles show a significant deflection, whereas alpha particles (being heavier) show a slight deflection
5. 25
6. **[any three from]** cosmic radiation, radon gas, rocks, living plants and animals, nuclear waste, medical
7. $3 \times 10^{-5}\,\text{Jkg}^{-1}$
8. gray
9. 6×10^{-4} Sv
10. with tongs; always pointed away from people; measurements to be made as quickly as possible; returned to lead-lined source holder as soon as practically possible

PRACTICE QUESTIONS (page 75)

1. a) Background radiation occurs both naturally through cosmic radiation and radioactive materials in rocks and soil **[1 mark]** as well as artificially **[1 mark]** through nuclear power and medical applications **[1 mark]**

b) $I \propto \frac{1}{d^2}$ $\therefore I = \frac{R}{d^2} \rightarrow R = Id^2$ **[1 mark]**

$R = 5308 \times (0.1)^2$

$R = 53.08$ **[1 mark]**

when $d = 0.25\,\text{m}$, $I = \frac{53.08}{(0.25)^2} = 849.3$

$\therefore I = 849.3 + 20 = 869.3 \approx 870$ counts per second **[1 mark]**

c) Use a Geiger counter to measure the count rate, C, at different distances, d, from the radioactive source **[1 mark]**. Determine the count rate, C_0, without the source to measure the background count rate **[1 mark]**. Determine the corrected count rate, $C - C_0$, at these various distances **[1 mark]**. As $C - C_0 = \frac{\text{constant}}{d^2}$, plot a graph of d (y-axis) versus $\frac{1}{\sqrt{C-C_0}}$ (x-axis), which will give a straight line **[1 mark]**.

d) The radiation is not detected at the window of the Geiger counter but somewhere inside the tube **[1 mark]**. The true distance or corrected distance represents a mean distance that is greater than the distance from the front of the tube **[1 mark]**. The y-intercept of the straight line will give a value for d_0 **[1 mark]**.

2. a) $E = 0.662\,\text{MeV}$
$$= 0.662 \times 1.6 \times 10^{-13}\,\text{J}$$
$$= 1.06 \times 10^{-13}\,\text{J} \text{ [1 mark]}$$

b) total energy $= nE$
$$= 2 \times 10^5 \times 1.06 \times 10^{-13} \text{ [1 mark]}$$
$$= 2.12 \times 10^{-8}\,\text{Js}^{-1} \approx 2 \times 10^{-8}\,\text{Js}^{-1} \text{ [1 mark]}$$

c) $t = 30\,\text{min} = 30 \times 60 = 1800\,\text{s}$ **[1 mark]**
total energy transferred $= 2.12 \times 10^{-8} \times 1800\,\text{s}$
$$= 3.81 \times 10^{-5}\,\text{J} \text{ [1 mark]}$$

d) $D = \frac{E}{m} = \frac{3.81 \times 10^{-5}}{5} = 7.63 \times 10^{-6}$ Gy **[1 mark]**
$W_\gamma = 1$
$\therefore H = W_\gamma D = 8 \times 10^{-6}$ Sv or 8μSv **[1 mark]**

e) $W_\alpha = 20$
$H = 20 \times 7.63 \times 10^{-6}$ **[1 mark]**
$H = 1.5 \times 10^{-4}$ Sv or 150 μSv **[1 mark]**
higher dose equivalent **[1 mark]**, therefore higher/greater risk of tissue damage **[1 mark]**

3. a)/b)

Counts	25876	14956	6481	3092	1089	784	139	138	
Time (s)	20	30	60	90	120	150	200	300	
Thickness	0	0.5	2	3	4	5	6	7	
Count rate (min⁻¹)	77600	29900	6480	2060	545	314	41.7	27.6	**[2 marks: –1 mark for each error or omission]**
In(count rate)	11.3	10.3	8.80	7.63	6.30	5.75	3.73	3.32	**[2 marks: –1 mark for each error or omission]**

c)/d)

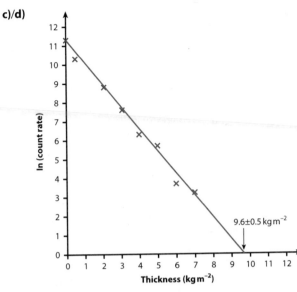

[4 marks: 1 mark for points plotted correctly, 1 mark for axes labelled correctly, 1 mark for straight line drawn, 1 mark for correctly marked x-axis intercept]

The thickness indicated at the x-axis intercept is an effective thickness of absorber that would stop most of the β⁻ particles [1 mark]

e) Count rates are very low and close to background levels [1 mark]; longer time needed for statistical accuracy [1 mark]

Radioactive Decay

QUICK TEST (page 78)

1. the probability that a radioactive decay will take place in unit time; equal to $\frac{\ln 2}{\text{half-life}}$; units of s^{-1}
2. the time taken for half of the radioactive nuclei to decay
3. an exponential function
4. $A = \lambda N$; Bq
5. $\lambda = \frac{\ln 2}{t_{1/2}}$
6. 1200 s
7. 1.2×10^9 atoms
8. carbon-14
9. [any one from] thickness of metal foils, non-destructive testing, monitoring flow rates
10. high-energy gamma radiation; caesium-137 or cobalt-60

PRACTICE QUESTIONS (page 79)

1. **a)** $^{14}_{6}C \rightarrow {}^{14}_{7}N$ [1 mark] $+ {}^{0}_{-1}\beta$ [1 mark] $+ \bar{\nu}_e$

   b) $t_{1/2} = \frac{\ln 2}{\lambda} = \frac{\ln 2}{4 \times 10^{-12}}$ [1 mark]

   $= 1.73 \times 10^{11}$ s [1 mark]

   $= 5490$ years ≈ 5500 years [1 mark]

   c) $A = 0.079$ Bq and $A_0 = 0.093$ Bq

   $A = A_0 e^{-\lambda t} \rightarrow e^{-\lambda t} = \frac{0.079}{0.093} = 0.8495$ [1 mark]

   $\therefore \lambda t = 0.1632$ [1 mark]

   $t = \frac{0.1632}{\lambda} = \frac{0.1632}{4.0 \times 10^{-12}}$

   $= 4.08 \times 10^{10}$ s [1 mark]

   $= 1292.5$ years [1 mark]

   ≈ 1300 years (2 s.f.) [1 mark]

2. **a)** $C = C_0 e^{-\lambda t}$

   $\ln C = \ln C_0 - \lambda t$ [1 mark]

   $\ln C = -\lambda t + \ln C_0$ [1 mark]

b)

Count rate (Bq)	7.8	7.3	6.6	6.2	5.8	5.1	4.6	4.3	4.3	4.2	3.3	3.2	2.7	3.2	2.4	
Elapsed time (s)	0	10	20	30	40	50	60	70	80	90	100	110	120	130	140	
Corrected count rate, C (Bq)	6.8	6.3	5.6	5.2	4.8	4.1	3.6	3.3	3.3	3.2	2.3	2.2	1.7	2.2	1.4	[1 mark]
$\ln C$	1.92	1.84	1.72	1.65	1.57	1.41	1.28	1.19	1.19	1.16	0.83	0.79	0.53	0.79	0.34	[2 marks]

c)

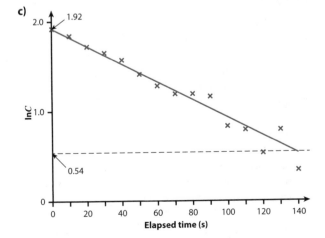

[3 marks: 1 mark for points plotted correctly, 1 mark for axes labelled correctly, 1 mark for line drawn]

d) gradient $m = \frac{\Delta y}{\Delta x} = \frac{1.92 - 0.54}{140}$ [1 mark] $= 0.0099 \approx 0.01$

$m = \lambda = 0.01 \, s^{-1}$ [1 mark]

$t_{1/2} = \frac{\ln 2}{\lambda} = \frac{0.693}{0.01} = 69$ s (± 5s) [1 mark]

3. **a)** 90 g of strontium-90 contains 6.02×10^{23} atoms, hence the number of atoms in 10 g of strontium-90 is

   $\frac{10 \times 6.02 \times 10^{23}}{90} = 6.69 \times 10^{22}$ atoms [1 mark]

   b) activity $A = \lambda N = \frac{\ln 2}{t_{1/2}} N$ [1 mark]

   $A = \frac{0.693}{28 \times 365.25 \times 86400} \times 6.69 \times 10^{22}$ [1 mark]

   $= 5.2 \times 10^{13}$ Bq [1 mark]

c) power $= AE$
$$= 5.2 \times 10^{13} \times 0.40 \times 1.60 \times 10^{-13} \, Js^{-1} \, [\textbf{1 mark}]$$
$$= 3.4 \, W \, [\textbf{1 mark}]$$

Nuclear Fission and Fusion
QUICK TEST (page 82)

1. the amount of energy needed to separate a nucleus into its constituent parts
2. iron
3. fusion
4. High energy is needed to overcome the electrostatic repulsion between the two protons
5. the difference between the mass of the constituent nucleons making a nucleus and the mass of the resulting nucleus
6. a simple way of converting mass (in kg) into its energy equivalent (in MeV); $1u = 931.3 \, MeV$
7. $^2_1H + ^1_1p \rightarrow ^3_2He + 5.5 \, MeV$
8. $^{235}_{92}U + ^1_0n \rightarrow ^{144}_{56}Ba + ^{90}_{36}Kr + 2\,^1_0n + energy$
9. No; fission of a given nuclide like uranium does not lead to a unique outcome
10. (a) $0.01888 \, u$ (b) $17.6 \, MeV$

PRACTICE QUESTIONS (page 83)

1. a) Binding energy is the energy needed or work done to separate a nucleus into its constituent protons and neutron [**1 mark**]
   Mass defect is the mass difference between the constituent protons and neutrons and the mass of the nucleus [**1 mark**]
   Binding energy can be seen as a mass defect; mass defects are given in units of 'u' or kg [**1 mark**] and binding energies given in terms of MeV or MeV per nucleon [**1 mark**]
   b) $^{56}_{26}Fe$ has 26 protons 30 neutrons
   mass of protons and neutrons
   $= 26(1.00728 \, u) + 30(1.00866 \, u)$
   $= 56.44908 \, u \, [\textbf{1 mark}]$
   mass of iron-56 $= 55.93494 \, u$
   mass defect $= 56.44908 \, u - 55.93494 \, u$
   $= 0.51414 \, u \, [\textbf{1 mark}]$
   binding energy $= 0.51414 \times 931.3 \, MeV$
   $= 478.819 \, MeV \, [\textbf{1 mark}]$
   binding energy per nucleon $= \frac{478.819}{56}$ [**1 mark**]
   $= 8.6 \, MeV$ per nucleon [**1 mark**]
   c) It is the most stable of all the nuclei [**1 mark**]
2. a) Induced nuclear fission is the process in which a heavy nucleus splits up into lighter nuclei [**1 mark**] by absorbing a neutron [**1 mark**] and releasing energy [**1 mark**]
   b) $^{235}_{92}U + ^1_0n \rightarrow ^{95}_{38}Sr + ^{139}_{54}Xe + 2\,^1_0n$ [**4 marks: –1 mark for each error or omission**]

c) Uranium-235 absorbs a slow neutron before turning momentarily into uranium-236 and subsequently dividing into two lighter nuclei and two fast neutrons. For fission to occur, slow neutrons are needed to sustain the chain reaction [**1 mark**]. The fast neutrons produced are slowed down (or thermalised) using a moderator such as graphite or water [**1 mark**]. These fast neutrons collide inelastically with the moderator nuclei, losing some of their kinetic energy [**1 mark**].
d) Thermal neutrons collide with uranium-235 nuclei, splitting them into two lighter nuclei and on average two fast neutrons [**1 mark**]. These fast neutrons are slowed down using a moderator so that a continuous chain reaction can be established [**1 mark**]. The chain reaction is controlled by ensuring that the correct amount of slow neutrons is involved in the fission process and this is achieved by neutron absorption using control rods [**1 mark**]. The fission reaction produces large amounts of energy, which is used to heat water into steam [**1 mark**] that drives the turbines to generate the electricity for the National Grid [**1 mark**].

3. a) Nuclear fusion is the creation of a larger nucleus from two nuclei of lower nucleon number [**1 mark**], with the release of energy [**1 mark**]
   b) (i) Most stable nucleus is iron ($A = 56$) but accept any value between 50 and 60 [**1 mark**]; between 8.5 and 9.0 MeV per nucleon [**1 mark**]
      (ii) Nucleon number less than $A = 56$; accept between $A = 0$ and $A = 55$ [**1 mark**]
   c) (i) positron; neutrino [**1 mark**]
      (ii) $^2_1H + ^1_1p \rightarrow ^3_2He$ [**2 marks: 1 mark for each side of equation**]
      (iii) The fusion of two nuclei of ^3_2He [**1 mark**] produces a nucleus of ^4_2He [**1 mark**] plus 2 protons and energy; these protons are then used in the initial step to continue the fusion process [**1 mark**]

Day 6

Telescopes
QUICK TEST (page 86)

1. $M = \frac{f_o}{f_e}$
2. Newtonian and Cassegrain reflectors
3. spherical aberration and chromatic aberration
4. the smallest angle required to distinguish between two points
5. Rayleigh criterion
6. CCDs
7. [**any two from**] very efficient; digital format; linear response to incident light; extends detection beyond the visible region

8. The Earth's atmosphere is totally opaque to UV radiation below 300 nm
9. The Earth's atmosphere absorbs radiation at these wavelengths
10. To protect them from their own thermal energy
11. The energy collected per second and is proportional to the (diameter)^2 of the objective lens, mirror or dish

PRACTICE QUESTIONS (page 87)

1. a)

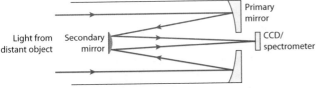

    [3 marks: 1 mark for correct position of primary mirror, 1 mark for correct position of secondary mirror, 1 mark for position of rays)

    b) Main advantage is that large, heavy, complex equipment/instrumentation can be attached to the base of the telescope [1 mark]

    c) The collecting power of a telescope is proportional to its collecting area, i.e. $\propto (\text{diameter})^2$ [1 mark]
    collecting time $\propto \frac{1}{\text{collecting area}}$ [1 mark]

    d) Let T_{CT} represent the collecting time for a Cassegrain telescope and T_{HST} the corresponding time for the Hubble Space Telescope; A_{CT} represents the collecting area for the Cassegrain telescope.
    $$T_{CT} \propto \frac{1}{A_{CT}} \rightarrow k \times \frac{1}{A_{CT}} \text{ [1 mark]}$$
    $$\therefore k = A_{CT} T_{CT} = \pi (0.3)^2 \times 60 \min$$
    $$k = 16.96 \text{ [1 mark]}$$
    $$T_{HST} = \frac{16.96}{\pi (1.2)^2} = 3.75 \min \approx 3.8 \min \text{ [1 mark]}$$

    e) Avoids atmospheric absorption within the visible region [1 mark]; avoids scattering by dust particles within the atmosphere [1 mark]

2. a) [any two from]
    CCDs convert light signals directly into digital format for computer processing
    CCDs are very efficient, at >70%, compared with film at ~5%
    CCDs extend detection beyond just the visible spectrum
    CCDs have a linear response to light input [2 marks]

    b) The critical stage when the central peak of one of the Airy discs is over the first minimum of the other Airy disc [1 mark], expressed as $\theta \approx \frac{\lambda}{D}$, where θ is known as the angular resolution [1 mark]

    c) $\theta \approx \frac{\lambda}{D} = \frac{510 \times 10^{-9}}{2}$ [1 mark]
    $= 255 \times 10^{-9} \approx 2.6 \times 10^{-7}$ radians [1 mark]

    d) Let 'x' be smallest feature on Moon
    $x = \theta L = 2.55 \times 10^{-9} \times 3.8 \times 10^8$ m [1 mark]
    $= 96.9$ m ≈ 100 m [1 marks]

3. a) collecting power $\propto$ area of dish
    $P_{GBT} \propto \pi (50)^2 \quad P_{LT} \propto \pi (38)^2$ [1 mark]
    $\therefore \frac{P_{GBT}}{P_{LT}} \propto \frac{50^2}{38^2} \approx 1.7$ [1 mark]

    b) 5 MHz $\rightarrow \lambda = \frac{c}{f} = \frac{3 \times 10^8}{5 \times 10^9} = 0.06$ m [1 mark]
    $\theta \approx \frac{\lambda}{D} = \frac{0.06}{100} = 6 \times 10^{-4}$ radians [1 mark]

    c) Connecting radio telescopes together and using interferometry [1 mark]; resolutions 10^3 times better than optical telescopes can be achieved [1 mark]

    d) Beyond these regions, radio telescopes are generally opaque to signals [1 mark] due to the Earth's atmosphere [1 mark]

Stellar Luminosity and Distance
QUICK TEST (page 90)

1. the total amount of energy it radiates per second, i.e. its power
2. $b = \frac{L}{4\pi R^2}$
3. +9.5
4. 10 pc
5. trigonometric parallax
6. $m - M = 5\log\left(\frac{d}{10}\right)$
7. standard candle
8. −6.69
9. $L \propto T^4$
10. an object that absorbs all of the radiation that falls on it and reflects none
11. $\lambda_{max} T = 2.9 \times 10^{-3}$ mK, i.e. metre kelvin
12. 5800 K

PRACTICE QUESTIONS (page 91)

1. a) the electromagnetic radiation emitted by a black body that extends over the whole range of wavelengths [1 mark], showing a characteristic form with a maximum at a certain wavelength [1 mark] that depends on temperature [1 mark]

    b) $T = 5800$ K
    $\lambda_{max} T = 2.9 \times 10^{-3}$ mK
    $\therefore \lambda_{max} = \frac{2.9 \times 10^{-3}}{5800} = 5 \times 10^{-7}$ m $= 500$ nm [1 mark]

    c) $L_\odot = \sigma A T^4$
    $= 4\pi r^2 \sigma T^4$ [1 mark]
    $= 4\pi \times (7 \times 10^8)^2 \times 5.7 \times 10^{-8} \times (5800)^4$ [1 mark]
    $= 3.97 \times 10^{26}$ W $\approx 4 \times 10^{26}$ W [1 mark]

    d) Solar constant is the intensity (or radiation flux) that the Earth receives from the Sun (in W m^{-2}) [1 mark]

e) $I = \dfrac{L_\odot}{4\pi d_{E-S}^2}$ **[1 mark]** where d_{E-S} is the mean Earth–Sun distance

$I = \dfrac{4\times10^{26}}{4\pi\left(1.5\times10^{11}\right)^2}$ **[1 mark]** $= 1415\,\text{W}\,\text{m}^{-2} \approx 1400\,\text{W}\,\text{m}^{-2}$

[1 mark]

2. a) Trigonometric parallax uses the Earth's orbital radius as a base line **[1 mark]** to determine the distance of nearby stars that move relative to more distant stars **[1 mark]**

b) $d = \dfrac{3.26}{\alpha}$

$\alpha = 0.768''$ (arcseconds)

$d = \dfrac{3.26}{0.768}$ **[1 mark]** $= 4.24$ light years **[1 mark]**

c) Apparent magnitude is the relative brightness of a star as seen by an observer **[1 mark]** and it is given by $m = -2.5\log b$ **[1 mark]**

d) $m - M = 5\log\left(\frac{d}{10}\right)$

$M = m - 5\log\left(\frac{d}{10}\right)$ **[1 mark]**

$m = +11.05,\quad d = 4.24$ light years $= 1.3\,\text{pc}$ **[1 mark]**

$M = 11.05 - 5\log 0.13$ **[1 mark]**

$\quad = 11.05 + 4.43$

$\quad = 15.48 \approx +15.5$ **[1 mark]**

e) $M_\odot = +4.83,\quad M = +15.5$

$M = M_\odot - 2.5\log\left(\frac{L}{L_\odot}\right)$ **[1 mark]**

$\rightarrow L = L_\odot \times 10^{-(M-M_\odot)/2.5}$ **[1 mark]**

$L = 5\times10^{-5}\,L_\odot$ **[1 mark]**

3. a) Standard candles are astronomical objects of known luminosity **[1 mark]** that are used to determine astronomical distances beyond those from the parallax method **[1 mark]**

b) $M = -6.2 \pm 0.2$ **[1 mark]**

c) $m = +18.2$

$m - M = 5\log\left(\frac{d}{10}\right)$

$+18.2 - (-6.2) = 5\log\left(\frac{d}{10}\right)$ **[1 mark]**

$24.4 = 5\log\left(\frac{d}{10}\right)$

$\log\left(\frac{d}{10}\right) = 4.88$ **[1 mark]**

$\frac{d}{10} = 10^{4.88} = 7.6\times10^4$ **[1 mark]**

$\therefore d = 7.6\times10^5\,\text{pc}$ **[1 mark]**

d) $d = 7.6\times10^5 \times 3.26$ light years

$\quad = 2.5\times10^6$ light years

$\quad = 2.5$ million light years **[1 mark]**

Conclusion: V1 lies in the Andromeda Galaxy and *not* in our Milky Way **[1 mark]**

Stellar Evolution
QUICK TEST (page 94)

1. a dense clump of clouds of dust and hydrogen gas formed under mutual gravitational attraction
2. nuclear fusion of hydrogen into helium
3. main sequence
4. a star in the later stages of stellar evolution with cooler outer layers, high luminosity and diameters 10–100 times that of the Sun
5. a compact stellar object with densities comparable to nuclear densities
6. the boundary of the black hole
7. 7 km
8. Type I are more luminous by two orders of magnitude; Type II show a plateau in their light curves
9. pulsars
10. because the gravitational force is so strong that not even light can escape
11. 3 solar masses

PRACTICE QUESTIONS (page 95)

1. a) [any three from] luminosity, temperature, mass, radius, age, chemical composition **[3 marks]**

b) x-axis: spectral class or colour index **[1 mark]**

c) a. main sequence star **[1 mark]**
b. red giant **[1 mark]**
c. white dwarf **[1 mark]**

d) (i) main sequence stars $\rightarrow$ nuclear fusion of H $\rightarrow$ He **[1 mark]**

(ii) when all the H in the star's core has become He; the outer layers expand rapidly to form a hot gas cloud $\rightarrow$ red giant **[1 mark]**

(iii) the outer layers dissipate as a 'planetary nebula', leaving behind the star's core **[1 mark]**

(iv) fusion in core produces carbon/oxygen and heats-up, forming a white dwarf **[1 mark]**

e) black dwarf **[1 mark]**

2. a) [any two from] they have a distinct spectrum; they have a different light curve; Type I supernovae have a much brighter light curve – two orders of magnitude greater than Type II; the light curve for Type I supernovae fades at a faster rate; Type II supernovae show a characteristic plateau in their light curve; Type I supernova explosions occur at the same critical mass **[2 marks]**

b) Type I supernovae have a well-defined standard luminosity **[1 mark]** that allows both apparent and absolute magnitude to be used to determine distance **[1 mark]**

c) When the core mass $> 3M_\odot$ the gravitational compression continues [1 mark], culminating in a gravitational field strength that prevents light from escaping [1 mark]; a black hole is formed [1 mark]

d) $M = 4M_\odot = 4 \times 2 \times 10^{30}$ kg

$R_S = \frac{2GM}{c^2} = \frac{2 \times 6.67 \times 10^{-11} \times 4 \times 2 \times 10^{30}}{(3 \times 10^8)^2}$ [1 mark]

$R_S = 11.9 \times 10^3$ m ≈ 12 km [1 mark]

e) The Schwarzschild radius represents the black hole's event horizon [1 mark]

Cosmology

QUICK TEST (page 98)

1. the increase in wavelength of light due to the source moving away from the observer
2. that the universe is isotropic and homogeneous
3. the cosmic microwave background radiation and the relative abundance of H and He in the universe
4. $v = H_0 d$; km s^{-1} Mpc^{-1}
5. an age for the universe
6. the red shift of distant galaxies based on the expansion of space itself
7. 0.0214
8. 6420 km s^{-1}
9. 14.45 billion years
10. Dark matter does not emit electromagnetic radiation and so is difficult to detect using current equipment
11. They show changes in temperature (energy-density) of the early universe sufficient for the formation of galaxies observed today

PRACTICE QUESTIONS (page 99)

1. a) Recessional red shift represents an increase in the wavelength of light [1 mark] emitted from an object due to its movement away from the observer (Doppler red shift) [1 mark] or due to the expansion of the universe (cosmological red shift) [1 mark]

b) By their shifts in the position [1 mark] of prominent absorption lines [1 mark]

c) H_0 represents the Hubble constant [1 mark], the reciprocal of which gives an estimation as to the age of the universe [1 mark]

d)

Galaxy	H_0	
NGC 3627	66.87	
NGC 2775	64.14	
NGC 6764	62.40	[1 mark]

mean $H_0 = 64.5$ km s^{-1} Mpc^{-1} [1 mark]

e) $H_0 = 64.5$ km s^{-1} Mpc^{-1}

$= \frac{64.5 \times 10^3}{3.1 \times 10^{16} \times 10^6} = 2.08 \times 10^{-18}$ s^{-1} [1 mark]

$t = \frac{1}{H_0} = 4.81 \times 10^{17}$ s [1 mark]

$= 1.50 \times 10^{10}$ years $= 15.0$ billion years [1 mark]

2. a) from graph: CaK $\lambda = 393.3$ nm [1 mark]

CaK shift $\Delta\lambda = 396.2 - 393.3 = 2.9$ nm [1 mark]

$\therefore z = \frac{\Delta\lambda}{\lambda} = \frac{2.9}{393.3} = 7.4 \times 10^{-3}$ [1 mark]

b) $z = \frac{v}{c} \rightarrow v = zc = 7.4 \times 10^{-3} \times 3 \times 10^8$ [1 mark]

$v = 2.22 \times 10^6$ m s^{-1}

$v = 2.2 \times 10^3$ km s^{-1} or 2200 km s^{-1} [1 mark]

c) $H_0 = 68$ km s^{-1} Mpc^{-1}

$v = H_0 d \rightarrow d = \frac{v}{H_0}$ [1 mark]

$d = \frac{2200}{68} \left[\frac{\text{km}}{\text{s}} \times \frac{\text{s} \times \text{Mpc}}{\text{km}} \rightarrow \text{Mpc} \right]$ [1 mark]

$d = 32.4$ Mpc [1 mark]

d) inaccuracies in determining the shift in wavelength [1 mark] and uncertainties in the value of H_0 [1 mark]

3. a) $H_0 = 68$ km s^{-1} Mpc^{-1}

$\rho_{crit} = \frac{3kH_0^2}{8\pi G} = \frac{3 \times 1.04 \times 10^{-39} \times 68^2}{8\pi \times 6.7 \times 10^{-11}}$ [1 mark]

$\rho_{crit} = 8.57 \times 10^{-27} \approx 8.6 \times 10^{-27}$ kg m^{-3} [1 mark]

b) $\Omega_0 = \dfrac{\text{density of matter in the universe}}{\rho_{crit}}$

If $\rho_{crit} = $ density of matter in universe then $\Omega_0 = 1$ [1 mark]

In this case, the expansion of the universe will eventually stop at some infinite time in the future [1 mark]

c) As density of matter $< \rho_{crit}$ then $0 < \Omega_0 < 1$ [1 mark] and the universe will go on expanding for ever [1 mark]

d) No consideration has been given for dark matter or the effects of dark energy [1 mark], which could have implications on the way the universe behaves in the future [1 mark]

Day 7

The Physics of Vision

QUICK TEST (page 102)

1. The cornea provides most of the focusing ability of the eye
2. The ciliary muscles control the shape of the lens and therefore make small adjustments in combination with the cornea to ensure that the eye focuses correctly
3. The retina contains light-sensitive nerve cells called rods and cones that receive light and transmit this information to the brain along the optic nerve
4. Rods are very sensitive to light, particularly low levels, but have no colour discrimination; cones are less sensitive but respond to narrow bands of wavelength to provide colour vision
5. Visual acuity is defined as $\frac{1}{\theta}$, where θ is the angle subtended at your eye by the smallest detail you can see
6. The fovea is an area on the retina that contains no rod cells resulting in a small region of enhanced visual acuity

7. Long-sightedness (hypermetropia) is when someone cannot focus on nearby objects; a convergent lens is used to bring the image to focus on the retina

8. the optical illusion whereby multiple discrete images (at a rate of about 24 Hz) appear to blend into a smooth and continuous image

9. an unevenly focused image on the retina formed by a non-spherically shaped cornea

10. cylindrical lens

11. power = $\frac{1}{\text{focal length}}$

12. 0.017 m or 1.7 cm

PRACTICE QUESTIONS (page 103)

1. a) long-sightedness [1 mark]; when the cornea–lens combination is not powerful enough to bring a nearby object into focus on the retina, and the image is focused behind the retina [1 mark]

   b) $u = 75\,cm = 0.75\,m$, $v = 20\,mm = 0.02\,m$
   power = $\frac{1}{f} = \frac{1}{u} + \frac{1}{v} = \frac{1}{0.75} + \frac{1}{0.02}$ [1 mark] = 51.3 D [1 mark]

   c) $u = 50\,cm = 0.50\,m$
   power = $\frac{1}{f} = \frac{1}{0.50} + \frac{1}{0.02}$ [1 mark] = 52 D [1 mark]

   d) need to increase the total refracting power by $52 - 51.3 = +0.7\,D$; power of lens = +0.7 D [1 mark]

2. a)

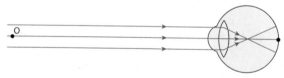

   O

   [2 marks for showing 2 additional and correct light rays]

   b) myopia or short-sightedness [1 mark]

   c) A: cornea [1 mark]; B: lens [1 mark]

   d) power = $\frac{1}{f} = 52\,D$, $u = 50\,cm = 0.50\,m$
   $\frac{1}{f} = \frac{1}{u} + \frac{1}{v} \rightarrow \frac{1}{v} = \frac{1}{f} - \frac{1}{u}$ [1 mark]
   $\frac{1}{v} = 52 - \frac{1}{0.50} = 50$ [1 mark] $\therefore v = 0.02\,m$ or 20 mm [1 mark]

   e) for an object at infinity, $u = \infty$ [1 mark]
   power = $\frac{1}{f} = \frac{1}{\infty} + \frac{1}{0.02} = 50\,D$ [1 mark]
   $\therefore$ the total refracting power needs to be reduced by 2 D; power of lens = −2 D [1 mark]; concave lens [1 mark]

3. a) a non-spherical cornea [1 mark]

   b) when one plane is in focus and another plane at a different angle is out of focus [1 mark]

   c) cylindrical lens [1 mark]

   d) the power of the lens [1 mark] and the angle of correction [1 mark]

The Physics of the Ear
QUICK TEST (page 106)

1. It is in this region that the sound signal is both amplified (by the malleus, incus and stapes) and any reflected signal from the inner ear is dampened

2. transmits vibrations to the fluid in the inner ear

3. 20 Hz to 20 kHz

4. frequency and intensity of sound

5. The threshold of hearing represents a sound intensity of $1 \times 10^{-12}\ W\,m^{-2}$, which occurs at 1 kHz; it defines precisely the sound intensity level of 0 dB

6. 90 dB

7. 140 dB; a jet plane taking off

8. a plot of hearing loss in dB against frequency

9. a unit of loudness that measures the intensity of sound with reference to a tone of defined intensity and frequency

10. used in sound level meters that provide a weighted output level to simulate the response of the human ear; used for environmental monitoring

11. the typical loss of hearing with age; affects high frequencies significantly more than low frequencies of sound

PRACTICE QUESTIONS (page 107)

1. a) Sound intensity is the power (energy per second) emitted per unit area [1 mark]; measured in $W\,m^{-2}$ [1 mark]

   b) Perceived loudness depends on the listener and is difficult to quantify [1 mark]

   c) I_0 represents the threshold of hearing [1 mark] and is defined as 0 dB on the sound intensity level [1 mark]

   d) sound intensity level = $10\log\left(\frac{I}{I_0}\right)$
   $10\log\left(\frac{I}{I_0}\right) = \frac{\text{sound intensity level}}{10} = \frac{110}{10} = 11$ [1 mark]
   $\therefore \frac{I}{I_0} = 10^{11}$
   and $I = I_0 \times 10^{11} = 1 \times 10^{-12} \times 10^{11}$ [1 mark]
   $I = 0.1\,W\,m^{-2}$ [1 mark]

2. a) A: eardrum or tympanic membrane [1 mark]
   B: ossicles [1 mark]
   C: oval or round window [1 mark]
   D: cochlea [1 mark]

   b) The tympanic membrane transfers sound waves from the outer ear to the middle ear or ossicles [1 mark]

   c) The fluid in the inner ear (perilymph) allows sound vibrations to pass to the basilar membrane in the cochlea [1 mark]

   d) Pressure waves in the fluid of the cochlea make the basilar membrane vibrate and resonate with a particular frequency [1 mark]; this causes a large amplitude of vibration that is picked up by hair cells attached to the basilar membrane [1 mark]; these movements trigger nerve impulses and these electrical signals [1 mark] are passed to the auditory nerve and to the brain [1 mark]

3. a) A phon is a unit of loudness level [1 mark] that measures the intensity of sound with reference to a tone of defined intensity and frequency [1 mark]

b) The loudness of a sound for a given person is measured by comparing the loudness from a standard sound source, which is placed next to it **[1 mark]**; the intensity of the known sound is adjusted until it sounds just as loud as the unknown source **[1 mark]**; if the standard sound source, set at 1 KHz, is measured to be say 70 dB then the unknown source is said have a loudness of 70 phon **[1 mark]**

c) a plot of hearing loss or hearing level in dB versus frequency **[1 mark]**.

d) shows progressive hearing loss **[1 mark]** due to age **[1 mark]** affecting higher frequencies the most **[1 mark]**

The Heart and Biological Measurements

QUICK TEST (page 110)

1. left and right atrium, left and right ventricle
2. left atrium along the pulmonary veins
3. the sino-atrial node
4. action potentials
5. Electrocardiogram or ECG
6. good skin contact by applying gel/removing dead skin cells/screening electrical leads
7. the depolarisation and contraction of the ventricles
8. the imbalance of potassium and sodium ions crossing the cell membrane that provides a changing potential difference
9. −70 mV to +35 mV
10. Nerve cell potentials spread very quickly (milliseconds) whereas cardiac muscle potentials act over seconds.

PRACTICE QUESTIONS (page 111)

1. a) P wave corresponds to the depolarisation and contraction **[1 mark]** of the atria **[1 mark]**; QRS-wave corresponds to the depolarisation and contraction **[1 mark]** of the ventricles **[1 mark]**

   b) T wave **[1 mark]**; corresponds to the repolarisation and relaxation **[1 mark]** of the ventricles **[1 mark]**

   c) pulse amplitude is 0.9 mV **[1 mark]**

   d) period of heart beat $T = 0.7$ s **[1 mark]**
   frequency of heart beat $= \frac{1}{T} = \frac{1}{0.7} = 1.429$ Hz ≈ 1.4 Hz **[1 mark]**
   pulse rate per minute $= 60 \times 1.429 = 85.7 \approx 86\,\text{min}^{-1}$ **[1 mark]**

   e) **[any one from]** heart rate would increase; time interval between beats would decrease; T would decrease **[1 mark]**

2. a) 'action potential' is the pattern or response of a changing potential difference **[1 mark]** that is transmitted along a nerve cell **[1 mark]**

   b) The action potential is generated by the movement of ions across the cell membrane **[1 mark]**

c)

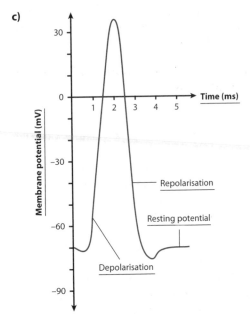

(i) 'Time (ms)' along x-axis **[1 mark]**; 0–5 ms **[1 mark]**; '(Membrane) potential (mV)' along y-axis **[1 mark]**; +40 to −90 (±10 mV) **[1 mark]**.

(ii) Depolarisation **[1 mark]**; Repolarisation **[1 mark]**; Resting potential **[1 mark]** [shown in correct positions to gain all 3 marks]

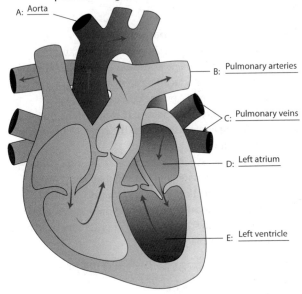

3. a) A = aorta **[1 mark]**; B = (pulmonary) arteries **[1 mark]**; C = (pulmonary) veins **[1 mark]**; D = left atrium **[1 mark]**; E = left ventricle **[1 mark]**

   b) shading shown on correct side of heart **[1 mark]**

   c) The sino-atrial node produces electrical signals (action potentials) **[1 mark]** from the right atrium to the left atrium, causing them to contract **[1 mark]**; the size, polarity and duration of these signals provides the rhythmic function of the heart **[1 mark]**

d) Action potentials of nerve cells are measured in milliseconds whereas those of cardiac muscles lasts considerably longer **[1 mark]**

Medical Imaging with Non-ionising Radiation
QUICK TEST (page 114)
1. magnetic resonance imaging
2. the absorption and emission of radio frequency radiation that shows the distribution of proton density within the body
3. advantages: no known side effects, high-quality images, contrast can be weighted; disadvantages: noisy, scans take a long time, expensive, bone imaging is poor, unsuitable for patients with pacemakers
4. sound waves above 20 kHz; using piezoelectric transducers/crystals where a potential difference is produced following deformation
5. the opposition to sound waves travelling through a material; depends on the density and speed of sound through the material
6. a high value of the reflection coefficient, which depends on the relative impedance of the two materials
7. 0.999
8. total internal reflection of light along an optical fibre
9. to protect the optical fibres and provide a boundary that allows total internal reflection to occur
10. 77°

PRACTICE QUESTIONS (page 115)
1. **a)** Ultrasound waves are sound waves (longitudinal waves) with frequencies greater than 20 kHz **[1 mark]**; ultrasound is produced by applying a potential difference across a piezoelectric crystal, which causes the crystal to deform **[1 mark]**; if the potential difference is alternating then the crystal vibrates at the same frequency **[1 mark]**
   b) When an ultrasound pulse meets a boundary between two different materials **[1 mark]** that have very different acoustic impedance **[1 mark]**, some of it is reflected **[1 mark]**; the reflected pulse is detected by an ultrasound scanner and these pulses are used to generate an image **[1 mark]**
   c) $\alpha = \dfrac{I_R}{I_I} = \left(\dfrac{1.7 \times 10^6 - 6.5 \times 10^6}{1.7 \times 10^6 + 6.5 \times 10^6}\right)^2 = 0.34$ **[1 mark]**

   $I_R = 0.34 \times I_I$ **[1 mark]**
   So 34% of the incident intensity is reflected **[1 mark]**
   d) **[any two from]** Ultrasound imaging has no known hazards; good for imaging soft tissue; ultrasound devices are portable and relatively inexpensive; non-ionising **[2 marks: 1 mark for each advantage]**
2. **a)** $n_{cladding} = 1.40, \quad n_{core} = 1.55$

   $\sin c = \dfrac{n_{cladding}}{n_{core}} = \dfrac{1.40}{1.55} = 0.903 \approx 0.90$ **[1 mark]**
   $c = 64.6° \approx 65°$ **[1 mark]**

b) reflection shown only at the boundaries **[1 mark]**; at least one reflection drawn showing (roughly) angle of incidence = angle of reflection **[1 mark]**
c) an incoherent or non-coherent bundle **[1 mark]**; there is no relative order to the fibres **[1 mark]**; simply works as a light guide to illuminate the object under investigation **[1 mark]**
a coherent bundle **[1 mark]**; optical fibres retain their relative positions at both ends **[1 mark]**; bundle transfers images from object to observer **[1 mark]**
d) This would lead to a smaller difference between the refractive indices **[1 mark]** and to a larger critical angle (hence more chance of refraction) **[1 mark]**
3. **a)** A large superconducting magnet is used to provide a uniform magnetic field **[1 mark]**; this field causes hydrogen nuclei in a patient's body to align themselves with the field **[1 mark]**; radio waves are then used to excite the hydrogen nuclei, which emit radio frequency signals when they de-excite **[1 mark]**; these signals are detected and computer-analysed to create an image **[1 mark]**
   b) Contrast is controlled by varying the length of time before pulses **[1 mark]**
   c) **[any two from]** no known side-effects; high-quality images for soft tissue, e.g. brain; images can be obtained for any part of the body **[2 marks: 1 mark for each advantage]**

Imaging with Ionising Radiation
QUICK TEST (page 118)
1. Known as braking radiation, it is the broad spectrum of radiation emitted by an X-ray machine
2. High-energy electrons promote electrons in a heavy metal atom and the subsequent decay of these electrons to lower levels (and the ground state) releases photons with well-defined energies dictated by the energy difference between the levels concerned
3. They take away (dissipate) the heat energy efficiently
4. (a) 1.4×10^{-14} J (b) 9.0×10^4 eV
5. 1.7×10^{-11} m
6. the thickness of material required to reduce the radiation intensity to half of its original value
7. computed tomography; **[one from]** expensive to build and use, or high radiation dose
8. A barium meal is a contrast medium that enhances the contrast between various tissues that have similar attenuation coefficients or atomic numbers and would otherwise be hard to distinguish
9. Images can be seen and recorded in real time

PRACTICE QUESTIONS (page 119)

1. a) **[any two from]** The anode is rotated so that the heat produced is spread over a greater area (volume); this avoids the risk of melting the anode; it also allows more X-rays to be generated **[2 marks: 1 mark for each explanation]**

b) The X-ray intensity consists of two spectra superimposed on each other **[1 mark]**: **(i)** a continuous spectrum of radiation, bremsstrahlung, as the electrons accelerate and lose kinetic energy **[1 mark]**; **(ii)** a characteristic line spectrum caused by electrons creating 'holes' and 'vacancies' in the ground state **[1 mark]** that are subsequently filled by outer electrons dropping down energy levels and emitting a photon in the X-ray region **[1 mark]**

c) When X-rays pass through matter they are absorbed and scattered **[1 mark]**; how much energy is absorbed depends on the atomic number of the material (and the energy of the X-ray) **[1 mark]**; bones, and hence fractures, show up in X-ray images because bone absorbs more radiation than its surrounding soft tissue **[1 mark]**

d) Half-value thickness is the thickness required to reduce the X-ray intensity to half of its original value **[1 mark]**

e) $I = I_0 e^{-\mu x} \rightarrow \frac{I}{I_0} = e^{-\mu x}$

If $\frac{I}{I_0} = \frac{1}{2}$ then $\frac{1}{2} = e^{-\mu x_{1/2}}$ **[1 mark]**

$\ln\left(\frac{1}{2}\right) = -\mu x_{1/2}$ **[1 mark]**

$x_{1/2} = \frac{-\ln\left(\frac{1}{2}\right)}{\mu} = \frac{\ln 2}{\mu}$ **[1 mark]**

$x_{1/2} = \frac{\ln 2}{0.57} = 1.2\,\text{cm}$ **[1 mark]**

2. a) A = fluorescent screen or photocathode;
B = fluorescent screen; C = anodes; D = X-rays;
E = visible light; F = evacuated tube; G = electrons
[5 marks: all 5 marks for all 7 correct; deduct a mark for each error]

b) A: The fluorescent screen converts X-rays into visible photons **[1 mark]**, and the photocathode at A converts these photons into electrons **[1 mark]**
C: The anodes are used to accelerate the electrons from the photocathode towards the screen B **[1 mark]**; they also focus the electrons to produce an image **[1 mark]**
B: The fluorescent screen at B converts the energetic electrons into light (visible) photons for viewing **[1 mark]**

c) **[any two from]** Fluoroscopy can be used to monitor dynamic processes such as fluid flow; gives lower dose of radiation; gives sharp, accurate images
[2 marks: 1 mark for medical application; 1 mark for explanation]

3. a) KE gained when accelerated $= qV = eV$ **[1 mark]**
$= 1.60 \times 10^{-19} \times 75 \times 10^3$ **[1 mark]**
$= 1.2 \times 10^{-14}$ J **[1 mark]**

b) $E = hf = \frac{hc}{\lambda}$

$\lambda = \frac{hc}{E} = \frac{6.63 \times 10^{-34} \times 3.0 \times 10^8}{1.2 \times 10^{-14}}$ **[1 mark]**

$\lambda = 1.66 \times 10^{-11} \approx 1.7 \times 10^{-11}$ m **[1 mark]**

c) CT scanning uses a narrow beam of X-rays **[1 mark]** that are scanned across a patient **[1 mark]**; a detector records the transmitted intensity at each position **[1 mark]**; the results are collected and digitised and an image is generated by computer **[1 mark]**

OR

An X-ray tube emits a finely collimated fan-shaped beam of monoenergetic X-rays across a patient **[1 mark]**; an array of detectors records the transmitted intensity **[1 mark]**; the source–detector array is then rotated and a new set of readings recorded **[1 mark]** and analysed by computer to produce an image **[1 mark]**

d) **[any one from]** scanning images can be recorded quickly; 3D scans; better image quality **[1 mark]**

Acknowledgements

The author and publisher are grateful to the copyright holders for permission to use quoted materials and images.

Cover & P1: © Shutterstock.com/nikkytok.

All other images are © Shutterstock.com and © HarperCollins*Publishers* Ltd

Every effort has been made to trace copyright holders and obtain their permission for the use of copyright material. The author and publisher will gladly receive information enabling them to rectify any error or omission in subsequent editions. All facts are correct at time of going to press.

Published by Letts Educational
An imprint of HarperCollins*Publishers*
1 London Bridge Street
London SE1 9GF

ISBN: 9780008179113

First published 2016

10 9 8 7 6 5 4 3 2 1

© HarperCollins*Publishers* Limited 2016

British Library Cataloguing in Publication Data.
A CIP record of this book is available from the British Library.

Series Concept and Development: Emily Linnett and Katherine Wilkinson
Commissioning and Series Editor: Chantal Addy
Author: Ron Holt
Project Manager and Editorial: Andrew Welsh
Cover Design: Paul Oates
Inside Concept Design: Paul Oates and Ian Wrigley
Index: Simon Yapp
Text Design, Layout and Artwork: Q2A Media
Production: Lyndsey Rogers and Paul Harding
Printed in Italy by Grafica veneta

MIX
Paper from
responsible sources
FSC™ C007454